PERSONAL BRANDING

BLOOPERS, BLUNDERS AND BOO BOOS

AND HOW TO CLIMB BACK!

A USER'S GUIDE AND WORKBOOK

C. Parker Williams, Ph.D.

A Fingertip Information Publication

Chicago

Personal Branding Bloopers, Blunders and Boo Boos . . . and how to climb back! A User's Guide and Workbook

By C. Parker Williams

Published by: Charmon Parker Williams
Fingertip Information Publications
Chicago, IL 60015
www.personal-branding-bloopers-blunders-boo-boos.com

First printing 2013
ISBN: 978-0-9895037-1-6

To Mom, Dad and Erick

You encircled me in love, supported my dreams, and made me believe I could fly!

To Ty, Spencer and Alex

You show unconditional love, accept me for who I am, and keep me grounded and focused.

TABLE OF CONTENTS

PROLOGUE

Close your eyes for a minute. . . Ok, I guess you can't read this and close your eyes at the same time. So just imagine this scene, in all its excruciating normality. It's morning, 5:45 a.m. to be exact. You get up, shove your feet into your slippers, scratch your rear end, and traipse into the bathroom. There's the mirror. . . You look into it and what do you see? A somewhat puffy face not yet presentable to the many coworkers and clients you will be conversing with in a couple of hours.

You shower, shave and . . . you know the routine . . . 60 minutes later . . . you walk out the door and drive your car to the commuter train line . . . step onto the platform. . . nod your head at a couple of commuters you recognize . . . At last the **train** arrives and you and several others board and begin the 49 minute ride out to the suburbs or in to the city. As the train rips through several neighborhoods, you view a blur of trees, buildings, people, cars . . . and then finally you notice your reflection in the window. Who is that person . . . anyway?

Moments later you walk through the doors of your company, hop on the elevator nodding at a few familiar faces. You are the last to get off, and as you edge to the front of the elevator, you see that familiar reflection again forming in the metallic elevator doors. Features are fading . . . and you enter the generic domain of endless offices and cubicles on your floor. You become absorbed in work. You prepare for meetings, sit in on conference calls, make a brief appearance at a co-worker's birthday celebration, and put out a few fires. At this point you are operating off of adrenaline. There are no mirrors in your office and so you don't think of your mortal being until your stomach growls and tells you it's time for lunch . . . or is it dinner time already? Commute back home . . . another 49 minutes . . . dinner . . . dishes . . . drill sergeant . . . demands . . . dumbbell routine while watching the nightly news . . . and then down for the count. Day in . . . day out . . .

Okay one, two, three . . . . Snap out of it! What's your assessment of the day?

"Quite productive. No interruptions. On target with deadlines. Managed to bridge a few tense relationships. Doing my job. . . and doing it well!"

Well guess what your manager and co-workers think.

"He's reliable, predictable, somewhat aloof, prefers to work alone. We wouldn't consider him a strong contender for the next level up."

Say what! Big disconnect? You bet!

All too frequently we have a perception about ourselves that differs from others. We may believe that we are doing well at work while others think we are just "so-so". We may even be misled into believing that what we are and who we are is noticeable to the many individuals we come into contact with each day when in reality they struggle with remembering how we have contributed or what we're interested in. Many of us are on autopilot for most of the day, and perhaps for most of our careers. Much of what we do or would like to do often flies under the radar, undetected by others. What are we doing or not doing that is causing this disconnect? How can we become more conscious of this? Why do our viewpoints often collide with others instead of coincide? And how can we promote ourselves without coming across as exploitive or self-serving?

You are about to join me on an excursion through the experiences of countless professionals, both ordinary and infamous, as we explore the answers to these questions. Many of these disconnects can be attributed to personal branding slip-ups. I promise to stand close by as we walk through simple and straightforward pathways that will help your personal branding mistakes become the exception and not the rule!

Getting the most from this book

During my career as an industrial/organizational psychologist, I have had the opportunity to conduct seminars and coach a wide range of professionals including recent college graduates, mid-career professionals, retiring executives and budding entrepreneurs. Through this process I've witnessed and heard several individual accounts about the many personal branding blunders presented in this book. I can say, unashamedly, that I have also committed some of the blunders described in this book. In the wake of these mistakes, I've learned to laugh at myself, look for the lesson, and move forward. We're all human; and the good news is that recovery is just one step away.

There is plenty of advice available about what you should do to create a personal brand, and we will revisit those tips in this book. However the focus for this book is on looking at what you should stay away from, the land mines to avoid, your blind spots, and how to take steps toward recovery if you have already made a personal branding mistake, as most of us have.

There are many bloopers and blunders you can commit with respect to personal branding. This book outlines 20 different mistakes that occur frequently. All of them may not be applicable to you. While this book is a fairly quick read, you may prefer to look at the list of branding bloopers in the Table of Contents and skip to the chapters that resonate most with you. You can always go back and review the remaining bloopers later.

The "Cases-in-Point" presented in the book are based on real scenarios and people whose names and identities have been changed, unless they are well-known public figures. Strategies for turning things around are provided for each branding blunder under "Road to Recovery". These tips are followed by specific exercises and worksheets you can complete and utilize for self-reflection, for soliciting input from others or for putting a plan into action. Some of the exercises are written for fun and entertainment, although there is still generally an underlying key message in these.

This book was purposely written on the light/humorous side to engage you and put you in a positive and proactive frame of mind. However personal branding is a powerful career management strategy, and one that should be taken seriously throughout your career. It is easy to become discouraged, however, by varying economic predictions and the employment outlook. Today, many professionals find themselves in "search" mode – searching for new jobs, for a new career, or searching for the secret to staying employed. Revisiting one's personal brand is part of the critical path to reinvention and "staying power."

What's in it for me, again?

To sum it up, this book was designed to be your user's manual and workbook. The information presented on the next 100 pages or so will:

- Help you learn from your and others' personal branding missteps
- Provide exercises for reflection and self-examination
- Guide you in crafting your strategies for change
- Introduce ways to build up your personal branding support system
- Prompt you to take action now!

COMING TO TERMS WITH
PERSONAL BRANDING

PERSONAL BRANDING DEFINED

As consumers, we all have familiarity with and preferences for specific brands. When choosing athletic shoes, we may prefer Nike or Adidas because of the look and feel. When purchasing a car, we may opt for GM over Kia because of the style of the cars. Or when selecting a hotel for a business trip, we may choose the Holiday Inn Express over the Ritz Carlton because of its affordability.

A certain expectation, emotion, and value come to mind when we think of specific product or company brands. This same experience is applicable to personal branding. Your brand is the perception that others have of you, demonstrated through the value you bring, how you make them feel, and how you are different from other similar products (or professionals). Your brand is your **Wow** factor. Similar to marketing professionals and brand managers you can be deliberate about defining your brand and how others perceive you. Your brand manifests in everything you do including your work, your social networks, your personality, your appearance, your environment, your collateral pieces and even your voicemail.

FREQUENTLY USED TERMINOLOGY

Throughout this book we will use certain terms that have been associated with product, company, and personal branding. Many of these terms are presented below:

Brand – Characteristics (e.g., name, functionality, look, etc.) that distinguish one company or competitor's product from another. A promise to deliver a clearly stated, unique and relevant benefit that is consistently expressed both tangibly and intangibly to differentiate one's offering from competitors.

Brand Promise – The specific and unique benefits or experience the brand intends to deliver to its target audience. Your brand promise should be unique, compelling and believable.

Brand Consistency – The degree to which messaging or practices align with the brand's identity and promise (or conversely detract from them). Consistency results from continually saying or doing things that enable you to demonstrate your brand.

Brand Dilution – The weakening of a brand by over-using it or over-extending it (e.g., applying it to conflicting products such as soft drinks and writing utensils).

Brand identity – The unique combination of factors that define the brand (name, color, logos, etc.). What people think and feel about you and what you have to offer; the emotional connection you make.

Brand image – Consumers' impressions of what the brand stands for and its ability to meet expectations. The brand's reputation.

Brand loyalty – From a target market perspective, this translates to the degree to which individuals consistently seek you out because they see value in your brand and/or want to align with it. If you were a product, consumers would repeatedly purchase you.

Differentiator – Any tangible or intangible characteristic that can be used to distinguish a brand from its competitors.

Personal brand equity – Refers to personal benefits that you as an individual build up over time because of your strong brand (your assets and ability to engender brand loyalty).

Personal branding - The act of creating or enhancing the image that you want others to have of you. Identifying how you want to be perceived by a particular group of people (i.e., target market) and developing and implementing a strategy that is consistent with that image.

Target Market or Audience – A particular audience the brand is trying to reach based on the audience's demographics (personal characteristics), psychographics (ways of thinking/opinions) or ethnographics (behaviors).

Top-of-mind – The brand that is at the forefront of a consumer's mind when considering multiple brands of the same product.

CREATING A PERSONAL BRAND

The process for creating or enhancing your personal brand is similar to the process used in industry; and as the diagram below illustrates, branding is an ongoing and cyclical process. There are several phases of activity that involve needs analysis, visioning and execution:

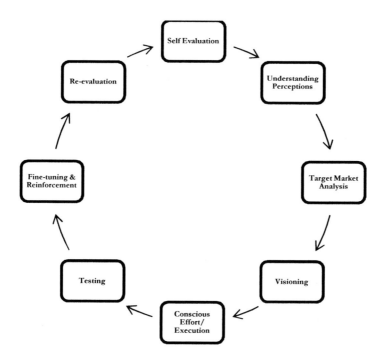

1. **Self-Evaluation** – Personal branding begins with a self-assessment of where you are today – what you think your unique offering is.

2. **Understanding Perceptions** – An essential component of understanding your brand is to seek out others who know you well (friends, co-workers, family) to get a well-rounded view (360 degrees) on how you are perceived.

3. **Target Market Analysis** – Your brand brings value when it matches the needs of your target market. A critical step in the personal

branding process is defining who your target market is and researching what their interests and expectations are.

4. **Visioning -** Creating a personal brand vision involves addressing the gap between where you are now and where you want to be. It requires you to think through the specifics of how you *want* others to perceive you.

5. **Conscious Effort -** Now comes the tough work. Creating a new or enhanced brand will require that you make a conscious effort to change behaviors and create new habits that align with your desired brand. Best-selling author, Steven Covey, suggests that it takes 90 days to create a new habit.

6. **Testing –** During this stage you will take your new brand out for a test drive. See if you get the desired results.

7. **Fine-tuning & Reinforcing Behaviors/Actions –** After paying attention to the feedback you are getting on your branding efforts, you may need to make slight changes to your behavior to keep on course toward achieving your brand vision.

8. **Re-evaluation –** At this stage you review your brand, continue to grow, develop, and evolve your brand to keep it current. Make major changes as a last resort. Remember your brand represents "You, Incorporated." It's the promise that people come to rely on you for.

As straightforward as the process above may appear, there are still many missteps one can take along the way, including neglecting to follow a structured process or not soliciting feedback, for example. In the following pages you will be introduced to twenty branding blunders that have significant consequences for career management, as well as how to turn these blunders around.

PERSONAL BRANDING

BLOOPERS, BLUNDERS AND BOO BOOS

AND HOW TO CLIMB BACK!

#1 HAVING NO BRAND AT ALL

*If you don't brand yourself . . . **Others Will!!***

WHAT IT MEANS

You have a brand whether you know it or not. You have either consciously shaped that brand or you have not focused on your brand. In some cases, your default brand is an effective one. Alternatively, a brand that you have deliberately crafted may be ineffective. Regardless of whether you are proactive or not, people will have a perception of you. Is it the perception you want them to have?

Branding is about shaping that perception to your advantage and being top-of-mind (at the forefront) as your co-workers and colleagues think about various projects. Given there is such a strong link between your brand and ability to manage your career, it would behoove you to know 1) what your brand is, and 2) whether or not it is effective. To leave this in the hands of others is a big risk that will eventually catch up with you.

Many of us believe that if we just "do a good job" then "everything will be alright." Doing a good job is probably the most misinterpreted concept in business. Performance and results are clearly important. However, these are givens and non-negotiable as you manage your career. Career and/or business success is a combination of performance, image, and exposure. . . and these components must simultaneously occur.

Some people are doing all the right things to brand themselves and manage their brands, but they are on automatic. They may not be aware or only slightly aware of what the connection is between personal branding and what they are doing. If you ask them what their brand is, they may not be able to tell you; but if you ask them what they do to promote themselves, market

11

their talents, or what they consider to be special or unique about themselves, they may be able to engage in dialogue with you.

Can you think of individuals you know who have successfully branded themselves? What about those who got branded by default – good, bad, or indifferent?

CONSEQUENCES

The risks you may encounter by not being deliberate about shaping your brand are many. You might get a label that does not align with your goals, interests, or values, perhaps even something you feel is the extreme opposite. You may be overlooked for opportunities, projects, and activities you really want that would be helpful to your career development. This can lead to frustration, which over time might cause you to disengage from your work, those around you, and your company.

Without your conscious input into branding, you lose control of your image. Consequently a reputation you do not want may spread like wildfire – into arenas you haven't even entered, simply through the word-of-mouth of others. On the other hand, you risk fading into the background if people are not clear on what you stand for and the value you bring to the table.

You will lose out on opportunities that translate into growth and financial reward if you aren't proactive about branding. Why? No one is thinking of you. Your name doesn't come up in succession planning meetings, or when decision makers are discussing who to develop, who to save in a merger or acquisition. Or when your name does come up, decision-makers are scratching their heads, trying to fill in the blanks, because not enough stands out about you, or trivial and unrelated things stand out. There simply is not enough information about you! Consequently, you get left behind or excluded since your value proposition is not known.

CASE IN POINT

I often tell a story in the personal branding workshops I facilitate of how I was part of a planning committee for a corporate wide celebration at a major consulting organization. There were about five of us who worked for a couple of months planning activities, reaching out to potential speakers and performers, and handling logistics around audio-visual, communication and catering. The weeks leading up to the final celebration included weekly trivia contests and educational displays. The speaker we secured was a world renowned individual, and we had a record turnout to the event – over 600 attendees. In short, the program and activities were a success and raised the bar for all future employee events.

Needless to say, our sponsoring executive was quite pleased with the outcome and wanted to ensure that senior leadership was aware of the individuals who had contributed to the success of this event. He crafted a wonderful and detailed email thanking us both collectively and individually and distributed this email to the CEO, the CEO's direct reports and other senior leaders. He thanked *Jean* for her leadership, *Lisa* for being the glue that held everyone together, *Terrence* for being a great team player and me for working humbly behind the scenes to bring quality to every aspect of the event . . .

My facial expression morphed from a wide grin to a jaw drop as I read over my acknowledgement again. On the surface you might think I'd be pumped up about being showcased to senior management, yet I was somewhat unsettled about being labeled humble. In fact, I didn't want anyone to think that I was content to work humbly behind the scenes. And while humility is a commendable attribute and may float someone's boat, it didn't float mine. If you knew me at all, you'd know I was the biggest ham deep within and so I didn't want to be branded as someone motivated by working HUMBLY behind any scene. I had been branded by default!

So, what to do? What to do indeed! This was a wake-up call for me. I started doing all I could within my role to ensure I stood out in front of my work. No longer would I design a program or workshop and enable others to present it. I raised my hand to participate in more of a leadership capacity on cross-functional task forces. I did all I could to ensure my work and I were more visible. Did it pay off? Yes it did! During the following year's corporate wide celebration, I not only helped with the planning, I emceed the event! Within one year of my personal rebranding campaign, I applied for a more senior level role and I got it! I credit my being top-of-mind and visible as part of the reason.

The Deliberate Brand

Everyone has a brand whether you are deliberate about it or not. The visual in this section highlights how involved or uninvolved we may be in shaping

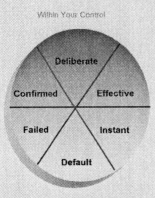

our brand. There are aspects of personal branding that are within our control -- these are on the upper half of the circle. Those aspects that define our brand that are circumstantial are on the lower half of the circle. Your **default** brand is the one that people attribute to you based on their perceptions, whether they be perceptions linked to your true identity or misconceptions. This is a brand that is based on circumstances.

The **instant brand** usually occurs when you first meet someone or some group. It is also circumstantial as it is the first impression that others have of you. As an interviewee, for example, you may impress your future employer in the interview with your knowledge, effective communication skills, and ability to relate your work-related experiences. When you leave, the interviewer may have formed an impression of you based on your presentation in the interview which, for example, may have been *credible, problem solver, professional and polished.* Your instant brand may or may not reflect your true capabilities or sustainable characteristics and will typically last through the honeymoon phase of your new job until you have had a chance to confirm it.

The **failed brand** is also circumstantial. This is a brand that actually hurts you within your target audience. They may believe that you are not right for a role or that you bring something that runs counter to their needs or expectations. Perhaps your style, ideas, or demeanor just do not fit in. Your brand may fail because you are presenting the wrong things, or it may be that you are not in front of the right audience — one that would appreciate your brand.

14

At the top half of the circle is those branding aspects that you can control. A **confirmed brand** would be one that is consistent and sustained. It may or may not be the same as the instant brand people associated with you. A confirmed brand is not necessarily good or bad. On the other hand, an **effective brand** is one that works successfully with a particular audience and typically arises out of someone doing their homework on the target audience's needs. **Deliberate** branding is the ultimate objective. It implies that you are implementing well thought-out actions and that there is a constant review and questioning of whether your actions support your brand. Being deliberate suggests that you realize that you are in charge of your career, in control of managing others' perceptions of you, and are consciously and strategically taking steps to shape those perceptions.

ROAD TO RECOVERY

People who are consciously managing their brand are paying attention to how they are perceived. If you have been branded by default, redefining your brand will initially require five key actions:

1. Find out how others view you.

   - Look at how you are described in emails.
   - Determine if there is a pattern to the types of projects to which you are assigned.
   - Ask others what the "word on the street" is about you.
   - Request feedback on a 360° survey or review the results of a 360° performance review you have received within the past year.

2. Identify the gap between how you are perceived and how you want to be perceived.
   - For example, are your managers, coworkers or others describing you as detail-oriented when you want to be viewed as strategic and visionary?
   - Where are your perceptions close to others'? Where are there big disconnects? Is there a total misconception about your interests and/or skills?

3. Identify two to three key things you can do to reinforce the brand you want.

    - Put together your list and run it by a couple of individuals whose opinions you respect.
    - This step is critical. You can do the analysis, but unless you develop a strategy and implement it, nothing else you have read or learned has any relevance. Branding cannot simply happen inside of your head. It is partially a mental activity, but you will gain traction much quicker if you commit to specific actions on paper. Create a time-based contract with yourself for a few things you will do over the next year.

4. Let others know what you desire.
    - Plant seeds with your managers, colleagues, mentors, etc.
    - Raise your hand and volunteer for assignments that will showcase skills others have overlooked.
    - Know what to say "no" to in order to stay loyal to your evolving brand. Steer away from tasks and assignments that maintain the brand you are trying to separate yourself from.

5. Evaluate whether or not your desired brand is catching on.
    - Ask for feedback on how your image is evolving within the workplace.
    - Take note of whether people are reaching out to you for the types of assignments you want.

EXERCISE

Visioning Exercises
- My Brand Objective
- Create a Personal Brand Statement

Worksheet: My Brand Objective

How do I want to be perceived?

	One year from now	Three years from now
What do I want to be known for professionally?		

How do I want others to describe me and my work?		

What major accomplishments do I want to have completed?		

What do I want to be my "differentiator" (the aspect that is most unique about me and distinguishes me from others)?		

How does what I've listed above support my career and personal goals?

Worksheet – Create a Personal Brand Statement

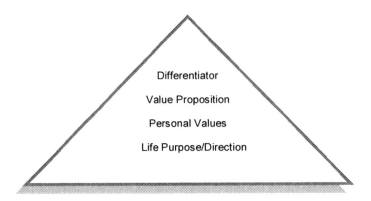

Create a concise personal brand statement (3 to 5 sentences) that includes:

- What you stand for (your purpose or direction in life).
- What you value/live by.
- Your value proposition to your target audience (e.g., problems you can help solve).
- What differentiates you from others?

Example: My purpose includes helping individuals realize their full career potential. I value honesty and open-mindedness and incorporate candor and a sense of collaboration into all of my interactions. I can provide information and coach others in a way that helps them understand their strengths and define strategies for reaching their goals. My brand is differentiated based on who I connect with (e.g., target audience is employees in transition), how I connect with others (one-on-one as well as via conferences and articles), and through my offer (helping clients reconcile competing work and non-work activities at each career stage).

My Personal Brand Statement

#2 DANCING THE NIGHT AWAY

A good name, like good will, is got by many actions and lost by one.
--Lord Jeffery

WHAT IT MEANS

Branding is as much about what you should do as it is about what you shouldn't. "Dancing the night away" is simply code for "how to destroy your credibility in one fell swoop." It is the mistake that many good-intentioned souls make when crossing that fine line between being sociable and being a spectacle. Depending on your brand objective, this blunder can stop the flow of opportunities dead in their tracks. Yes, you may become more popular on a social level, but this could put your career efforts in a coma! As Janet Jackson might put it, "It's all about control."

Networking is a critical component of branding, but it must be distinguished from "net playing" or "not working". Every venue in which you are visible provides the opportunity to either reinforce your brand or chip away at your brand. Remember self-branding is a marketing activity. It is the process in which you impress upon your target audience or those who can connect to what you have to offer and it can happen in almost any venue. Is branding something you need to think about every time you step out the door? Well, if there is a chance you might run into someone from your target audience, then the answer is yes . . . within reason.

Like a walking billboard, you are a continual advertisement of your brand!

For example, let's say you have a well-known brand at work as being strategic, visionary, and organized. Co-workers would reasonably expect you to be well-rounded enough outside of work to demonstrate other aspects of your personality. So if they were to see you in a grocery store, going up and down aisles, appearing somewhat relaxed and orderly about how you shop for items, wearing jeans or something else casual, there probably wouldn't be a disconnect with your brand at work.

However, if someone from work saw you running, "helter skelter," from one end of the store to the next, looking confused, asking numerous people throughout the store for assistance, they might, at minimum, think you are having a bad day, but in all probability would wonder who had taken over your body. This behavior would most likely chip away at your brand of being strategic and organized.

People expect you to show different behaviors in different settings -- within limits. They wouldn't expect brand "Dr. Jekyll" to morph into brand "Mr. (showing his) Hyde." Put another way, they wouldn't expect brand "strategic leader" to turn into brand "having a melt-down in the grocery store."

CONSEQUENCES

When others you interact with in a professional setting observe big disconnects in your behavior in more casual settings, they begin to question your character and capability. This could result in:

- You and your brand not being taken seriously
- Missed opportunities because others can't predict how reliable your behavior will be in front of their colleagues
- Word getting out to people who weren't at the venue, adversely affecting their perception of you
- Lessened opportunities to further build relationships with people who only know about your social persona

CASE IN POINT

We all know about the power of networking and have probably gone to a social event with business and professional colleagues. Some of these social gatherings are rather informal, intimate, and even downright raucous.

Hopefully, you have a good sense about who you can let your hair down with. But I am here to tell you, once you let it down, you won't be seen quite the same again.

Does this sound like you? Patsy had a group of close friends from work with whom she hung out periodically. There was a lot of fun, teasing, and joviality. Patsy came out of her shell quite a bit at these parties, as did all the other turtles in the room. Patsy thought that these periodic parties would be a good place to try to drum up new business or at least get referrals. So she brought her business cards and a brochure she had mocked up to one of the parties she attended. So far, so good. Many people leverage informal parties as business networking opportunities. Let's see how the night transpired.

The party was a "make your own margarita party" and the tequila was flowing. An hour into the party Patsy was on her second drink. The music was lively and the night was young. Patsy was feeling quite confident and decided to talk business. She connected with about five people in the room, talked about the new business she was trying to start and handed out her business cards and her brochure . . .

Fast forward to the next morning . . . mid-afternoon, Patsy is sitting on her balcony nursing tomato juice and aspirin. . . and feeling pretty proud of herself for killing two birds with one stone at the party the night before – business and pleasure. As she recalls the night, she was witty, charming, charismatic even, and painted an irresistible picture of her talents and business plan. She remembers at least half of the people she spoke with nodding their heads enthusiastically and promising to connect with her on upcoming business opportunities within the companies in which they worked. She sends follow up emails to everyone to stay at the forefront of their minds.

Two weeks later – no word from anyone, but this is not surprising in the business development cycle. One month later – still no word. Three months later – no word and Patsy decides to send additional emails and reach out via phone, as well as set up luncheons. But lo and behold, a friend is throwing another party on the beach and "what good luck!" she will see most of the same people there. The theme of this party is "Drop it like it's hot." Patsy and the rest of the attendees had a chance to show their skills in "Limbo" and the "Beyoncé Bounce." Well Patsy was not to be shown up and walked home with second prize that evening. Can I get a Woo Woo!

During this party, she again approached her colleagues and talked about her business, was a bit more direct, and inquired if there were any opportunities they were aware of. Again, she recalls heads nodding, and folks promising to keep her in the loop when opportunities arose. This time one month went by when a good friend, Linda, told her about a project at a downtown bank that was pulling in three individuals to work on a short term project. This was right up her alley; and the Program Manager, Larry, was someone she had hung out with at the previous two parties. Patsy was confused. "Larry knows I do this. Why didn't he call me?" Patsy decided to give Larry a call to inquire if there was still time to get in on the project. Larry fumbled for a minute, and then let Patsy know that he had totally forgotten that she was in that line of work and that he had already selected the contractors, but would keep her in mind next time. Six months later Linda called Patsy again to ask if Larry had called her about an upcoming project at his company for which he needed referrals. Linda said she had recommended Patsy. So why didn't Patsy get the call? Hello?

The moral of this story is fairly obvious. Unless you are in the entertainment industry, your prospective customers and clients will not be impressed by your dancing on the tabletop . . . even if they are on the chair waiting to get up there next!

Patsy's view of herself ➔ fun loving, resourceful, savvy businessperson, great networker.

Larry's and others' view of Patsy ➔ Party animal!! Lots of fun! Love hanging out with her. Not someone I would want to showcase to my boss. Hey, she might slip up and say anything!

So how does Patsy redeem her credibility?

ROAD TO RECOVERY

You may feel that you can never regain credibility under these circumstances. The ability to do so depends on three factors -- scope, frequency, and recency. Your receiving the benefit of the doubt is linked to how well people know you and know your work. People may be more forgiving if they have seen other examples of your behavior (scope). However if they see you morph into an out-of-control state on more than one occasion (frequency) this will definitely chip away at your credibility and any professional brand you are trying to build – unless your brand is a stand-up comic. The more (recent) the occurrence, the more memorable.

1. Learn the lesson and move on. Take time to reflect on your behavior and think back to when you began to lose control. What was your motivation for acting out? Was it the intake of too much alcohol? (In many cases, this is the main culprit). Were you just trying to unwind after a demanding week of work? Have fun, but keep poised in public, let your hair down at home. Were you trying to show someone up? (You probably succeeded . . . but not in a good way). Did you drink too much, because you felt shy and out of place in the setting? There are probably other shy people feeling the same way about networking. Take notice and reach out to one or two of these individuals to converse and connect with. Focus on learning about them and making them feel comfortable and you will be less conscious about yourself. A relevant quote from Maya Angelou is applicable here. *"I've learned that people will forget what you said, people will forget what you did, but people will never forget how you made them feel."*

2. Lay low on the party circuit. Eventually people will forget or be less critical about what you did.

3. Reach out to a new audience who has not seen you in action. You may need to impress a new group who can then begin to speak on your behalf.

4. Build up points, by showing up in venues that build your credibility. This includes volunteering for special task forces at work, volunteering for community work, appearing on panels, sharing your expert opinion in meetings or in written communications, etc. In due time you will see your credibility rebuild.

EXERCISE: Networker or Net Player?

Are you a networker, net player, or not yet on the court? For each item, circle the response that best describes you.

---

a. I have an elevator speech
b. My elevator speech becomes slurred after 10:00 p.m. (or happy hour)
c. I don't know what an elevator speech is.

---

a. I make it a point to say and remember the names of people I meet.
b. I've come up with a simple system for remembering everybody's name. It's "Hey Baby!"
c. What people? I rarely go out.

---

a. I ask questions to learn something new about people I already know and don't know, like "What kind of interesting projects have you been working on lately?"
b. I ask questions to get to know people better like, "What's your Zodiac sign?"
c. I spend every minute possible talking about myself and don't worry about asking others questions.

---

a. I hand out business cards that include what type of service I provide.
b. I hand out business cards on which I handwrite my home phone number and marital status.
c. I don't have any business cards.

---

a. I carry a tin of breath mints with me to each function.
b. I carry a pack of Hubba Bubba bubble gum to each function.
c. I try not to stand too close to others while talking.

This exercise is primarily for entertainment purposes.

Scoring: Like I need to tell you . . .

a responses – Networker
b responses – Net player
c responses – Not yet in the game

3 BEING LESS THAN AUTHENTIC

---!---

If your success is not on your own terms, if it looks good to the world
but does not feel good in your heart,
it is not success at all.
--Anna Quindlen

WHAT IT MEANS

So much has been said and written about authenticity. There are many
words you can substitute for authenticity – real, genuine, true, bona fide.
The opposite would be fake, perpetrator, imitator, or hypocrite. You know
who I'm talking about!

How is authenticity demonstrated? Is it through following your bliss? Being
true to yourself? Saying any fool thing you want because you're over 50?

Yes and no. Individuals described as authentic, bring themselves to the table,
whatever that is, and they are willing to express or share themselves with
others, in spite of who may disagree or question. This involves the ability to
communicate confidently on where you stand, how you feel and think about
a particular issue.

Authenticity does not mean that one has license to be rude, in order to make
a point. Civility, sensitivity, and sensibility are still important interpersonal
factors.

Being true to your values, ideals, and goals is at the heart of authenticity, as
well as having the common sense to know that not everyone thinks or feels
like you. However there are probably many with whom your message, your
life experience, will resonate.

27

Being "less than authentic" is akin to forcing a square peg into a round hole. Here are examples of how it manifests:

- Going along with a plan you don't agree with
- Smiling when you are seething inside
- Trying to represent something that is not inside your heart because you feel you "should"
- Holding back the real you for fear of:
  — Being rejected
  — Being unpopular
  — Being controversial
  — Being fired!
- Representing yourself as something you are not or building up a lot of brand equity in something you don't value.

CONSEQUENCES

Being less than authentic takes a toll on one's physical and mental functioning and creates internal tension. In psychological terms, this can be referred to as "cognitive dissonance" which occurs when there is a disconnect between what you believe and what you are doing. In order to reconcile this, either your behavior or attitude will need to adjust.

Dissonance or discord is often strong when we hold a belief about our self-image and then do something against that belief. For example "I believe I am an honest and forthright person, but I always tend to tell my team mates what I think they want to hear."

- To resolve the conflict, and resulting tension, we can take one of three actions:

  - Change our behavior (being more candid with our team mates).
  - Justify our behavior by changing the conflicting thought about ourselves. (I am not hung up on being honest or candid with my team mates)

- Justify our behavior by adding new thoughts about ourselves. (I am honest but value avoiding conflict more so)

- Unreconciled cognitive dissonance can contribute to stress and ultimately to depression.
- Additionally behaving in a manner that minimizes our true values and interests will lead to lack of fulfillment in our career and our lives.
- It is downright energy draining to maintain an image that does not reflect who we are. (It is almost like "passing" for something you aren't.) For example, a gay person "passing for straight" must constantly watch his conversation, lest he give away clues to who he really is. He will always experience some degree of paranoia that someone will figure out who he really is and expose him. It's the same with someone sustaining a brand that is not reflective of what or who they are at the core. There is always a possibility of slip-ups and break-downs – reverting to one's true self.
- Consequently you will experience a loss in brand integrity once people find out you're not the "real thing."

If the behaviors you are portraying feel uncomfortable or too forced, you will not have long lasting success in displaying them. A sustainable brand is one that highlights your strengths and interests *while* it meets the needs of your target market.

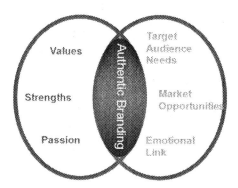

CASE IN POINT

In a 2004 interview with Renetta McCann, chief executive of Starcom North America, she provided a memorable description of her brand that speaks to the heart of authenticity and subsequently sustainability. Renetta McCann is very much in tune with the concept of authentic branding. In her role at the time, McCann was ultimately responsible for the largest office within Starcom MediaVest Group, one of the top brand communication networks in the world. McCann has earned a reputation for cultivating Starcom into one of the top strategic planning "think tanks" in the industry and has acquired an extensive collection of awards and honors during her career.

In describing her personal brand McCann indicates, *"Over time it's occurred to me that I have built a brand that says, "When you engage me, I will give you ideas, be brutally frank, and will be real focused on problem solution. I don't know that this is unique, but when I bundle these together, clients are amazed that I don't get bogged down with ego level issues. I have an ego, but I don't convey that I'm out for me first."*

"I developed my personal brand over time. I had to develop a style that was going to be effective in a client service setting. My clients want to know how my presence will enhance their bottom line. And in somewhat of a Pavlovian manner I have developed a style that works with clients as well as works internally with employees."

McCann adds, *"Your brand is most powerful when it taps into who you really are. Branding is not necessarily defined by your profession. You need a focal point. Pick something you can stick to throughout life. I am the same person at work as I am at home. So when my kids approach me with questions, I give them ideas. I am brutally frank; and I am focused on problem solving."*

"This notion of brand consistency is the same with packaged goods," suggests McCann. *"Starbucks, for example, has taken 'flavored water' and branded it as "an experience". They took this same concept at 'T-Mobile' and it was successful because it was consistent with their brand. Product and, similarly, personal brands can evolve and grow, but it has to be done in a way that is consistent with the individual."*

ROAD TO RECOVERY

How do you know if you are being authentic, if your brand is consistent with whom you are? Here is some food for thought.

1. Get to know you.

- How is "you" expressed? Instead of trying to change it, build on your strengths.
- Hone in on what you want out of life and identify those things that you are not willing to compromise.
- Create a personal vision statement.
- Think about how far you are willing to deviate from this vision.

2. Monitor how you feel in different situations.
- Are there specific settings in which you feel you are suppressing who you are or what you believe?
- Practice bringing a bit of you, the authentic you, to every situation.
- Understand that adapting to a situation does not mean changing your values or the core of "you".

3. Identify your target audience.
- Who needs to be aware of the work you do, your brand?
- What need can you fulfill for them?
- What type of brand would be relevant to this audience?
- Does this match your interests and skill sets?
- Are the behaviors valued by your target audience something you are already doing?
- What do you need to start, stop, or continue doing to build or enhance your authentic brand?

4. Focus on someone's brand you admire.
- Think about what drew you to them? Is it because they are likable, strong, controversial, down to earth, or successful?
- Why do you feel their brand is authentic?
- Think about what they represent, do, say, and endorse that reinforces their brand.
- What do you have in common with them on a superficial level?
- What elements that you see in them do you want to build within your brand?

Examples of Personal Brands

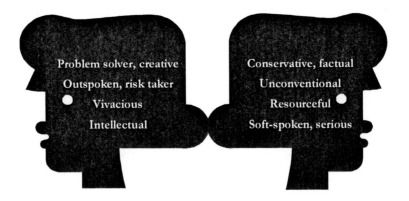

Problem solver, creative
Outspoken, risk taker
Vivacious
Intellectual

Conservative, factual
Unconventional
Resourceful
Soft-spoken, serious

EXERCISE: MY TWO FACES

Is what you are doing to promote yourself consistent with who you are? Complete the two worksheets below from two perspectives.

1. First, think of how you present yourself in the workplace or group situations in which you are involved. What do you believe is required to be effective?

2. Secondly, reflect on how you feel most comfortable behaving. What do you feel is a true reflection of who you are?

3. After you have completed both profiles, compare them and determine how different or similar they are.
   a. Where is there alignment? Where is there a disconnect?
   b. What do you believe your brand requires?

Profile 1 – How I Present Myself

Which of the characteristics below best define how you present yourself?

1 Look at each pair of characteristics below and determine at which point on the continuum you **CURRENTLY OPERATE** and place an "X" there. For example if you believe that you present yourself as being balanced between being task oriented and relationship oriented you would put an "X" in the middle (3).

①

	1	2	3	4	5	
Relationship Oriented						Task Oriented
Strategic (Long-term focus)						Tactical (Short-term focus)
Supporter						Leader
Independent						Collaborative
Methodical						Spontaneous
Diplomatic						Candid
High Energy						Calm
Self-promoting						Modest/Humble
Action Oriented						Analytical
Gregarious						Reserved
Traditional						Unconventional
Talkative						Quiet/Reflective

Profile 2 – The Authentic Me

Which of the characteristics below best define the truer reflection of your authentic self?

2 Look at each pair of characteristics below and determine at which point on the continuum you would **PREFER TO OPERATE** (because it represents your true strengths, interests, values and goals) and place an "X" there.

3 After you have completed Profile 2, compare each item to Profile 1 and calculate the point difference.

②   ③
Point difference between profiles 1 and 2

Relationship Oriented	. . . . 1 2 3 4 5	Task Oriented	_____
Strategic (Long-term focus)	. . . . 1 2 3 4 5	Tactical (Short-term focus)	_____
Supporter	. . . . 1 2 3 4 5	Leader	_____
Independent	. . . . 1 2 3 4 5	Collaborative	_____
Methodical	. . . . 1 2 3 4 5	Spontaneous	_____
Diplomatic	. . . . 1 2 3 4 5	Candid	_____
High Energy	. . . . 1 2 3 4 5	Calm	_____
Self-promoting	. . . . 1 2 3 4 5	Modest/Humble	_____
Biased toward action	. . . . 1 2 3 4 5	Analytical, explorative	_____
Gregarious	. . . . 1 2 3 4 5	Reserved	_____
Traditional	. . . . 1 2 3 4 5	Unconventional	_____
Talkative	. . . . 1 2 3 4 5	Quiet/Reflective	_____

After you have completed both profiles, compare them and determine how different or similar they are.

- Look at the items where there is a 2 point difference or more. These are the areas to be concerned about as they indicate that you are deviating away from your authentic self.

- For those items with a 2 point or more difference:
  - Place the characteristics you are closest to from Profile 1- *"How I Present Myself"* at the top part of the iceberg on the next page.
  - Place the characteristics you are closest to from Profile 2 - *"The Authentic Me"* worksheet below the waterline in the iceberg.

A sample scenario might look like the following:

You have a two or more point gap on the following items:

- Supporter/Leader
- Relationship Oriented/Task Oriented
- Talkative/Quiet

Supporter, Task Oriented and Quiet are on the "How I present myself Worksheet." Consequently these would appear at the top of the iceberg.

What People See

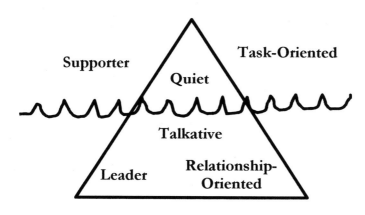

What People Don't See

My Iceberg: What are people seeing and what is hidden under the surface?

What People See

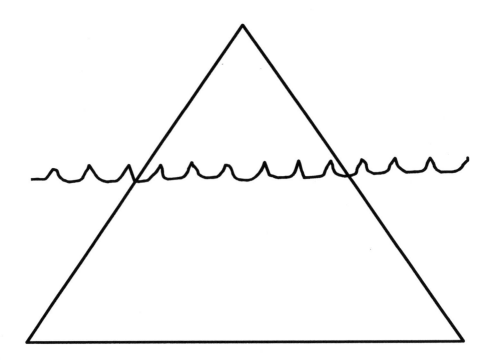

What People Don't See

Once completed, this visual will provide insight into areas that might be causing tension for you, and remind you of those hidden aspects of your personality and character that you need to incorporate into your role and your personal brand.

When green is all there is to be, it can make you wonder why, but why wonder. I'm green and it'll do fine, it's beautiful, and I think it's what I want to be.

--Kermit the Frog

#4 THE CHAMELEON

I don't know the key to success, but the key to failure
is trying to please everybody.
--Bill Cosby

WHAT IT MEANS

Being a chameleon refers to changing your brand as often as you change your environment so that you blend in.   The whole point of branding is to stand out, to be noticed, to differentiate yourself, to be consistently you . . . not to switch back and forth to what you think the people around you are, or to camouflage yourself.

Being a chameleon goes way beyond being flexible or adaptable. These two attributes are social skills that everyone should have in their arsenal. Chameleons try to please everyone, or at least they try not to offend anyone. However, branding is not about trying to appeal to everybody or get everyone's business. It is about carving out a niche and focusing in on a particular target audience.

CONSEQUENCES

Playing the chameleon dilutes your brand's integrity. You may think others appreciate you for having a changeable nature, but you will find that behind your back they will label you as inconsistent, unreliable, wishy-washy, if they notice you at all! Strong brands are not afraid to go against the grain. In fact this behavior is necessary to their survival.

Inhibiting expression or pretending to be something that's not inherently you is a drain on your energy. This constant change of behavior does nothing to build a strong, memorable brand. It only raises questions about your true worth. People will wonder what value you bring to the table.

CASE IN POINT

BUT I ALREADY STAND OUT!! I'M JUST TRYING TO BLEND IN! There are many motivations that may lead to playing the chameleon. You may not want to "stand out" because you want to "fit in." This might apply to someone who is the only woman in the room, or the only person of color in the room, or the one with the strong accent. Maybe you're the youngest in your work group, or perhaps the oldest. You might feel uncomfortable with how you look, not comfortable with your weight, height, etc. Well guess what? YOU ARE GOING TO STAND OUT ANYWAY! People notice things that are different. Your visible difference is the beginning of a brand of sorts. So you might as well leverage it. Be thankful you are being looked at versus being overlooked! Your difference isn't necessarily going to go away. If you think so you are as out of touch with reality as "Annie" in the movie "Bridesmaids" when she thought that putting on sunglasses would conceal her identity as she tried to sneak back into first class.

Branding is about breaking out of your comfort zone, to some extent. Do you want to be remembered for being the only woman in the room or the man with that funny name and accent; or do you want to be remembered for being the person who had valuable points to contribute, or one who challenged the group's thinking, or brought new energy to the discussion? It's a beneficial exercise to think through how you want to be remembered in every situation - that is how you reinforce your brand.

"Do I really need to be deliberate about how I come across in In EVERY SITUATION?" Yes, at least to some degree. In a business setting where you are there to contribute (such as a meeting or panel discussion) the need for monitoring how you come across is fairly obvious. A situation where you are there to learn (e.g., training class or conference) provides another opportunity to manage your "presence". In a learning setting, it's not advisable to hog the time to illustrate your brand, but you could use the

opportunity to make an authentic connection with others – to bring something personal about yourself into the discussion, particularly if you are in front of your target audience. Specific things you can do to be memorable in this setting include:

- Playing devil's advocate (challenging in a diplomatic way) when everyone seems to be in agreement
- Sharing a brief example of a professional experience that relates to a learning point the instructor is making
- Making sure you are heard – speaking audibly, clearly and engaging others through eye contact
- Reaching out to someone during a workshop break to ask a follow-up question and stimulate further thinking. *"What did you think about the presenter's remarks on . . . ? Here's my reaction. . ."*

So how do we get caught up in playing the chameleon? Here's one scenario. Let's say that what you really believe to be your differentiator or value proposition is that you are outspoken, passionate, a risk taker, and you use this to help work teams solve problems. This brand has served you well in community organizations, at church, and with your peers. However, around your manager, and her peers, you tone down your passion and defer problem solving to someone else, and take on a persona you feel will be more agreeable. So you "switch lanes" to come across as more conservative and factual, while inside you are about to boil over with out-of-the-box ideas. Then when you are around senior leaders, your true brand becomes even less visible. You switch into the sagely observer, the "yes-person" brand.

Some of you may think "switching lanes" is simply a way to be political. However, there is a difference between being political and fading into the background. Being politically savvy involves understanding the hierarchy, influencers, communication norms, your audience's needs and preferences, and the impact of alternative courses of action. This is important intel to have as you decide on appropriate actions and build your brand. Being political does not require you to go unnoticed.

Self-Monitoring and Unconscious Chameleons

Self-monitoring theory is a contribution to the psychology of personality, as proposed by Mark Snyder in 1974. The theory describes the extent to which individuals are concerned with managing impressions and the process through which people regulate their behavior so that they will be perceived by others in a favorable manner.

A "high self-monitor" is someone who is concerned with how they are perceived by others and will change their behavior in order to fit different situations. Conversely, "low self-monitors" do not share a similar concern for situational appropriateness. Low self-monitors tend to express themselves in a manner consistent with their beliefs, attitudes, and dispositions regardless of the social circumstance.

In a 1992 research study, Tracy Alderman hypothesized and concluded that within Snyder's two self-monitoring styles (high and low) there exist four subtypes which manifest in meaningfully different ways. These four subtypes were found through crossing self-monitoring with social desirability (or the need to obtain social approval and the tendency to act in socially appropriate ways). They include:

- **Conscious Chameleons** – (Individuals who are high in both self-monitoring and social desirability). This is someone who is highly in tune with what others think of him and who also has a strong need for approval.

- **Instrumentalists** (Individuals who are high in self-monitoring and low in social desirability). This is someone who is highly in tune with what others think of her but who does not have a strong need for approval.

- **Unconscious Chameleons** (Individuals who are low self-monitors and are high in social desirability). This includes those who do not tune into how they are presenting themselves but have a strong need for approval.

- **Self-Presenters** (Individuals who are low in both self-monitoring and social desirability). Those who do not tune into how they are presenting themselves and could care less what others think fit into this category.

ROAD TO RECOVERY

Stepping out of your camouflage requires observation, focus, and reflection.

1. Be strongly entrenched in who you are . . . just know how to be flexible. What does that mean? Demonstrate that you are open to others' ideas, but make sure you also contribute your own.

2. Many of the pointers for being authentic apply here. In addition, you will benefit by identifying those situations where your behavior change is a stretch -- where you don't feel good during or afterwards.
    *   Change your behavior in those situations to what is more authentic to you, and take note of peoples' reactions.
    *   Change your environment or social networks and test your authentic tendencies with a new audience.

3. Identify what makes you switch lanes.
    *   Start by thinking about the people you hang out with (for business) with whom you feel good. In all likelihood, the conversation is balanced in terms of give and take. They listen to you. They share. No one is ego tripping. Or perhaps the people you feel most comfortable around are those that consistently, yet respectfully challenge you, get you to see a different point of view, help you learn new things about yourself and the context in which you operate.
    *   Now think about those people you are trying to impress upon that you don't feel comfortable with, but you hang out with them anyway (to get business, to get an entrée to someone else). What are you expressing in these situations that is not true to who you are? Hint. Are you smiling, when you secretly want to wring someone's neck? Are you agreeing, either silently or vocally, just to avoid creating waves?

EXERCISE: Flexible, Political or Chameleon?

Can you tell the difference between behaviors that suggest you are being flexible, political, or a chameleon? Test this out with the examples below.

	a. Being flexible	b. Being political	c. Being a chameleon
1. Expressing my opinion and demonstrating my openness towards opposing views			
2. Voicing an opinion I believe will resonate most with the group I am in			
3. Sharing my opposing view one-on-one with a leader/team member in order to enable him/her to save face			
4. Listening carefully and observing verbal cues and adjusting my delivery method to my audience			
5. Watching my words carefully so as not to make anyone uncomfortable			
6. Dumbing down my vocabulary so as not to appear smarter than the group I am with			
7. Dressing somewhat more conservatively for a meeting with clients			
8. Wearing eyeglasses (even though I don't need them) when addressing a group of professors so that I will come across as an "intellectual"			
9. Accepting an invitation from my manager which requires me to dress up (even though I don't like it) to attend a company sponsored gala			

Answers: 1.a 2.c 3.b 4.a 5.b 6.c 7.a 8.c 9.b

#5 FOOT IN MOUTH SYNDROME

!

If you have made mistakes, even serious ones, there is always another chance for you. What we call failure is not the falling down but the staying down.
--Mary Pickford

WHAT IT MEANS

You put your foot in your mouth, or perhaps you should have to have kept your thoughts silent. You said or did something that has damaged your reputation because it was offensive to someone and heard in public or went viral on the Internet. Or maybe you did or said something that just went against the image you are trying to build. Perhaps it was an attempt at a joke or some utterance that did not make any sense.

CONSEQUENCES

"Foot in Mouth" represents a very expansive category of behaviors and offenses that range from immediately forgettable to unforgiveable. In some cases these behaviors might actually be illegal, unethical, or perceived as immoral.

- As many know, being offensive is one of the fastest ways to ruin your reputation unless like comedian, Don Rickles, you make your living by doing so.
- Depending on the severity, this could be a potential career ender, particularly if you put your organization at risk, from a liability stance.
- At minimum, you could lose respect from friends, family, and strangers.

CASE IN POINT

You might think a one-time offense or questionable remark might not count for much, but you could build a line that wraps around the Coliseum with one-line offenders. Remember Don Imus' offensive references to female

43

players on the Rutgers Women's Basketball team or former Vice President Dan Quayle's misspelling of the word "potato."

And then there are those who had their 15 minutes of fame and botched it. Vanessa L. Williams' infamous expose in Penthouse Magazine resulted in her losing her title as Miss America, yet her acting career has certainly restored itself. Another pageant contestant also made it into the "Foot-in-Mouth" hall of fame. When asked why she thought one-fifth of Americans couldn't locate the United States on a map at the 2007 Miss Teen USA pageant, contestant Lauren Caitlin Upton, Miss Teen South Carolina, gained instantaneous notoriety for providing a rambling and non-sensible response. She certainly wasn't the first pageant contestant to do so, but given social media, she became one of the most recognized. According to YouTube, video clips of her response on the website have had over 78 million views and it was the site's most viewed video during the month of September 2007.

Upton's story is worth noting because she took lemons and made a hefty pitcher of lemonade in a relatively short period of time. She owned up to her faux pas. As a guest on NBC's *The Today Show*, Upton told Ann Curry and Matt Lauer that she was overwhelmed when asked the question and did not comprehend it correctly. She then utilized her air time to give a more well-thought out response.

Upton was able to laugh at herself and capitalize on it. She has since signed a deal with Donald Trump's modeling agency in New York City and has appeared on several network and cable shows. Upton attended the 2007 MTV Video Music Awards, where she performed a parody of her famous response. She also appeared on an episode of the TLC series *King of the Crown* and on a 2009 Comedy Central's episode of *Tosh.0* and MTV show, Ridiculousness. She did not let her public misstep paralyze her. Conversely she rode the wave while it was high.

ROAD TO RECOVERY

There are a number of directions we can take to rebuild our brand, after we have done something offensive or questionable.

1. Come back with a sincere apology. Talk to your stakeholders (whomever they may be) about how you have learned from your mistake and how you plan to make amends or avoid the offense in the future.

2. Lay low, do the time, and raise your EQ (emotional intelligence quotient). Build awareness around the issue in which you committed the offense. Address your blind spots with education and feedback you solicit from others. People who see you are sincerely trying to make amends or learn from the situation will applaud you. So make your recovery efforts known.

3. Laugh at yourself and campaign your humanness. Take your "show" on the road, like so many celebs do. Capitalize on it. Speak to it. Educate others on it. Make your mistake a valuable teachable moment for others. Turn lemons into lemonade!

4. An opposite approach to the one above would be to move on and encourage others to move on as well. This would be more relevant if what you said was senseless but not so much offensive. So if the embarrassing situation comes up in conversation, you validate it and flip the script. Agree that, "yes I said that; that came out of my mouth." If someone wants to harp on it, show disinterest. "Ok we've all done something stupid. Let's talk about that interesting project you are working on." When people see that they cannot provoke you, eventually they will move on as well.

EXERCISE: Name it! Own it! Reframe it! Move forward!

What Noticeable Mistake did I Make?	How Can I Turn this into a Positive?

What is my comeback strategy?

Do this	By when?	Results I expect to see
Stop doing this	By when?	Results I expect to see
People I should **start** associating with to rebuild my image	By when?	Results I expect to see
People I should **stop** associating with	By when?	Results I expect to see

Make sure you consider who needs to see your comeback plan in action – your target audience.

#6 WALLOWING IN THE "DEAD ZONE"

!

A setback is a setup for a comeback
--Bishop T.D. Jakes

WHAT IT MEANS

This blunder is a close cousin to "Foot in Mouth." However, it is not so much about what you said or did on one or more noticeable occasions. It is more about a continual trajectory your career has taken down the road to nowhere and the inertia that keeps you there.

Let's say you took on a risky role. Perhaps you started off as the golden child at work, but over time your reputation took a nosedive based on any number of factors -- your lack of political savvy, a new boss, your exclusion of some key players, or the continual selection of mediocre performing coworkers for your team. Perhaps it was your demonstration of too much enthusiasm, emotion, or attitude. In the final analysis, your target audience wasn't impressed and started spreading their opinions about you all too readily. This is the opposite of the halo affect – where you can do no wrong. On the contrary, everything you touch seems to turn to rubbish. You are drawing criticism at every turn.

Well jump out of the trash bin! Brush off the smell of dead fish! Get up and move on! Easier said than done? You bet . . . especially in today's economy.

CONSEQUENCES

While changing venues may be difficult, the unwillingness to make a move has unwelcome consequences.

- You develop a strong brand alright . . . one of being a failure, "has been", or "n'er do well."
- Your self-esteem suffers and you may stop believing in your ability to do anything effectively. You become increasingly pessimistic as the dialogue inside of your head turns into an on-going and self-deprecating soliloquy.
- All of your energy is focused on pleasing, proving . . . pointless!
- You may overlook potential opportunities because your mind shuts down to any changes.

CASE IN POINT

Actor, Mickey Rourke, known for *The Pope of Greenwich Village*, *Diner* and *Rumble Fish*, had all but vanished by the early 1990s. Rather than land the kind of starring roles he was once famous for, the self-destructive actor disappeared from the acting front and became infamous for a professional boxing stint and his run-ins with the police.

In an Internet posting of a CBS interview with Rourke he offered the following, "*Once you've been somebody, really, you have a career and you're a nobody, and you're getting older, you're living what's called a state of shame. I went through that in the movie business, you know? You are alone."* . . . "*It took me to lose my wife, my house, my career, my respectability,*" Rourke said. "*I had to fall all the way down.*"

Rourke began to regain visibility and credibility with a leading role in 2005's *Sin City*. However, it was his performance as washed-up pro wrestler Randy "The Ram" Robinson in director, Darren Aronofsky's 2008 flick *The Wrestler* that brought him back to the spotlight. The role, which mirrored his own life in many ways, earned him a Golden Globe and an Academy Award nomination in 2009.

ROAD TO RECOVERY

So what can you do as you are working out your exit and reentrance strategy?

1. Come up for air and exhale.
   - Take a vacation; get away from your toxic environment.

- If you feel you cannot get away from your situation, embrace the monster and make peace with it. Live in the "now" focusing on what you can control.

- As you transition, you may have to get comfortable with being uncomfortable for a while.

2. Read articles about famous and not so famous comebacks – these may inspire you to get off your rusty butt and end the pity party.

3. Do things that will make you feel good about "you." At this stage, the audience you will need to impress most *is* you.

   - Learn something new and develop your skills by taking an online course or a series of webinars.

   - Set short-term goals (things you can complete within two weeks) and celebrate when you achieve them.

4. Seek feedback from trusted sources; someone who can be candid, knows you, and has seen you in action. Find out:

   - Where others may have wanted more information or less

   - What you did that was not clear or was confusing

   - What was perceived as offensive, insensitive or poor judgment on your part

EXERCISE: Lessons Learned

Don't let this lackluster moment in your career define you. Step outside of it. Look at it for what it is worth.

- Identify at least three great things that occurred during this time period and feel good about those three things.

- Identify three things you would have done differently, if you had to do it again, and learn from those.

- Identify three things that you felt led to your derailment, but that you wouldn't have done differently (e.g., play politics, or show less emotion); and use this as feedback for what environment and activities to observe carefully or avoid in the future.

- In what business setting do you think your approach, style, and expertise add value?

#7 HEAD IN SAND SYNDROME

Advice is what we ask for when we already know the answer but wish we didn't.
--Erica Jong

WHAT IT MEANS

Your head is in the sand when you are being oblivious to your brand, or ignoring feedback. It is the delusional belief that "If I can't see anything, then that must mean no one else can see it either." Or "If I haven't heard anything, that must mean there is nothing to hear." "Hear no evil, see no evil, say no evil. Everything must be fine." Hah!!

At the root of this syndrome is fear -- fear that you won't like what you hear, fear that those you are trying to impress are "underwhelmed," or may not even like you, fear that you might need to change something about yourself.

It may be that your ego is so big you can't pull it out of the sand. You are right and the world just does not get it! It would be too upsetting for your protective way of being to hear anything to the contrary. However, when it comes to your career or business it is critical to understand your stakeholders' needs, wants, desires, and preferences. This has to be factored in regardless of how opinionated or committed you are to approaches that you have created.

If your target audience is not giving you feedback, solicit it. Feedback is a gift! Even though you may not like what you receive, you can leverage it to change your direction, clarify expectations, or determine if there is another audience that might value your approach more.

CONSEQUENCES

Keeping your head in the sand prevents you from understanding how others perceive you. Consequently you develop a false sense of security that things are going well. You run the risk of overlooking things because you are not aware of your blind spots; and in this case ignorance is not bliss! When you finally do seek feedback and make changes it is too late to make a difference. You neglected to pull your head up soon enough to avoid the train wreck. The devastating impact on your career can lead to lowered self-esteem or a state of apathy.

 **Candid Feedback is a Gift**

Some people don't mind giving you direct feedback. But there are others who will sugarcoat it. The way you frame your request will make the difference. For example, you can tell individuals that given a specific project you are working on, you want to know what impact it's having on others and would like to know where there are opportunities for improvement and what you are already doing well. This gives them a framework for sharing good and critical feedback. Giving them forced choice options helps as well – Ask others to give you the "good, the bad, and the ugly."

Another way to get candid feedback is to place someone in the "messenger" role. Here, you would ask something like *"What's the word on the street about me?" What are the people you have access to saying about me – good and not so good?"* This enables your colleagues to share candid information more easily since it is assumed that it originates from another source. They may truly be giving you information from other sources or this could be their way of giving you their personal insights.

When people offer feedback, accept it as you would a gift, graciously, even if you don't like or agree with it. Remember these perspectives are reality from the individual's point of view. This is not the time for debate. If you choose to do so, the person you approached will be less willing to give you candid feedback in the future.

CASE IN POINT

Cal was a recent hire to a large insurance company. He was in a project manager position within one of the regional Information Technology units. After six months, he felt a bit uneasy as he was not making a lot of progress on a special project he had been given. However his manager, nor anyone else, had made much comment other than to ask how things were going. Cal decided that no news was good news. Throughout the year, his manager teamed him with other more tenured employees to help him gain traction on his project. Cal did not have a problem with this as it enabled him to reach the deadline set for completing the project. Six months later, during Cal's annual performance review discussion, he was floored by the low ratings he received. In addition, his manager suggested he move into a different position with less responsibility.

Who was at fault here? Certainly Cal's manager should have provided ongoing feedback throughout the year. But Cal also had the responsibility of soliciting feedback when none was provided. No news may only mean that your manager is uncomfortable giving bad news.

ROAD TO RECOVERY

Ready to pull your head out of the sand?

1. Have a conversation with the crabs or other sand creatures, and then pull your head out. Translated – Have a "tough love" conversation with yourself. Ask yourself what you are hiding from and why you think it is safer to be in the dark. Think through what you think the worst case scenario would be if you were to seek feedback as well as the benefits you might receive.

2. Identify three people you can trust and schedule a date each month in which you will reach out to them to connect, as well as solicit feedback. Have some specific questions in mind.

3. Don't be so hard on yourself. "Rome was not built in a day." Ease out of ignorance or your state of bliss into an increasingly more realistic realm. You will most likely need to use some sort of self-

motivation technique to help you on your journey and adjust to the light. Establish some milestones (e.g., setting up feedback meetings) and reward yourself along the way. Keep in mind that it typically takes a few months to solidify a new habit. You may be testing out new behaviors that go outside of your comfort zone.

4. For the bull-headed egoists . . . ah . . . not so fast. Don't skip past this section, even those of you who think you're descendants of Mother Teresa. It is easy to move through life in your own head; most of us do. It is more commendable to be able to understand and empathize with others. In the long term this understanding will enable you to work more effectively with others improving their perception of you and your brand.

This is a two part process. The first part involves being self-aware and noting the impact that you have on others. The second part requires looking at the world from someone else's point of view -- getting inside of their head. If you are very egotistical, this exercise might be tougher for you, but it is not impossible. You may not care much about what others think about you. Or you may make faulty assumptions about what others think of you based on the limited data you receive and how you filter it.

A useful exercise for building awareness is provided on the following page.

EXERCISE: Total Recall – Two Views of Reality

Practice this exercise with someone you can trust. It could be a family member or friend. Here's a role-play to work through. Bring up a situation that the two of you were involved in sometime in the recent past. Ask them to write down their take on it and then ask them to write down what they thought your take on it was. You would do the same. Go through this exercise for another two or three situations. You should probably see a theme emerging shortly – that the "reality" (of any situation) is in the eye of the beholder.

Situation:

My recollection of the situation and how effectively it went
I thought . . .

My assumption of your recollection of the situation and how effectively it went
You probably thought . . .

#8 NOT ADDRESSING THE ELEPHANT

IN THE ROOM

!

You are the handicap you must face.
You are the one who must choose your place.
--James Lane Allen

There may be those of you reading this who are still not on board with branding. Let's take a few minutes to address this hesitation for it might stem from your subconscious mind. You cannot genuinely commit to branding until you surface these potential objections. Why might you be hesitant to brand?

Does branding seem inconsistent with what you value or feel is the right thing to do?

Do you feel that there is something inherently wrong with promoting yourself? You would not be alone. Many individuals have acknowledged that it doesn't feel right to toot their own horn. It feels like bragging and showing off. I can fully understand this perspective. I know how much of a turn-off it is to be around people who do nothing but talk about themselves – their accomplishments, their children's accomplishments, their next projects, their hopes, dreams, their problems. . . shut up already!! And you probably do not want to be thought of in that regard. Let me state this clearly. Branding does not equal bragging. Branding transcends bragging. In other words . . . Branding is not limited to talking about yourself, although that is one component. The goal is for others to be talking about you, playing you up, talking about your value in a way that reinforces your brand and nets you the outcomes you want.

Is it your cultural upbringing?

Gender, generation, geography and genetics all play a role in your identity and how you express yourself. In general I find that men appear to be more comfortable with sharing their accomplishments than women. Generation X and the Millennials seem to latch on to self-promotion more so than Baby Boomers and Traditionalists. And while this might be my imagination, Easterners and Southerners appear to talk more about themselves than Midwesterners. The point here is that our upbringing and even the era in which we were born all contribute to our socialization – how we behave within society and what we feel is appropriate to express. Our behaviors were most likely influenced and reinforced by our family, communities in which we grew up, and institutions we attended (such as school, church and work). Think about some of the messages you received early on that may have shaped the way you feel about personal branding.

Is it because of your religious beliefs?

As I was facilitating a branding workshop, one of the participants asked the question, *"Okay, let's just put this on the table. What about those of us who feel branding goes against our religious beliefs? God should be given the glory for our skills and talents."* The room came to a quiet hush and then five more heads in succession started nodding and looking to what I would say next.

This is how I feel about that. You can not acknowledge or convey to others God's role in your life unless it is demonstrated through you – unless you let YOUR light shine. In fact I would go as far as to say that you do a disservice to all that you believe in when you don't let this energy flow through you. If you have a special talent or gift, use it and allow others to benefit from it. Who would believe that it is possible for faith to carry you through insurmountable obstacles, to walk in to where doors were currently closed unless they see you in action? How can you inspire others unless you tell them your story? This is how I believe you give God the glory. The Higher Power that you believe in is expressed through you!

COMMON MYTHS ABOUT BRANDING

I need money to brand

Branding does not need to be an expensive endeavor. At work it may require raising your hand for the right assignments. During and after work, it may mean that you spend more time networking. At most it may require an update to your collateral pieces (e.g., resume, business cards, etc.) or wardrobe. It is primarily an investment in your *time* to reflect on what you have been doing and to solicit input from others on how this is received. It requires planning, observing, and connecting with others.

I need a publicist

For professions that are in the public eye, such as entertainers, professional athletes, and/or politicians, this may be true. For the rest of us, a publicist is not a requirement, perhaps a nice-to-have, but not a necessity. In fact the many people that are already a part of your network can serve as publicists for you by speaking on your behalf, introducing you to new people and inviting you into different venues.

I need to be a professional

For those who are in entry level jobs, clerical jobs, labor jobs, or have not yet started your careers, personal branding is still a relevant topic. What value you bring and how you differ from others in similar roles will always cross the minds of the individuals you come into contact with. Unless you have a uniquely specialized skill set that is difficult to find, there will always be competition.

Your wow factor might be your personality, the creative touches you incorporate into your work, or your resourcefulness and problem solving capabilities. Whatever it is, you will benefit from identifying it and leveraging it to your advantage.

I don't need to brand if I already work somewhere

We work in a global economy where companies are restructuring and reinventing themselves on a more frequent basis and calling upon their employees to be more agile. They are no longer wed to holding on to talent on a permanent basis. They have adopted outsourcing and other "shrink and grow" strategies. Organizations sustain and develop individuals that can contribute to their core business processes and those that can help innovate so that their offers are more competitive. Consequently individuals must continually reinforce, redefine and/or reinvent their value proposition to align with the direction of the business.

Branding can also translate into increased financial rewards. If your value proposition is clearly known, you have negotiating power. Organizations will do more to attract you, retain you and invest in your development.

I can't effectively brand if I am an introvert

While being introverted might imply you are more self-reflective, draw energy by spending time alone, and may not be entirely chatty, it does not mean you can't display your value or make an emotional connection with people. Many people who are introverted have been quite successful positioning and distinguishing themselves based on their talents. In fact, according to a 2006 article in USA Today,

> " . . . *four in 10 top executives test out to be introverts. . . The list of well-known corporate CEO introverts reads like a Who's Who, starting with Gates, who has long been described as shy and unsocial, and who often goes off by himself to reflect. Others widely presumed to be introverts include Warren Buffett, Charles Schwab, movie magnate Steven Spielberg and former Sara Lee CEO Brenda Barnes.*"

While who you are and what you bring must be visible to others, this can be done in many ways including through written and email communication, or in one-on-one meetings. Networking with others is necessary, but this does not mean you have to be the social butterfly of the event. Know who you want to connect with and why, make sure to surround yourself with individuals who can speak on your behalf by letting them know about your accomplishments and what you are interested in, and plan your time wisely.

Be prepared to share something about yourself with strangers (e.g., your elevator speech*) and then get to know them. This will help you hone into their interests, needs and what you share in common. While effective communication skills are critical, personal branding does not have to involve an ongoing tirade of networking functions and large-group presentations.

If I am doing well in my role, I don't need to brand

Famous last words! Today's golden child is tomorrow's step child. If you are doing well, most likely it expands beyond performance. Take note of the things you are doing well with regard to your image and exposure. Also keep in mind that as you evolve within your career, your target audience may change and have different perceptions about you and expectations of you.

Branding is for companies or business owners

Savvy career management involves you thinking about yourself as your own entity – Me.com – even if you have an employer. View yourself as a free agent who can pick and choose what team you would like to be on. To do so, you must still stay at the forefront of the league's conversations in order to stay marketable. What have you done for the league lately?

You are a product; and consequently you can easily be removed from the shelf or to a more obscure position at any time. Gone are the days of cradle to grave employment. Your career sustainability is dependent on you taking an active role in career management which involves deliberate and conscious personal branding. View yourself as the CEO of You, Incorporated!

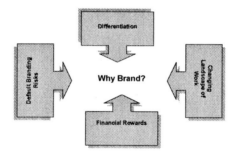

Regardless of whether you are active about promoting your brand or not, people will have a perception of you, your work, and your worth. If you don't brand yourself, others will. Is the perception that is "out there" the one you want? Creating a self-brand is a way to manage those perceptions -- a way to set the record straight!

Going Up?

*An elevator speech is a short pitch about yourself that can quickly catch the attention of your audience and be delivered in about 30 seconds. This speech is often used at networking and other social events. It should convey something about who you are, what you do, and the benefits and unique aspects of your business, job or projects you are working on. Your overview should be memorable and help you create a connection with the individual(s) you are speaking to.

EXERCISE: My Elevator Speech

Create two versions of your "elevator speech" and practice rehearsing them until it feels comfortable.

For people who know me

For those I am meeting for the first time

#9 MISLEADING PACKAGING

!

. . . you can learn as much — or more — from one glance at a private space
as you can from hours of exposure to a public face.
-- Malcolm Gladwell, Blink 2005

WHAT IT MEANS

Appearances count. As much as we wish they would not, they make a difference and people's opinions of us will be based on these visible impressions until they get to know us at more than a superficial level. It's the packaging that creates the anticipation, the expectation that a certain quality of service will be provided or that a certain type of experience will be had. Think of products you buy. You either go for packaging that is recognizable, and therefore predictable, or something that appeals to you emotionally. Packaging that is congruent with the product within it relieves or reassures us. Packaging that is not may either pleasantly surprise us or leave us scratching our heads. Think about the initial reaction you may have had when Heinz began marketing its ketchup in funky purple, green and blue hues.

Well at the time, my pre-teen son was in love with this product and requested it every time we passed by its shelf in the grocery store. As for me . . . I cringed at the thought of the product. I had flashbacks to my son squeezing the ketchup bottle over a plate of fries and green or purple stuff oozing out on to the crispy potatoes. Yuck! I couldn't imagine anyone wanting to put that combination in their mouths. This was such a huge disconnect for me. Now, I imagine someone could become just as grossed out over seeing something "blood red" oozing out of a bottle onto a plate of fries. But I associated this with being "normal" and even "desirable." The younger market Heinz was trying to appeal to probably thought the concept was "groovy." The more mature market, on the other hand, might have had some reservations about using ketchup that wasn't red.

For consumer goods, memorable and appealing packaging has wording that is clear, with an engaging design, and colors that are typically vivid and energizing or subtle and calming, depending on the product. For individuals, packaging includes several elements. It is reflected in:

☐ Your personality
☐ Your communication style
☐ Your appearance
☐ Your resume and other collateral pieces
☐ Your work environment (office, desk)
☐ Your associations (those you hang out with).

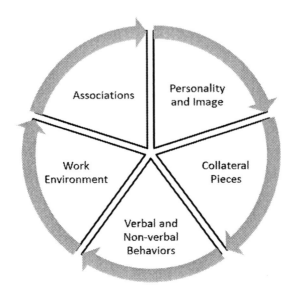

CONSEQUENCES

When your packaging conflicts with what you are trying to brand, people may feel that you cannot deliver on something that you really can and they, consequently, will not seek you out for opportunities that you are interested in. Or conversely, if you are representing something totally disingenuous, people will think that you can and want to deliver on something that you are really not interested in and will ask you to do things that are not personally fulfilling, engaging or beneficial to your career development. The bottom line is that people may bypass you for relevant opportunities if they come to the conclusion that what you present, visually and behaviorally, disconnects from what they think you should be presenting.

CASE IN POINT

I once worked for an organization where one of my colleagues had a reputation of being the consummate project manager. We will call her Doris. Doris was known for providing exceptional direction to cross functional teams, leading them through process improvement efforts in a systematic and efficient manner and meeting and exceeding expectations for completing projects under deadline. She displayed a blend of seeing the big picture, understanding all the little details, and helping to guide others through projects. Doris was sought after to lead projects for both internal and external clients.

I scheduled a meeting with Doris to get her insights on a project I was working on. She worked in another building and I volunteered to come to her office. When I arrived, I poked my head in to let her know I was there, and then had to do a double-take! There was Doris sitting in the middle of heaps of files about to fall over. . . on the floor, on her desk, on her credenza and, oh my! It was "A HOT MESS!"

During the course of our meeting, Doris spun around in her chair, like a whirling dervish, going from desk to credenza, to stacks on the floor looking for notes on slips of paper, in file folders and . . . "you name it." I had to remind myself several times to close my dropping jaw, to disguise my amazement. Needless to say, this was a big disconnect for me. How did she pull it off -- this icon of a project leader? My expectation was that her office would be neat and organized with efficient filing systems, where information was readily accessible. The packaging (her office) was not consistent with the reputation (her brand). I walked out with a big question mark over my head. It made me think back to an article interview I had with a Senior VP at Kraft. In this interview she shared with me that advice can come from anywhere and that early in her career a custodian once gave her some sagely advice that stuck with her. The custodian looked around her office and then tactfully told her that when he cleaned up the offices of other executives, the rooms were already spotless. All of the senior leaders had offices that looked a certain way. Neatness and order were a part of the leadership brand and this was reflected in their work environment.

ROAD TO RECOVERY

Is your packaging consistent with the brand you are trying to convey? How can you transfer those "***Appeal***" concepts to "Brand You"?

1. Pay attention to both your verbal and nonverbal behavior. Does it match the role or brand you are trying to project?
2. Dress the part. Make sure your attire aligns with the professional image you are trying to portray. Take a good look in a long mirror -- every day!
3. Attend a workshop or webinar on dressing for success.
4. Take inventory of your surroundings, your affiliations and networks, and your collateral pieces (e.g., business cards, resume, web-site). Do these reflect professionalism and add to your credibility?
5. Think of people whose brand you admire. What is it about them that stands out? Think beyond the skills or talents they have and focus on the way they deliver or express themselves.
6. Get feedback from others that see you on a regular basis – Ask the question – *"Do you think the way I present myself is consistent with my brand"* or *"What about the way I present myself – my clothes, appearance, body language, vocal tone – reinforces my brand of being a _____ and what takes away from that brand?"*
7. If you have the money, you may want to retain an Image Consultant if you are in a highly visible or public role.
8. You could also hire a communications coach to give feedback on how effectively and confidently you express yourself. A good friend or colleague could play this role, as well.

EXERCISE: Make-over Survey

Survey five individuals on what they would suggest you do if you were to get a makeover that was consistent with the professional role you are in or are seeking.

Suggestions	What I will commit to
Individual #1 _____	
Individual #2 _____	
Individual #3 _____	
Individual #4 _____	
Individual #5 _____	

#10 IGNORING YOUR TARGET MARKET

!

Think like a wise man but communicate in the language of the people.
--William Butler Yeats

WHAT IT MEANS

In analyzing your brand's effectiveness, it is important to understand who your target market is. Your target market or audience includes those individuals to whom you are trying to sell your product. In personal branding, your product is you, and so your audience consists of the individuals with whom you need to impress, gain visibility and access to, gain trust, influence, and stay top of mind.

Evolving Needs - The needs and interests of this audience will tend to evolve over time. There is also the possibility that your target audience may change altogether. Depending on your role in your organization, your target audience may have started out as your manager and co-workers. It may have evolved to include other functional areas, internal or external clients. As your career matured, the audiences you needed to impress may have extended to senior executives, boards of directors, and possibly the national or global community. Understanding who you are trying to influence or "sell to" is a critical first step in revisiting your personal brand's effectiveness.

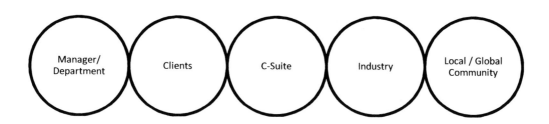

69

CONSEQUENCES

As you evolve in your career the major stakeholders that have an interest in what you do may change. Consequently the activities, outcomes, image that you conveyed with a former target audience may no longer be relevant, influential or effective. Your stakeholders or target audience may likely change if you get a promotion, change professions, move to a new business unit, location, or company.

Even if your target audience stays the same, their needs will likely change over time. Your inattention to this will diminish your brand's value and your audience will doubt your interest, expertise, and credibility.

Your single-mindedness on your career interests without consideration of your target audience is what marketers refer to as "marketing myopia." This phenomenon takes place when a company or individual becomes "product-oriented" instead of "customer-oriented" focusing on what they have to offer as opposed to what the customer wants and needs.

CASE IN POINT

Debra had a role as an internal communications consultant for her company's community outreach and public relations division. She supported the division by preparing various communication pieces including press releases, internal newsletter content, policies, strategy documents, program protocols, and other related materials. The director for the division was scheduled to take three months off for parental leave. Debra was asked to step in as interim director, which would require her to be a spokesperson to employees and all levels of management within the company, as well as to external stakeholders. She would need to sit in on daily meetings, evening dinners, present updates at external events, as well as coach senior leaders on what to present. Debra was familiar with the role given that she was currently the one to prepare all of the written communication for these meetings and presentations. She was flattered to be able to step into the role and viewed this as a chance to demonstrate her leadership skills.

After the first couple of weeks of performing in the role, the VP for Debra's area called her into his office to give her some feedback. Apparently, he had been receiving comments from internal employees that Debra did not demonstrate a "leadership presence" in carrying out her new responsibilities. She was a bit puzzled as she knew that the content of her messages was on target. Her VP mentioned that her delivery style appeared a bit to informal and casual for senior managers and for the public. He also indicated that the amount of information provided was a bit too detailed, and that she was not as respectful as she could be of her audience's time constraints. He suggested that she work with another Division Director and a communications coach during the remainder of her interim assignment in order to think through what she could do differently.

Debra's main misstep was in neglecting to study and seek feedback from her new target audience (senior management and the public) as well as minimizing her need to understand her company's definition of leadership. She made the assumption that what worked in her previous role would work in her new interim role as director.

ROAD TO RECOVERY

In defining where you can add value for your target audience, you must first identify where the need exists. This question can be answered after analyzing the organization's internal environment and external marketplace.

1. Focus on your target market's pain points. Ask yourself:
   - What business problems need to be solved?
   - What business needs aren't being met?
   - How can I take advantage of new trends and changes in the industry?

2. The process outlined above parallels that of conducting a SWOT analysis – identifying the Strengths, Weaknesses, Opportunities, and Threats – of the industry or profession within which you work. Additionally it is imperative that you understand the current as well as strategic direction of the overall business in which you are working.

3. Interview a few individuals from your target audience to get their perspective on needs and opportunities.

4. Build awareness by attending industry conferences, joining professional groups or social media networks, and reading trade publications.

EXERCISE: Target Market Analysis

Use the worksheet on the next page to identify your target audience and their current and future needs. Assess yourself against these needs and determine where there is a match or gap. For those areas in which there is a gap, write down a few things you can do now to close the gap.

WORKSHEET: Target Market Analysis

Who is in my target audience? _____

Target Audience	Self-Assessment	Match? ✓	or Gap? ✓
General skills and services needed by target audience?	Do these match my skills, strengths and talents? ☐ Yes ☐ Partially ☐ No		
What's unique about my offer?	Is this visible to my target audience? ☐ Yes ☐ Partially ☐ No		
Unmet needs (opportunities) within my target audience?	Do I have solutions to offer? ☐ Yes ☐ Partially ☐ No		
Overall culture and image within my target audience?	Is this compatible with my personality, values? ☐ Yes ☐ Partially ☐ No		
How do I anticipate my target audience changing in the next few years?	Will I need to modify my brand? ☐ Yes ☐ Partially ☐ No		
With what new issues will this audience be concerned?	Do these match my skills, strengths and talents? ☐ Yes ☐ Partially ☐ No		

Action Plan for Closing the Gap

Gap area	Two to three things I can do now to close the gap

#11 LETTING YOUR BRAND BECOME RUSTY

The problem is never how to get new, innovative thoughts into your mind, but how to get old ones out. Every mind is a building filled with archaic furniture. Clean out a corner of your mind and creativity will instantly fill it.
--Dee Hock

WHAT IT MEANS

What has your brand done for you lately? This is a question you should be asking yourself on a regular basis. Why? Because great personal brands, like great company and product brands stand the test of time. The owners of these brands know when to adapt to ensure they maintain the appeal necessary to captivate their target markets.

Going through the exercise of building a personal brand is a thorough process, but it is not a one-time event. It involves understanding and appreciating what you stand for, what you have to offer, and what your target audience wants. It requires that you get feedback on top of feedback on how others perceive you, to determine if others' perceptions mesh with how you are attempting to portray yourself. It requires a lot of thinking and testing -- thinking about what differentiates you from others, how to make that come to life, and then testing how effective you are at it.

CONSEQUENCES

Your brand is not meant to be changed like an article of clothing. Similar to your personality it should be somewhat stable in your life. However given the changes in the world of work, communication, and technology it stands to reason that you will need to either fine-tune, expand or modify your brand at some point in your career. If your brand has not done anything for you

75

lately, like any endangered species, it has the potential to become extinct, invisible, and out of print! People will not seek you out for things that you have interest or passion around. You may be marketing yourself in a way that no longer resonates with your target audience. They will move on to the next more refreshing brand. You'll become just another commodity.

For example, your brand of being "detailed oriented," "efficient" and "no-nonsense" may serve you well if you are a statistician or mechanic. However if you move into a role where you are now managing people or running a business unit, you may need to expand your brand to include "leader" "effective people developer," and "strategic." Sometimes enhancing your brand equates to demonstrating different skill sets. If you don't currently have these skill sets, you may need to work on acquiring them.

How do you know if your brand is not working anymore? There are probably clear markers when your brand has failed. However, you may need to do some additional digging to determine if your brand is rusty or stagnant. A stagnant brand has no traction. While it may not be a career ender for you, it does not work for you, either. Some indications of a stagnant brand are: individuals are not reaching out to you (the product) as often; you seem to be overlooked when promotions, assignments, or networking opportunities come about. People aren't aware of your contributions. You are chosen for the same type of non-growth projects time and time again. Like the careers of some actors – you may have been typecast!

CASE IN POINT

We can look at the automotive industry for numerous examples of brands that have disappeared or are on the verge of extinction. As an example, GM's Hummer was an SUV based on the design of a military vehicle known as the High Mobility Multipurpose Wheeled Vehicle, or "Humvee." During the early 2000s, the Hummer was a popular vehicle, but it was also highly criticized. People in smaller vehicles felt intimidated by the enormous size of hummers on the road. The Hummer like many large vehicles was adversely impacted by the 2008 recession. Its substandard gas mileage was an issue for consumers, demand dropped; and so GM ultimately discontinued production of the brand for the civilian market.

There are many brands that are not flexible enough to be sustainable over time. This presents corporations with the opportunity to introduce new brands or energize current brands. Introducing a new brand takes significant lead time and this is also true for a personal brand. Ongoing monitoring of your brand's impact and effectiveness along with regular "refreshes" will help you stay from behind the eight ball.

ROAD TO RECOVERY

How do you resuscitate your brand? In general, it is advisable to think about your goals and the direction your career is taking on an annual basis. Performance development and planning discussions with your manager or an executive coach can facilitate this.

1. Additionally, set aside some time alone (e.g., a long weekend) reflecting on all aspects of your life and identify how the career piece of the puzzle is fitting in. During this reflection, you can ask yourself whether or not your personal brand is effective, has failed, or has just become stagnant. In all likelihood, you may need to start with whether or not you even have a brand.

2. Aside from the annual review of your brand, other times your brand should be revisited include when you have transitioned to a new role, have moved to a new company or business unit, or have received consistent feedback that does not connect with the impact you feel you are making.

3. While a career setback may signal the need to reevaluate your brand, it does not always mean that you need to change your brand. It may mean that you need to reinforce it and bring it back to life. Dig deep to understand what contributed to the setback. Was it performance related, skill related, or political? How much was within your control? When the reasons begin to point to your overall visibility, or lack of, your effectiveness in connecting with key stakeholders, or the level to which people understand what you do and stand for, you then have reason to suspect that your personal branding efforts have missed the mark. There are many branding assessment tools to help you with this process.

EXERCISE: What has my Brand Done for me Lately?

I can tell my brand is working because:

I don't think my brand is working because:

My brand needs: (which one of the following):	Two or three things I can do to accomplish this:
☐ Expansion	
☐ More focus	
☐ Rebuilding	

#12 IGNORING YOUR CYBER BRAND

!

When I took office, only high energy physicists had ever heard of
what is called the Worldwide Web....
Now even my cat has its own page.
--Bill Clinton

WHAT IT MEANS

Are you using rusty tools to sharpen your brand? Are you overlooking the opportunity to leverage online tools and social media? The tools to which we have access, to connect with others and make visible our personal brand, have evolved exponentially in the last couple of decades. At the end of March 2013, Facebook announced that it had 1.11 billion monthly active users. If it were a country it would be the world's third largest in terms of population, making it bigger than the U.S. In 2012, Twitter boasted that it hosts more than 400 million tweets per day. One hour of video is uploaded to YouTube every second. Users accessing the web through mobile devices have almost doubled every year since 2009. The Internet and social media will enable you to reach thousands upon thousands of individuals and, equally, enable them to reach you. This can serve to strengthen your emotional connection with your target audience. As an example, social media played a pivotal role in the 2008 and 2012 presidential elections.

People can learn a lot about you with the touch of a keystroke. Recruiters, athletic coaches, potential and current clients and customers, friends, former classmates, your relatives -- the list goes on. Is what they see on the Internet favorable to you and your brand?

Do yourself a favor. Stop right now and Google® yourself . . . Alright, get your mind out of the gutter. Search for both "web information" and "images." What do you find? Do you find anything? Most likely, there will be some extraneous information that is not related to you given someone may have the same first or last name as you. But how much relevant information did you find, and was it positive, negative, or neutral?

There are several discoveries that individuals can make about you when they do a search on your name or company.

Components of your online brand or identity

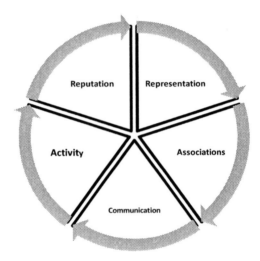

Components of your online brand include:

- **How you are Represented** – who you are, what you do, your professional and personal profile

- **Your Associations** – who your friends and colleagues are (e.g., Facebook friends, Linkedin contacts); what they are posting on your site; sites you have visited and liked; organizations, online professional discussion groups and chat groups you belong to

- **Your Communication** – what you have to say, blog responses, professional engagements you are speaking at, what you saw happen at the game three minutes ago, photos, and videos you have created or have been tagged in

- **Your Activity** – conferences you've attended or spoken at, articles you've written, campaigns you have funded, what you did on vacation

- **Your Reputation** – what are others saying about you, e.g., LinkedIn testimonials and endorsements, tweets, etc.

CONSEQUENCES

The profusion of blogs, tweets, YouTube videos and online discussion forums can allow angry customers, jilted lovers, jealous rivals, or carefree friends to define your identity and potentially destroy your professional brand. Whether valid or not, these comments can have far-reaching effects. In the world of large retailers and customer oriented businesses, this phenomenon is referred to as "groundswell."

Additionally, if you are not managing the content that you place online, you may dilute your brand by sending inconsistent messages, mixing up your personal and professional identities. At minimum you may miss opportunities to showcase your accomplishments and expertise within networks that are relevant to your career aspirations. And at a basic level, you will lose out on one of the best time-saving and efficient ways to reach your target audience, en masse.

CASE IN POINT

I decided to Google® a classmate. He had become a well-known artist in his field. I linked on to his website and perused his gallery. What I saw was incredible and breathtaking. I was so impressed with how talented and successful my classmate had become since graduation. Wanting to see more of his work and what events/openings he had planned, I decided to further search under his name on the Internet. By chance I came across a blog forum that he was a part of. I began to read through the comments, assuming that the participants were talking about art or something related.

To my surprise I found that my friend was engaged in a back and forth debate with a couple of bloggers in which he used extreme and profane language. It caught me off guard. In an instant my impression of my classmate changed 180°. *Who was this person? How unprofessional! Doesn't he know that anyone and everyone has access to these comments?*

I thought a bit about how eccentric artists can be, but ultimately, my discovery brought my classmate down a couple of levels from the pedestal that I had placed him on.

Research suggests that negative information is more memorable than positive information – even if it is only a fraction of what the person represents. Consumers, clients, and employers also tend to make decisions based on the most recent information they have received.

The moral of the story -- negative press takes on a life of its own! Be careful what you say and what you place online as it will live on into perpetuity on the World Wide Web. It will come to represent who you are. If you are trying to control "you" as the brand, you will need to be mindful of the vast array of comments and photos that can either contribute to your brand or destroy it.

ROAD TO RECOVERY

There are several things you can do to create or clean up your on-line brand.

1. Create a brand presence, but use caution in determining which tools you will use and what accounts you will set up. The grid below gives a quick glimpse of online tools that might be useful in your personal branding campaign.

	Description	Useful for:
Facebook	Largest social network site	• Networking, finding old friends and classmates, sharing personal and family photos • Advertising
LinkedIn	Popular social network for business professionals	• Professional Networking • Sharing your bio and accomplishments • Posting presentations you have given • Joining professional discussion

	Description	Useful for:
		forums • Identifying job opportunities • Discovering sales leads and connecting with potential business partners
Twitter	Social media account that allows you to post and receive messages (tweets) to a network of contacts, as opposed to sending bulk email messages	• Networking • Asking and answering questions • Sharing up to the minute developments on what you are doing (e.g., thoughts on a conference session you are sitting in on) • Inviting others to receive your tweets • Following other members' posts • Alternative news source (e.g., information on the 2012 Summer Olympics and presidential campaign were popular tweets)
Voice over Internet Protocol, e.g., Skype	Communication protocols that allow for the transmission of voice, video and text over the Internet	• Allowing users to communicate with others over the Internet • Meetings across several locations • Virtual training and presentations • Connecting with others long distance as an alternative to the telephone
Email Blasts	Electronic mailing of information typically to a large distribution list enabled by special software or a third party service provider (e.g., Constant Contact)	• Starting your own newsletters • Press releases • Distribution list management • Event updates and invitations
YouTube Podcasts and video-casts	Website which enables you to upload, view and share digital audio and video media files	• Creating a video resume • Sharing a presentation or series of presentations on an area of expertise • Alternative news source
Big Tent, etc.	Group collaboration and communication tools	• Group/team collaboration • Scheduling • File sharing
Web-site or Personal Web-page	A site accessible on the Internet which contains a set of related web pages displaying information, graphics and/or videos about a company, product, or person, etc.	• Posting your personal profile, bio, resume • Highlighting your business and selling your services/products • Utilizing as a blog forum

	Description	Useful for:
Blogs	A web log or online discussion forum initiated by you that allows for responses from others on specific topics	• Demonstrating your insights and expertise on a subject. • (You will need to keep it up to date and be responsive to those who post comments on it.)
Mobile devices	Such as your smartphone, tablet, or other PDA	• Managing and accessing all of your online accounts from wherever you are • Quickly responding to emails • Advertising

Remember you don't have to do everything at once. If you start a blog, people will expect you to keep it up to date. If you use Twitter, you may need to check into it every day, possibly multiple times during the day. A lot can happen in an hour.

2. Clean up your information. If you find there are damaging comments about you on the Internet, there are a couple of things you can do:

- For sites you are responsible for you can delete postings, hide comments, unfriend "friends," or cancel memberships.

- It is advisable to keep your professional brand and personal brand separate to some extent. If you are trying to create a serious professional brand, be mindful of what you post (e.g., personal photos, controversial blog posts, etc.) as all of these irrelevant items will pop up when someone does a search on your name, and will consequently dilute your brand strength.

- Use a fictional name for your personal blogs or postings so that you can remain somewhat anonymous.

3. Add more favorable web content so that the "cream" (or positive information) rises to the top (of the search results).

- Enter more blog comments that showcase your expertise. Link these to your personal web page.

- Add links from your web-site to other relevant sites and web-articles about the latest trends in your industry.

- Write short articles or "op ed" pieces and publish on sites like ezine articles and ask.com.

4. You can also leverage an Internet Reputation Management firm to manage your web content if you are willing to spend money. Charging anything from a few dollars to thousands of dollars a month, companies such as International Reputation Management, Naymz and ReputationDefender assure their clients of better results on an Internet search, by saturating the web with positive postings, pushing the positive items up on the first page of the search results and burying the negative items deeper down.

EXERCISE: Social Media Game Plan

WORKSHEET: Social Media Game Plan

Start with manageable bytes!!

Social Media Tool	How I plan to Use it	By When

13 FLYING SOLO

---!---

Learn to regard the souls around you as parts of some grand instrument. It is for each of us to know the keys and stops, that we may draw forth the harmonies that He sleeping in the silent octaves.

--Anonymous

WHAT IT MEANS

This is a collaborative world. In many situations, especially those involving your career advancement, you cannot move mountains alone. It is imperative to work with and through others. Similarly, personal branding is not a solo activity. You don't have to do everything by yourself. When you look at product and company brands, there's a lot of support in place for creating and sustaining the brand. There are publicists. There are multiple distribution channels and numerous ad campaigns. As an individual you can enjoy the same system of support. In fact in order to have a successful brand it is advised that you take full advantage of all of the support networks within your life. You need other people to help spread the good word about you. So what different groups should you reach out to as you develop and enhance your brand?

Your brand champions or publicists – These are the people in your life that have access to target audiences that you would like to impress upon but with whom you currently don't have any interaction. So for example, if you are aspiring to reach senior leaders in your company, but are not invited into their meetings, you should identify someone who can speak on your behalf that does have access. This might be your manager, a mentor, another co-worker, or possibly someone outside of the organization you know who has a social relationship with someone on the leadership team. You can begin to have regular conversations with this individual to plant seeds about what you are interested in, accomplishments that you have achieved, so that they can, in turn, begin to share that with others. You can get feedback from this individual, as well, on the evolving perception that senior leaders have of you. The power of alliances is exponential. There are probably only one or two degrees of separation between your circle of colleagues and the individuals you would like exposure to.

Personal advisors – This is another group that can help you as you are branding yourself and will most likely include some of the same individuals as your brand champion list. Your personal advisor's role is to provide feedback and insights on relevant opportunities that leverage your strengths. This person might be a mentor or a coworker in your unit. It could also be a friend. It is generally someone who knows enough about you to offer some personal coaching. Your manager or supervisor can play this role to a great extent. You can also leverage a professional coach. Someone who plays this role should, at minimum, have had the chance to see you in action in a number of different settings.

Your networks – Another important part of your support system is your network. Branding and networking go hand-in-hand. George Fraser, author of "Click: Ten Truths for Building Extraordinary Relationships", talks about three types of networks: 1) personal networks – which include family, close friends and individuals who can support you; 2) operational networks – groups that help you get various tasks done - these groups change throughout your life; and 3) strategic networks - groups that you are trying to penetrate, individuals who are doing what you want to do (e.g., senior leaders, mentors, etc.). Fraser asserts that successful leaders spend over half of their time cultivating, nurturing and building relationships.

Whatever network we are talking about, your goal should be to spend a devoted portion of your time in these networks. There's no way you can be a brand, if people don't know about you – your product, your service, or what you have to offer; and people are not going to know about you unless you are visible in some way. Now if your brand is expressed through writing, for example, you can reach a lot of people without seeing them. But what keeps you top of mind is your ability to create an emotional connection through periodic interaction, preferably face-to-face. This humanizes you and helps to build and sustain the relationship. *"Who ya gonna call"* when an opportunity arises? -- the writer whose work you respect or the writer whose work you respect and with whom you just finished chatting with after a presentation. People do business with individuals they like, trust, and admire. Even in this era of technology and social media that enables us to go months on end without face-to-face meetings, it is important not to minimize the "power of presence."

CONSEQUENCES

There are risks and consequences in trying to brand all by yourself. One includes myopic thinking or tunnel vision. If you are not getting ideas from other sources, connecting with others, and obtaining feedback, you can develop narrowed thinking around your offer. There might be several things you are doing to dilute your brand that you are not even aware of because you are not getting feedback. You really can't be sure if you are hitting the mark unless there is some sort of acknowledgement within your network and target markets.

You may be offering things that others don't need or you may neglect to tap into a talent you have that would open up new opportunities. Additionally, flying solo results in you missing out on the opportunity to expand your target audience through the connections your colleagues, friends and relatives have.

There are certainly aspects of personal branding you can do alone, particularly those that require self-reflection. However much of branding involves others. Let's borrow from an industry example and look at the branding of a new car model. There are numerous activities that include people outside of the car manufacturer, itself. The manufacturer will organize focus groups to enable experts and the general public to give insight on the new car concept. Then there are tests and product trials to make sure the car is delivering what it was built to provide. Surveys are generally distributed to evaluate the customer's satisfaction with the product. Similarly, you need a structured process, interaction and feedback loop with your target audience to test your brand's effectiveness.

CASE IN POINT

Naomi recently started her own business selling IT consulting services. She was very excited and had done quite a few things right such as developing a business plan and setting aside a year's salary. Naomi created a company identity with business cards and a web-site. She defined her list of services and scheduled several one-on-one meetings to let people know what she was doing. So far, it sounds like she is off to a good start in terms of promoting and marketing herself, right? This activity resulted in her obtaining a couple of initial meetings with companies who could be potential clients; but after five months she still had not received any call-backs.

What Naomi was not doing was as long as the list of things she was doing. In her one-on-one meetings, she talked about what she could offer, but did not take advantage of these opportunities to get feedback on whether or not this was of value. She also was not in the habit of asking the person she was with to spread the word or send her materials on to others. And, perhaps one of her greatest sins was in not following up after the meeting.

Naomi was also putting all of her marketing "eggs in one basket," the one-on-one meetings. While individual meetings can be an effective approach, the typical cycle of business development suggests that any solid contracts from a prospect could be six months to two years out.

Naomi was advised to be more visible on the conference circuit. She found a national IT conference and in looking at the agenda, thought, *"I probably should be presenting at this conference."* She decided to go, and hand out some of her business cards. As she was sitting in on the workshops and general sessions, she realized the wealth of information she was receiving about her industry, its current challenges and opportunities; and wondered if she needed to revamp her service offerings. There were ideas afloat that she had never entertained. Furthermore, she had a chance to interact with her peers and her competition and look at their websites and promotional materials. She also had the opportunity to talk to a lot of people who weren't aware that she had started her own business. Through this experience Naomi learned that even though she had a solid offering that was based on her expertise and experience, she still needed to be more diligent about being visible, networking, and leveraging professional conferences to stay abreast of trends. She has since joined a few local professional organizations at which she volunteers to speak or help coordinate events and has significantly increased her exposure and access to company decision makers.

ROAD TO RECOVERY

The road to recovery requires being disciplined about scheduling time to connect with others, to seek advice, to share what you are doing, and to be visible to your target audience.

1. Attend conferences that align with your profession and industry as well as conferences that don't so that you can stand out as offering something unique. Let's say you are an independent training consultant and go to a national conference sponsored by the American Society of Training and Development (ASTD) thinking you will drum up business. Well guess what? About 6,000 other people are there with the same thought in mind and a lot of these individuals are affiliated with large publicly traded organizations. You can best leverage this type of conference for professional

development, networking, presenting, and potentially for identifying any firms who are looking for contract trainers or employees.

Another option, however, would be to go to a conference that is not comprised of training professionals. Perhaps it's the American Society of Hospital Pharmacists or the International Society of Architects. These are industry conferences where you will be the one who offers a different set of skills. You'll stand out because of the different types of questions you'll ask in the workshops. You can leverage networking receptions to share who you are, what you do, and the perspective you bring. You'll be memorable because of your difference!

2. Begin communicating more via email or social media to stay in touch with those in your target audience, particularly those it is difficult to see on an on-going basis. Send annual holiday greetings. Send occasional links to information you think they would be interested in.

3. Calendaring: Schedule networking meetings on to your calendar on a regular basis. Ensure you have a least one to two meetings a week to connect with others within and outside of your organization. These meetings don't have to be expensive lunch meetings; they can be over coffee. Use these meetings to ask for input on your approach or ideas as well as to plant seeds about your accomplishments and interests. Make sure your discussion is a two-way street and that you also take time to ask about things your colleagues are doing.

EXERCISE: My Brand Publicists

Who are my current brand champions (those connected to people/groups I would currently like to gain access to)?

Name	Role	How I can best leverage this relationship

Who are my future brand champions (those connected to people/groups I would eventually like to gain access to)?

Name	Role	How I can best leverage this relationship

EXERCISE: The Power of Alliances – Six, no wait . . . two degrees of separation

As you complete this worksheet, start by listing the target people/audiences you are trying to reach①. If you personally know someone who has a direct relationship with them, place the name of the person you know in the slots above the 1° mark. If your friend or colleague does not have a direct relationship with the target person or group, determine if the person you have a close relationship with is two, three, or four levels removed from the person with whom you are trying to connect②.

Brainstorm with your direct contact on ways to gain access to your ultimate target audience.

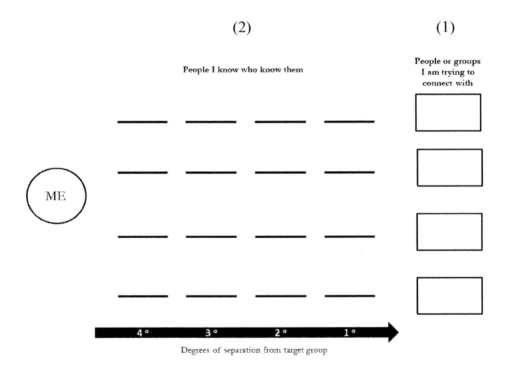

Degrees of separation from target group

#14 TIME MISMANAGEMENT

!

One of these days is none of these days.

--English proverb

WHAT IT MEANS

Many of us get so immersed in our work and the day-to-day that we don't take time to think about our careers and the direction we are heading. Consequently we neglect to promote and market ourselves so that we can continue to attract opportunities or move into a new career area. There are also those of us whose personal branding activity can be described as occurring in "fits and starts" – where we are not gaining any traction because of our inconsistent efforts.

CONSEQUENCES

If you are not able to gain any traction, you may never get around to developing a robust brand that is remembered by anyone. People may wonder what you are doing because they never hear about the things you have accomplished or the things that you are interested in. Life will continue to go on as it is. That may be a good thing in your book because it is familiar and comfortable. But if you are mismanaging time around personal branding, you probably are mismanaging time around other career development activities as well.

Here's a riddle for you.
If a tree falls in the middle of the forest, and nobody is there to hear it, does it still make a noise?

If no one is aware of your brand, no matter how much you are doing . . . it flat out **DOES NOT EXIST.** A very critical piece of the **branding equation** is exposure to others. You may believe that you are doing all the right things to maintain your brand consistency and integrity, but if the right, and I stress **RIGHT** people aren't aware of what you are doing, you are making "**NO NOISE, NADA**".

CASE IN POINT

"Leave it to Larry" - Larry was an independent consultant who would often partner with other small businesses and contractors in his work. When working with a team of individuals, Larry was known for being responsive and getting things done in a crunch. Consequently, a few of his consulting partners, who were less organized, would call Larry, at the 11th hour to take over something that needed warp speed turn-around. Larry didn't mind at first, but as he got busier, he noticed that with all the interruptions to his planned schedule, he didn't have time to plan and develop business on his own. His role on these projects was usually tangential versus highly visible and subsequently the clients were not aware of his great talents. Larry wanted to change things so that others would respect his time. Basically, he wanted advance notice and more time to focus on his own business development agenda.

ROAD TO RECOVERY

The reality in this situation is that others aren't always ready to change when we are. And so we have to take matters into our own hands. What could Larry and we do differently to have more control over time and be more visible with our target audience?

1. "What gets measured gets done!" One way to get things done is to create a to-do list and establish a measurable timeframe for completion. So put personal branding on your schedule. Start off by setting aside an hour on two or three days of the week, where you

commit to working on personal branding. Set a date, perhaps a recurring weekly or daily event with a 15 minute reminder just like you would any other calendar event.

2. Give your personal branding meeting an agenda. Your first session could simply involve sketching out what you're going to do within those one-hour time slots. One day might involve you completing your self-assessment, thinking about how your target audience has changed, and going through a few exercises presented in this book. Another session might involve connecting with people to let them know what you are doing, or creating collateral pieces (e.g., updated resume, bio, or brochure).

3. What you do is up to you. The main point is to set aside structured time and document what you plan to do. Research has shown that people are more likely to achieve goals that they document on paper. It's not enough to just keep these thoughts in your head because that is where they will stay. Put your personal branding "to do" plan on paper where you can see it, touch it, change it, manipulate it, and go back and CHECK IT OFF once you have done it!

EXERCISE

How many plates are you juggling? Where are you spending and spinning your time? Use the worksheets on the next couple of pages to work through this.

1. Use the worksheets on the following pages to list the things you do on a weekly or monthly basis and indicate the percentage of time you spend on each. Put "working on personal branding" on the list as well. Initially you may find that you have a big fat zero next to this category. Below is an example which shows how someone might divide up 100% of their time at work during a typical month.

How I Currently Spend My Time

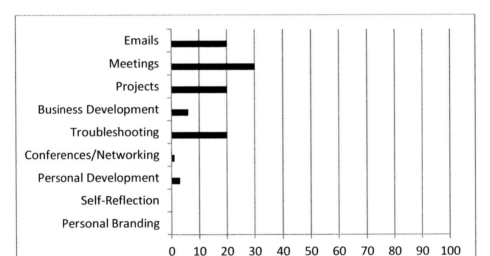

2. Once you have established this list and indicated your current time allotment, then create your ideal list. Indicate what you would like to be doing and how much time you would like to be spending on activities. Be realistic. It should be the same list or shorter than your original one. It could also be an entirely different list if you feel you are not involved in the activities that you need to be at this point in your career.

3. Compare the two lists. Identify the gap and determine what you are going to need to do differently to transition from where you are to where you want to be. One activity might include putting action items on a schedule. Another might be learning how to say no. Better managing your time could be as simple as not answering the phone every time it rings. Controlling interruptions and distractions go a long way when you are trying to find extra time in your day.

WORKSHEET:

How I Currently Spend My Time

Activity	% of Time Spent	10	20	30	40	50	60	70	80	90	100
Personal Branding											
Total	100%										

WORKSHEET:

How I Should be Spending My Time to Reach My Goals

Activity	% of Time Spent	10	20	30	40	50	60	70	80	90	100
Personal Branding											
Total	100%										

#15 SPREADING YOUR BRAND LIKE BUTTER

Happy is the man who can do only one thing;
in doing it, he fulfills his destiny.
--Joseph Joubert

WHAT IT MEANS

In your quest to be viewed as an expert, avoid trying to boil the ocean with your brand – being everything to everyone. This happens when you raise your hand for everything. "Ooh, I can do that! Ooh, Ooh, I can do this too! I'm good at everything!"

This behavior suggests that you have not found your niche or a body of work in which you have developed expertise or a strong interest. It is particularly observable in freelance consultants who are chasing the money. Sometimes this manifests as always jumping on the same bandwagon as your competition. Given the unpredictable cycles of income, it's not hard to understand why independent consultants and contractors may diversify and accept projects that are not really aligned with their areas of expertise. While this may lead to expanded business, if done too frequently, it will result in a lower quality of output. Before long the "Jack-of-all-trades" may find he is stretched beyond capacity and stressed out!

CONSEQUENCES

While it is important to be a generalist in some professions, you must know your limitations. Not having a niche or focus dilutes your brand. Those you are trying to reach will not know what it is they should consider you for. Because of this uncertainty you may miss out on opportunities.

Burnout is another consequence. Constantly trying to play catch-up while learning and implementing can become very draining. After a while you lose interest in what you are doing and lose that spark that gives you creative energy. Overpromising on results will frustrate you and your clients. Eventually you will not be taken seriously on anything.

Is there an upside to being a "Jack or Jill-of-all-trades"? Depends on what profession you are in. But for the most part consumers want to know where to shop for what. They begin to question you if your shingle suggests that you are "one-stop shopping" for everything. It would be like going to a business that offered oil changes, tarot card readings, and pedicures . . . . although, I am sure if someone tried hard enough, they could find a common theme here.

CASE IN POINT

A lesson can be learned by looking at some of the major brands that moved into product areas much better left alone. In many cases brand extension was the issue, where customers felt that the expanded offerings missed the mark. In others, consumers did not see brand consistency or a unifying factor across the products.

Harley Davidson Perfume - Harley-Davidson customers are known for their loyalty. However, this iconic motorcycle brand stretched this loyalty a bit too much when they began to expand their offering to T-shirts and cigarette lighters and then to aftershave and perfume. These new offerings did not appeal to Harley-Davidson's customer base. They had spread their brand too thin.

Bic Underwear – Bic's brand capitalizes on disposable products and convenience. This was effectively marketable for razors, lighters, and pens. When they began to market disposable underwear, customers weren't buying it. There was too much of a disconnect between the underwear and Bic's other products.

The Disciplined Pursuit of Less

In an August 8, 2012 Harvard Business Review Blog, author Greg McKeown addresses "The Disciplined Pursuit of Less." He introduces the "clarity paradox" as an explanation for why successful organizations and people don't automatically move to the next level to become very successful. This clarity paradox can be defined in four phases:

Phase 1: When we *really* have clarity of purpose, it leads to success.
Phase 2: When we have success, it leads to more options and opportunities.
Phase 3: When we have increased options and opportunities, it leads to diffused efforts.
Phase 4: Diffused efforts undermine the very clarity that led to our success in the first place.

McKeown's recommendations for getting back on track include:
- Use more extreme criteria with our career choices (e.g., What are we absolutely passionate about that fits our market's needs?)
- Give ourselves permission to eliminate the non-essentials (e.g., the activities that are "cluttering" our lives).
- Beware of the "endowment effect" which is defined as the tendency to value an item or opportunity more once we own it. We should be asking ourselves "If I did not have this opportunity, how much would I be willing to sacrifice in order to obtain it?"

ROAD TO RECOVERY

The road to recovery involves finding your sweet spot and a unifying factor across what you have to offer.

1. Think of a few things you are interested in. Link these to activities that are compatible and that leverage your skills and talents. If you are interested in a number of vastly different activities, don't forget you can always have hobbies. But in terms of shaping your career, remember, focus and alignment are key.

2.   Look to see if there is an underlying theme in the different things you like to do. Perhaps you are into programming and you also like public speaking. These two activities could certainly be combined. Programming and dance choreography . . . not so much, unless you are creating choreography electronically. There are often underlying themes to some of the work-related things that we do. Perhaps the theme is creating, whether that be a new service, new product, article, or program. If this is the case, find a way to shape your brand under the umbrella of creativity or design.

3.   When you find yourself tempted to take on new assignments that you know are going to be time-consuming and draining, think about whether it is absolutely necessary to do so. Does the payment outweigh the costs of your time? Would it help you fine-tune your craft and your brand? Will others view the assignment or work that you are doing as compatible with your brand? Do you want people to continually reach out to you for these kinds of assignments? If you've answered "no" to any of these questions, run for the hills when these opportunities surface!

EXERCISE: Analyzing My Strengths

Use the following worksheet to create a list of competencies (knowledge, skills, abilities and other characteristics) that are required in your profession. Place an X where relevant in the columns identifying if what you have listed is something you are good at, interested in, spending a lot of time doing, or needed by the target audience you are trying to influence.

WORKSHEET: Analyzing My Strengths

List of Competencies Relevant to my Profession	① This is one of my strengths	② This is something I enjoy doing	③ This is something I currently spend a lot of time doing	④ This is something I know my audience values	Total Number of X's in this row
•					
•					
•					
•					
•					
•					
•					
•					

Analyze the patterns in your completed matrix.

- Do you believe everything is a strength? Do you enjoy doing everything? How are the skills related? Are there certain things you are doing that are diluting the overall brand you are trying to build?

- Look across each row to see where you have a check mark in both columns 1, 2 and 4. These areas are where you can contribute most. If there are several rows where each of these three columns is checked, select the top three you would prefer to do.

- Use this information to think about where and how you can fine-tune your brand.

#16 IGNORING YOUR COMPETITION

!

A computer once beat me at chess,
but it was no match for me at kick boxing.
Emo Philips

WHAT IT MEANS

Let's pretend for a moment that you are going into business as a retail department store or a gourmet coffee shop – like Sears or Starbucks, for example. You wouldn't dare launch your business without finding out what your competition is doing, where they're located, who their customers are, and what distinguishes them. A major component of branding involves intelligence gathering on industry trends and practices. In your case, the competition may not be other businesses, but other professionals in your industry. Perhaps it's every other pharmaceutical rep in the region or every business analyst within the company. It could be every physician assistant in the hospital, or every auto shop owner in the county. It's not enough to know what you have to offer and what you plan to do. You must also be aware of what your competition is doing if you want to differentiate yourself and stand out.

CONSEQUENCES

At minimum you might find that you are offering the same service to the same audience, and in the same location. Perhaps there is a broad enough pool within your target audience for many competitors to coexist. For example, when I think of Human Resource professionals, financial advisers, and attorneys there's probably a large population of people and companies who need these services. But, while individuals and organizations may require and use your services, they have no obligation to stay loyal to you. At any point in your career you may be competing against others to find, keep, or advance within your profession. Situations where this is especially relevant include during company restructurings, where decisions must be made about who to keep and who to let go. It is in your best interest to make sure decision-makers know and appreciate your differentiating factor. This awareness helps you to stay competitive and marketable.

CASE IN POINT

Olympian Gold Medalist, Usain Bolt, most likely took a refreshed look at his competition in 2012 when Yohan Blake ran a personal-best of 9.75 seconds to upset Bolt by .11 seconds in the Jamaican Olympic Trials. Paying attention to the competition helps us keep our game at its best. If one competitor has raised the bar by offering something new and different this will have an impact on our customer's expectations. This does not mean that you have to jump on every bandwagon that your competitors are. Ultimately, you will need to strike a balance between paying attention to what is out there, what is in demand, and charting your own path.

ROAD TO RECOVERY

Understanding what your competitors do can provide you with basic knowledge on what you should be able to offer, at minimum.

1. Find out who and where your competition is? Where is your competition? Go to their place of business. Sit in on their meetings if they are co-workers. You can attend conferences and listen to their presentations. You might even be able to sit in on roundtable discussions with peers within your profession to collectively share ideas. Additionally, reading professional trade magazines is a great way to stay abreast of trends within the industry. This competitive analysis is a critical component in shaping your brand and identifying varying ways to enhance it.

2. To differentiate yourself you could use a different twist on what you do or establish a niche market within the broader target audience. For example if you are an auto repair shop owner you might decide to focus on trucks and SUVs, or target large companies which have fleets of vehicles vs. individual customers.

3. Many companies minimize the competitive factor by partnering with, collaborating with, or buying out their competition. Individuals can do this as well. Often independent consultants get together and join forces to either take on larger projects or to bring to the table additional skill sets that complement each other. I have partnered with a number of other independent consultants and generally the arrangements have been fulfilling and profitable. Within these partnerships we outlined how each of us would contribute to the project. More often than not I have found that working with someone who has different skills and expertise than I do provides for the best partnering relationship, because we are not trying to compete in each other's space.

EXERCISE: Analyzing My Competition

WORKSHEET: Analyzing My Competition

Use the worksheet below to compare your brand to your competition's. This could be other professionals in similar roles within your company or industry. Under the "Me" column, jot down a few descriptive words that address the category in that row. Do the same for your competition. Then place a check in **either** the "strength" or "weakness" column based on how you think you compare to your competition.

In the final column, estimate the importance of each competitive factor to your customer or target audience on a scale from 1 to 5. 1 = not very important; 5 = highly important.

Competitive Analysis

Category	Me	My Competition	Strength? √	Weakness? √	Importance to Target Audience
Areas of Expertise					
Years of Experience					
Credentials					
Image/ Reputation					
Visibility/ Exposure					
Target Audience					
Access to Target Audience					
Self-Marketing Techniques					

Look at how you have completed your competitive analysis grid and reflect on the following questions:

- Who is your competition?
- In areas that are of high importance to your audience, how do you compare to your competition?
- What is your competition doing that you aren't?
- In what areas do you have an edge on your competition?
- Are your target audiences the same?
- Do you have the same level of visibility as your competition? If not, why?
- What can you learn from your competitors?

Now, write a short paragraph stating your competitive advantages and disadvantages and specific things you can do to become more competitive or to differentiate yourself.

#17 THINKING YOU ARE TOO OLD TO BRAND

---!---

To be seventy years young is sometimes far more
cheerful and hopeful than to be forty years old.
- Oliver Wendell Holmes

WHAT IT MEANS

Branding is not confined to the young professional, or for just generations X, Y and Z. Branding is important for Baby Boomers and beyond. Branding is simply making one's mark and defining one's path; and that can happen at any age. Sadly, though, many people fall prey to the notion that they are too old to begin something new or to realize a long-held dream. New directions and personal bests have been achieved by countless individuals in the latter stages of their lives. Takichiro Mori was an economics professor until he left academia at age 55 to become a real estate investor, and subsequently *Forbes*' two-time reigning "world's richest man." In 2010, at age 88, Betty White was at the top of her game and became the oldest person to serve as guest host for Saturday Night Live. Both Pablo Picasso and Georgia O'Keefe were still painting at the age of 90, and chemist, Paul Walden, was still giving chemistry lectures. Personal branding can help us move into new territory or revitalize our careers. It is a tool for people at all stages of their career, for those considering an occupational change or "encore career" as Marc Freedman, CEO of Encore.org describes it; and even for those ready to retire.

Due to a combination of factors (including increased health and longevity, decreased retirement savings, caregiving responsibilities for parents, and attempts not be a burden on their own children) adults over 60 are continuing to pursue their careers. Some are going back to school to repurpose themselves, while others are starting their own businesses. Some are trying to transition from the corporate setting to a non-profit setting.

115

There are also those who are solely looking at how they can become more active within their communities. Whatever new journey we are talking about, this transition can be a challenging time. It provides an opportunity to rethink one's approach to self-branding and marketing.

CONSEQUENCES

There are many things to think about when recreating or sustaining a personal brand. For those who are over 50, the exercise is similar in many ways to those who are under 50. But unless you accept that branding and staying marketable are important, you run the risk of getting stuck in a rut from which you may not be able to climb out of, of resigning yourself to unfulfilling roles that you see no escape from. Worst case scenario, you may find yourself unemployable. This is different and more concerning than being temporarily unemployed for it implies that your skillset and talents are no longer relevant or of value within your profession.

When you neglect attention to branding just because you are seasoned in your career, you run the risk of being forgotten and overlooked. Additionally, you may cease to inspire those who previously looked up to you or respected your contributions. You decrease the "currency" previously accumulated for your professional legacy. This may not matter to some; but there are many of us who are concerned about our legacies. As psychologist Erik Erikson indicates, in our late 50's and 60's, we enter a stage of life where we must reconcile "integrity versus despair." At this stage we tend to reflect on our past hoping to feel good about our accomplishments, that there was some purpose to our lives, and that we were able to give back to others in some way. Otherwise we may experience anguish and despair.

CASE IN POINT

It was the third time in a week I had received a call from a professional colleague of mine, Diane. I sat down and braced myself as I prepared to listen to the same oratory I had heard earlier in the week. *"I don't know what I'm going to do! I've been on interview after interview. I don't think anyone's going to hire me. I'm just too old. They either tell me I am too experienced or that I don't have a specific skill set that they're looking for. But I know that's code for "we just don't want your old @#! up in here."*

116

Ok. I had had enough. *"Diane"*, I said, *"if you don't stop your whining and complaining, I am going to reach through this phone and choke you. I hope you don't go into your interviews with this "sour grapes" attitude. I know you are smart enough not to say anything, but your facial expression probably gives away everything you are feeling inside. Now the journey may be long. But, suck it up! Do what you have to do. You might have to take something temporary in the meantime. But you are a survivor. I know you are a survivor because you have managed to befriend senior leaders in your former organization through restructure after restructure. You have great people skills, great technical skills, and great contacts. Right now you just have to do something that's going to make you feel good about YOU. It's just a matter of time before you land somewhere!"*

Well the next time I heard from Diane, she had landed a job, slightly less in pay, but very fulfilling, and a close commute from her house. She was ecstatic, as this new job enabled her to contribute her skills, work with a new team from whom she could learn and update her skills, as well as achieve work-life balance. *"What did you do differently?"* I asked. Diane wasn't sure. *"I don't know. I started reaching out to people I have worked with before, because I knew you weren't going to take my calls any more, and before I knew it someone was telling me about an opportunity at XYZ Company and this person happened to be on the hiring team. What luck! He knew my track record, was impressed by it, could speak on my behalf, and here I am!"*

Diane had refocused her nervous energy into action and it ultimately paid off. She also took a bite of reality by reexamining her list of requirements for her ideal job.

ROAD TO RECOVERY

For those of you who are 50 and over, remember you didn't get to this point in your life without learning something. You are a resilient human being that has had to adapt and bounce back time after time. It's time now to reflect back on all of the value you bring to the table.

Many of us mistakenly think that all employers are looking for younger individuals to fill open positions. While this may be true in some scenarios, companies realize that age brings with it professional maturity, substantive work and life experience, and often the ability for the employee to hit the ground running. That is precisely what you can emphasize as a strength as you transition to a new job or career!

1. *Take inventory.* A self-assessment is the place to start. Begin by listing the major accomplishments you have achieved during the course of your career. From this list, you should be able to identify the strengths that you have and unique aspects about yourself that may help you to stand out from others. You'll also need to review information that updates you on industry trends so that you can determine whether you need to update your skills or seek out a new target audience.

   The second part of taking inventory involves reflecting on your dreams and finding a sweet spot between what you have always wanted to do, what you are currently competent to do, and where there is a need within your target market. This is a very important step in shaping a brand that will lead to a fulfilling and relevant role.

2. *Be open to change.* Whether you are unemployed, frustrated in your current role, stuck in a rut, or ready to retire, this is the time to think about new horizons. How do you want to spend your time? Having a plan is essential. Being flexible will also be critical as you think about how you want to transition at this stage in your life. Perhaps you were in a senior manager role in your last organization. If you cannot find a comparable role, an option is to accept a senior level professional role where you can still demonstrate leadership but may not be responsible for people management. You may also need to be flexible about salary expectations. Sit down and list out your financial needs and how this will translate into your salary and benefits. Remember to include items like health care, retirement, long-term care, tuition reimbursement, etc.

   If you're not planning to change organizations, this might be a time to raise your hand to lead or to take on different or more complex projects.

   Perhaps you are fine with your current role and assignments, and want to make a different kind of impact within the organization. Mentoring and coaching younger employees may be a fulfilling activity at this stage. Keep in mind, you are not too old to reach out to mentors for yourself, particularly if you are trying to transition into a new arena. Another option is to share your expertise on a non-profit advisory board or become active in a community organization for whose cause you feel passionate about.

3. *Update your skills.* It is critical to stay knowledgeable about trends within your field and industry. This is critical no matter what stage of your career you are in. The conundrum is in finding the time. The prevalence of online classes in almost any subject you could dream of helps employed adults with time management challenges. If you are not seeking a degree you can, periodically, take individual courses to brush up on your skills. Webinars and podcasts are also ways to enhance your knowledge on an industry related topic. These events are offered by companies and professional organizations all of the time. Your own company may offer these webinars and this is an excellent way to stay in the loop on what is going on in other parts of the company.

4. *Build up your confidence.* Your image is driven in large part by the aura or energy that you project. This aura is tied to the level of confidence that you have in yourself and how you generally feel about yourself. Others can sense your level of confidence and respond to this energy.

As an example, I am reminded of a former co-worker of mine who I'll refer to as "Mr. Red Carpet." Whatever setting or venue he showed up in – whether familiar or unfamiliar, he owned the space. His aura was "I belong here!" And people rolled out the red carpet for him. This energy was projected with senior leaders, clients, the community, you name it. I recall trying to get into a particular event with him during a national conference. Our tickets were supposed to be waiting for us at the box office. However there was some communication slip-up. I then noticed the person at the ticket counter sizing up "Mr. Red Carpet" and the next thing I knew, we were in! I have observed several other similar examples like this and must conclude that "Mr. Red Carpet's" confidence and resulting impact on others are most likely rooted in how he personally feels about himself.

So what things make you feel good about yourself? It is often the little things. I recall reading a discussion item from one of my graduate students who was talking about ways to cope with stressful situations. She talked about wearing your fancy panties on days when you want to wow others. Obviously there is no need to show anyone your fancy panties, but just knowing that you have something on that makes you feel good or special can make a difference. When we feel good we project an aura of confidence.

You may want to work on achieving small milestones while you are reinventing your brand. This is another way to build your level of confidence. Finish that article. Clean out that closet. Take that trip. Take that class. The mind is an interesting tool that we can use and shape as we choose. As we master and complete more of our mini goals, we stimulate our minds in positive ways. Reaching our bigger goals becomes much easier, because we have strengthened our "Can Do!" muscle.

Positive affirmations work for many. Stand in front of the mirror and tell yourself how brilliant you are, what strengths you have, what you're going to accomplish, and then pat yourself on the back when you do so.

5. *Enhance your energy.* Part of society's obsession with youth, aside from their beauty, motivation and adaptability, is their high energy level. What employer does not want someone who is driven and brings high energy to the task? You can bring drive and energy too! Your energy may be even more focused and impactful because of all of the insights you have gained over the years. Whatever your personal brand is, your employer or clients will want to see that you bring energy, a sense of urgency, and can reliably deliver on results. This may be a bit challenging if you have been in a slump for a while, or feel tired and depressed.

So let's talk about things that will increase your energy. No secret here. Eating right and exercising. Eating healthy on a regular basis promotes overall well-being and energy. Exercise increases the blood flow throughout your body and circulation to your brain. This enhances cognitive functioning, enabling you to better focus, create and analyze concepts, and express yourself. A high energy level comes across as interest, as confidence, as credibility. Begin now to make small changes to increase the energy in your life.

Doing something you are passionate about is also a way to generate energy. Ideally this passion would stem from aspects of your job; however this is not always possible. Make sure you develop interests outside of your job that you can look forward to – a hobby, a personal goal, a fulfilling relationship. Schedule some predictable pleasure into your life!

Additionally, identify the things that zap your energy. One common energy zapper is a lack of sleep. Research has found that most adults in their fifties get between four to six hours of sleep, nightly, when what we really need is at least eight. In the book, "Power Sleep," author, Dr. James B. Maas speaks to the debilitating effects that the lack of sleep has on our bodies. The effects are cumulative and lead to dysfunction as well as disease. The good news is that this dysfunction can be combatted by getting adequate amounts of sleep on a regular basis.

These principles, many of which were learned when we were young, may seem trivial but are important, back-to-basic tactics as you seek to energize your brand.

6. *Repackage.* What people see on the outside will influence what they think about your abilities, effectiveness, and credibility. As we age we need to be disciplined in how we project ourselves. To project a youthful, high-energy brand, pay attention to your wardrobe, hair, grooming, make-up, facial expressions, and your posture. For example, there are many of us who unintentionally slump our shoulders. There are others of us who seem to wear a continual scowl on our faces when listening to others. These nonverbals (whether intended or not) suggest rigidity and chip away at a youthful, energetic brand. You may want to seek advice from others

to get a sense of what they think about your total look and how it meshes with the brand you are trying to project. Ask a trusted source to observe you in different settings and provide an appraisal. Perhaps your look is too casual, too formal, or too rigid.

Take a look at individuals who are viewed as successful in the areas that you are interested in. How are they packaging themselves? What could you do to add a spark to your visual image – one that is appealing and professional?

7. *Network, network, network.* As we mature in our careers we may slow down on attending industry conferences and keeping our professional memberships current. This reduces our visibility and access to others. It also limits our exposure to new ideas and opportunities. Seasoned veterans are often in demand if they stay relevant, and part of staying relevant includes staying connected to others. Get back in to the swing of things with both your professional and personal networks. This one behavior change will probably net the most return in terms of advancing your personal brand.

EXERCISE: Tough Love Conversation

Use the space below to reflect on your current reality and articulate your vision for change.

What are my concerns about getting older?
What has worked for me in the past, when I had to go through a period of change?
What is my vision for what I would like to be doing/contributing in the next five to ten years? How do I want to be perceived by others?
What changes do I need to make now in order to make this vision a reality? What might I need to give up in order to move on?

Reinvention Plan: Three new behaviors I will commit to in the next few months to enhance my brand so that it matches my vision.

Action	Start Date	Completion Date

18 THINKING YOU ARE TOO YOUNG TO BRAND

!

Every artist was first an amateur.
--Ralph Waldo Emerson

WHAT IT MEANS

In my facilitation of workshops for high school and college students, one thing has become crystal clear – you are never too young to have or work on your brand. In fact many corporations collaborate with academic institutions to develop the "workforce for tomorrow" and a major component of this is training on career development and professional image building. When students in my workshops are asked to think of their personal brand, a wide range of responses come up. Many labels are comical or perhaps exaggerated depictions such as "smooth," "invincible," or "superwoman." Some are self-deprecating, such as "goofy," "clumsy," or "nerd-boy." And of course there are those in the session who cannot think of a way to describe themselves. For these students it is generally a light bulb moment to hear that their fellow classmates definitely had a word or two in mind when thinking of them.

Thinking of my own children's brands, I can reflect back to when one of my sons was in middle school. We often got called in for parent-teacher conferences. We soon learned that our quiet, unassuming child who could focus on building a Lego® metropolis for hours on end was the "class clown," a brand he was to carry all through middle school. Fortunately as he moved into high school he used his comedic and extroverted talents to lead organizations and participate in student presentations. Whew! We were quite glad his brand had evolved! There is a season for everything. And for all of you reading this that are high school and recent college grads, know that an important element of your future career success we'll be linked to the personal brand that you begin to shape today.

CONSEQUENCES

The high school and college years (while filled with protracted study) are the fun years; but they are also the years in which additional aspects of our character develop. During this stage of development we are influenced by our peers. We seek to create and sustain intimate relationships, and begin to think about being industrious and starting our careers. As all of this is occurring, we need to be mindful of the lasting impressions we are making through the behaviors we exhibit. Our instructors and classmates could be future employers or co-workers, or be needed to provide a reference. Consequently, your brand of being a party animal on the college campus will clearly need an upgrade prior to shifting to the workplace. Now is the time to let others see that you are well-rounded, and have more to contribute than just your fun side.

Research suggests that an impression is formed within the first seven seconds of meeting a person. For those graduates going into interviews, this is an important concept to understand. Lack of awareness around this has costly results. How you package and present yourself will affect your ability to impress and influence others' initial perceptions of you. Once you begin to engage in dialogue during the interview, your ability to connect with the interviewing team and demonstrate something memorable will help you stand out among the multitude of other job candidates who have the required qualifications. When a job offer is made, the initial impression formed of you will be compared against your performance and image you build within the organization. Bottom line, there will always be a need for you to manage this impression or your personal brand.

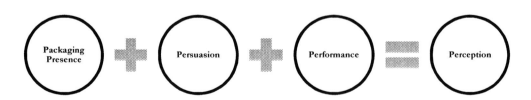

CASE IN POINT

At one point in my career I was helping MBA graduates from some of the top tier business schools land jobs with coveted firms on Wall Street. As I was calling one of the candidates to set up an interview I was forwarded to his voicemail. I gasped at what I heard! His recorded message said something like *"The love god is out at play. Leave a message and I'll get back to you today."* To add to the mood, he had Barry White's seductive music playing in the background! While this type of message might be okay for friends, it was clearly inappropriate for the Goldman Sachs, Morgan Stanleys and other potential employers who would be calling to set up interviews. This type of behavior causes employers to question a candidate's judgment and, as a result, they may not make it to the first stage of the selection process.

ROAD TO RECOVERY

At this stage of your life, the world is your oyster. It is full of possibilities and opportunities. If you have not thought about career development or shaping a brand, you are not alone, for even professionals who are seasoned in their careers may not have put a lot of thought into their personal brand. You will be ahead of the game if you start to manage your brand now. Many of the exercises in this book will be beneficial for you as you think about shaping your personal brand. These exercises can be a supplement to the information and tools your school career centers have on career development.

Some of the things you as the student or recent graduate can do now to shape your personal brand include:

1. *Effectively manage your academic activities.* Several hundred thousand graduates will be looking for jobs within any given year. How do you differentiate yourself from them? How do you prevent yourself from being viewed as a commodity? For some employers, the school you come from is a distinguishing factor, or your grade point average, or how effectively you were able to balance academic studies, a part-time job, and participate in relevant student organizations. Make sure your academic record and extra-curricular activities reinforce the image you are trying to portray.

127

2. *Get the attention of your future employer.* What you look like on paper will be the first impression a potential employer has of you. Make sure your resume is persuasive. I have heard of many unique approaches used by job hunters. One student indicated that she sent her resume along with a pizza delivery to the HR Department to make sure it did not get thrown to the bottom of the pile. This is one tactic, but it may not always meet the desired results, particularly given the fact that most resume submittal is now done online. Sending in a resume that has been recommended by an employee who works with the company will have a stronger impact, particularly if that individual's reputation is highly credible within the organization. This is an example of brand association. Your brand builds equity or value because it is associated with another employee's brand that is valued by the organization.

There are several guides on how to find a job, how to write a winning resume, how to leverage your contacts, and how to interview. With respect to branding, make sure everything associated with your job search is credible, consistent, and relevant. This includes your Facebook page and any other electronic information that exists about you.

3. *Conduct a self-assessment.* This is a critical step in any career planning one undertakes. Conduct an inventory of your strengths and identify areas for improvement. At this point you don't have to share this with anyone. It is an exercise to help you hone in on what to promote about yourself and where you may need to make some adjustments. Think about any internships or full or part-time jobs you have held as well as talents you have demonstrated in other venues such as community work, professional organizations, church, at home, at school, etc. List your strengths and how you have applied them. List any feedback you have received on development needs.

You should also list the things you value, are interested in, and what you want to avoid. It might be revealing to take a personality inventory to get a sense of your temperament, style of communication and how this meshes with various careers. There are numerous career planning assessment tools available. Descriptions of many of these (like the Strong Interest Inventory, which measures your interest in a broad range of occupations, work activities, leisure activities, and academic subjects) can be found at www.career-lifeskills.com.

4. *Explore opportunities.* Talk to your friends and their friends or family about the jobs they are in. Attend career fairs. Read career profiles of various individuals in magazines or online media. Does the job sound like something you might want to do? Then get more information on it. There are several career sites on the web that provide this type of information.

   Determine what your desired role requires - Next, identify the competencies and other success factors required for the role you are interested in. You may need to do some research to complete this list. Look up the job requirements on ONetonline.org (a database which provides descriptions of thousands of job titles). Talk to your career counselor at school. If you have graduated, you can still leverage these career center services as an alumni.

   Schedule "informational interviews" with professionals who are already in the role. This will enable you to get an inside view of the work, work environment, people you will be interacting with, and the personal factors that are successful for the role.

5. *Analyze the bridges and gaps.* Now look for the points of connection, as well as the gaps between where you are relative to where you want to be. Consider your skills, experience, and interests. Is the career path you have chosen to pursue one that would be fulfilling, where you think you could ultimately be successful? You may not know this for certain until you try the job out.

6. *Dip your foot in the pool or at least get it wet.* During the early stages of your career, getting experience is key. Internships and work through "temporary agencies" are a great way to get your foot in the door of

an organization. But the job is not the only way to get the experience. You may also be able to develop the skills you need in other settings. For example:

- Volunteering your services to a community, civic, or social organization
- Conducting committee work within a professional organization
- Taking on leadership positions within various student organizations

Another tactic you will want to use to get your foot in the door is to make yourself visible in forums where professionals in your desired field congregate. This sends the subtle message that you are "one of them."

"Birds of a feather . . ."

This would include joining professional organizations within the industry you are trying to move in to and attending conferences. It would also include arranging to present in these forums on topics in which you are knowledgeable.

Writing for magazines or other publications your target audience reads is another related strategy for building visibility. And today, anyone can submit an e-article or start a blog online about a particular subject.

Managing one's career and brand is an endeavor that requires reflection, direction and persistence. Much of it breaks down to the fine art of networking, image building, and demonstrating competence. The more your name is known in your desired arena, the higher the odds of you connecting with someone who is willing to give you that first chance.

EXERCISE: Timeline of Accomplishments

Use this worksheet to identify your major accomplishments and skills. Think of organizations you led or participated in during school, part-time jobs you held or volunteer work you completed. Your list might include things like student council president, varsity athlete, high score on SAT, volunteer work at a nursing home, strong team player, project leader, etc.

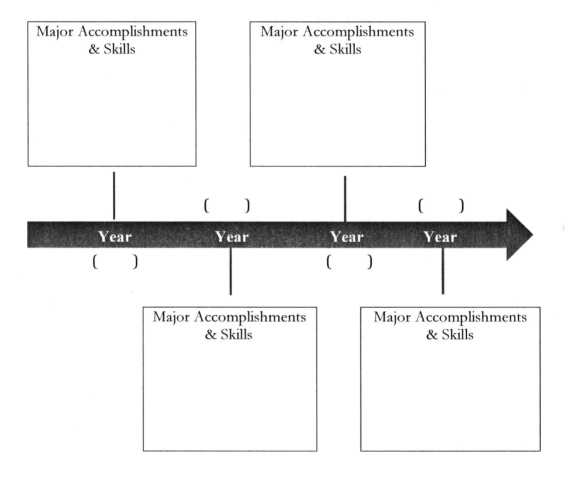

EXERCISE: Me in Five Years

How do I want to be perceived?

	Five years from now	Three things I need to do to achieve this
What do I want to be known for professionally?		
What major talents and accomplishments do I want to be associated with?		
How do I want others to describe me and my work?		
What do I want to be my differentiator, my brand?		

#19 STANDING IN THE SHADOW OF SOMEONE ELSE'S BRAND

!

We carry within us the wonders we seek without us.
- Sir Thomas Browne

WHAT IT MEANS

Many of us associate ourselves with individuals who are popular, successful, or have dazzling personalities. Perhaps this person is our manager, a business partner, a public official, or some other person we work with or support in some kind of way. Our role and responsibilities may be important, yet they revolve around helping this individual. We may even be viewed as indispensable to this person. Somewhere along the way, however, our identity has become intertwined with theirs. When others think of us they think of "Joe" or "Jolene." This phenomenon applies to many of the vice presidents who have served. Spouses of famous and high profile celebrities also fall in this boat.

Those of you who have a "helping brand" – are generally accommodating and willing to provide support to others. You have attributes that attract people to you; possibly talents or capabilities they are lacking. For example, you may be resourceful, creative, a good writer, or problem solver. At minimum you probably have good interpersonal skills and can remain calm in stressful situations. Because of this you are invaluable and constantly sought. You may also be continuously busy. On the surface nothing is wrong with this unless your work goes unrecognized by a broader audience. The person you support is in the spotlight and may even get credit for your work. Some of this may be justified. But in order to fully demonstrate your value, there is a need for you to grab some of the spotlight for yourself.

CONSEQUENCES

You may feel that you have an easy way riding on the coattails of the highly visible. Perhaps this is fine with you and your brand association is where you want it. You are learning something. This person is mentoring or sponsoring you. Fine and dandy! The benefits you receive from this individual, however, do not obligate you to stand in their shadow. If you continue to do so, you run the risk of not being sought for projects that you want to lead, reaching your potential, or leading a fulfilling life. People will view you as the go-to person; but it will be the go-to person to get to Joe or Jolene. You may feel that you are "standing in the shadows of love," but you are simply standing in the shadows!

CASE IN POINT

Al Gore epitomizes what it means to come out from the shadows into the spotlight. He is probably one of the most visible brand makeovers today. Gore went from being one of the most un-notable vice presidents in our time to a Nobel prize winner. The American public and the world at large saw him rise like a phoenix from the ashes. While he was visible as a vice president, he was not popular. After leaving the White House he went through an agonizing presidential election loss to George W. Bush.

As many former vice presidents do, Gore went into private industry. Here he met with a number of successes including the launching of a profitable cable TV station, the acquisition of a number of businesses including an investment management firm. But it was when he reached back and blew the dust off of a set of slides he had prepared on global warming that he got America's attention. The independent film on which he collaborated and appeared in, "An Inconvenient Truth", was praised and recognized by a Nobel prize in 2007. Who knew that this former "veep" described by some as "wooden" and the "robo-candidate" could reenergize his fans and critics and rise to the heights of visibility that he did. He focused on things that he was passionate about; and in his words his makeover was less the result of a conscious strategy than it was a few smart initiatives coming together at the right time. This is an enlightening example of preparation meeting opportunity.

ROAD TO RECOVERY

Coming out from the shadows may be as simple as deciding to do so.

1. You can start by balancing your time so that more is directed to creating your own visibility. Now is the time to reflect on what your vision is. What is it that you want to do that you are not doing? Think of your target audience. Are they in the same venue that you operate in now?

2. Begin to do more things independently. Start a project. Schedule presentations where you are out front. Send emails on YOUR behalf. Make sure you take credit for YOUR work and showcase what YOU can do. There are probably several opportunities for you to do so. Start small if you have to, but start, and do so alone.

3. Begin to reduce the amount of time you are seen with your high visibility associate. This doesn't mean that you have to relinquish your relationship with this individual. He or she may even be able to help you with connections. Just make sure that when you meet with and engage these connections, you are doing so on your own.

EXERCISE: Coming out from the Shadows

Respond to the questions below to help you identify why you are in the shadows and how to come out.

Whose shadow am I standing in?

Why? What is gratifying or fulfilling about this? How is this helping me achieve my career goals?

What about this role is dissatisfying?

What can I start doing now to become more independent and visible?

What target audience am I trying to reach?

Who else can I reach out to in order to help me increase my visibility?

138

#20 NEGLECTING TO LEAVE YOUR BRAND LEGACY

!

If I have seen further it is by standing on the shoulders of giants.
-- Sir Isaac Newton

WHAT IT MEANS

Your brand is bigger than you; and it can live on past the time you spend in any particular role. It can influence and inspire numerous others to live to their potential and explore new directions. What impact are you here to make upon others? What footprint will you leave behind? Personal branding has an unselfish, altruistic quality. It can do as much good for you as it can for others.

CONSEQUENCES

The implications of not leaving a brand legacy are far reaching. At a personal level, it may be frustrating that we're not remembered for our contributions. Yet who can we blame? Did we do what we could to shine a light on what we had to offer? Were we trying so hard to fly under the radar that a mystery remains around what we actually did? What effect does our acceptance of this way of operating have on our families, work colleagues, on those who thought they knew us? At minimum, those who thought we didn't contribute much will continue to think so. For those who missed the opportunity to know what we were about and what we did, it is a loss for us as well as for them.

Did we miss the opportunity to inspire a son or daughter, or younger sibling because we did not share those aspects about ourselves that we are passionate about? Creating a brand legacy does not have to be about

139

boasting or bragging about our life accomplishments. It can simply be about making sure our story is shared with others.

CASE IN POINT

Icons like Gandhi, Martin Luther King, Jr., Steve Jobs and numerous others all left indelible imprints on our global society. They were not necessarily trying to be different; as much as they were trying to **make a difference**, and their legacies have and will continue to endure the passage of time. I've worked in companies, where someone who had been gone for years was still spoken of fondly because of the impact they had with the people they worked. It might have been someone who wasn't afraid to speak out on unpopular issues, or someone who paved the way for new employee programs. Perhaps it was a leader who truly walked the talk and had a connection with employees at all levels.

Most likely, there are individuals who have had a major and positive impact on you -- whose words, deeds and style you remember. Think of who these individuals are. What is most memorable about them?

ROAD TO RECOVERY

If you haven't done so in the past, you can start now to be more deliberate about the actions you take in your life. You can devote time to defining your legacy and involving yourself in activities that will strengthen it.

1. Your legacy may be as simple as being a good role model for authenticity and purpose. Everyone is unique in some way. We all have "gifts differing." Being yourself should not be a struggle, and if being yourself is all you are remembered for, then job well done!

2. Be a mentor. Take time monthly to connect with others who are early in their careers. You can meet one-on-one or with a circle of individuals over lunch. Listen to their challenges and share your insights. Your perspective will be valued and you will most likely learn something from this exchange as well.

3. Tell your story.   There are several ways you can share your experiences and perspective on life and work.   Write a book. Start a blog. Create a video.   Teach a class. Participate on a workshop panel.   Your words may be the very ones to inspire someone who is facing similar challenges or who is at a similar crossroad as you were at some point in your life.

Civilization survives because we leave future generations a path to walk upon. We leave them our knowledge, our insights, our hopes, dreams, and sometimes our fears.   But we leave them something.   Your goal does not have to be as lofty as leaving the entire society something.   Start with those around you, your family, your friends, your colleagues.   These are individuals who you can touch and inspire by making small differences in your own life. Yes – your own life.   Your attempts at self-improvement, no matter how ultimately successful you are, are testimonies and sources of inspiration to those that are watching you.   And believe me . . . others are definitely watching you!

Be the change you want to see in the world.

--Mahatma Gandhi

EXERCISE: My Brand Legacy

Who are my brand benefactors (those whose lives I want to impact)?

What do I want to leave them?

What would I envision their tribute to me to say (e.g., the difference I made in their lives)?

What can I do on a daily, weekly or monthly basis to create this legacy (e.g., mentor, etc.)?

Action	How Often?

EPILOGUE
TURNING YOUR SHIP AROUND

Several examples of branding missteps have been presented throughout this book. There were also many exercises, tools and worksheets contained herein that you can go back and use to craft your personal branding action plan. None of the tools in this book, however, will work if you don't work them. The best advice in the world cannot substitute for a lack of action.

In order to move forward without feeling overwhelmed, here are some points to consider as you are turning your ship around and creating momentum in a new direction.

- It takes time to create a new habit, so **set aside some time each day** to work on your personal branding plan. Your brain can rewire itself to sustain new habits through sufficient practice and support.
- Pick one or two things to work on (**start small**)
- **Write it down**.
    - Use the worksheets in this book to develop a vision of how success will look and then develop the plan to get there.
    - Create a checklist of new behaviors, something you can pull out and look at several times throughout the day.
- **Reward yourself** along the way for changed behavior.
- If you are stepping into new space, some behaviors may initially feel uncomfortable. **Experiment** and find what works for you.
- **Reflect** on your personal branding experience and jot your thoughts down in a journal. This information can be looked at from time to time to extract ideas on what is working well and to identify better approaches.
- Remember to **leverage others** along the way. The impact you can make with and through others is bigger than the impact you can make by yourself. Personal branding is a contact sport!

Bon Voyage! Enjoy the journey!

REFERENCES

Alboher, Marci. (2012). The Encore Career Handbook: How to Make a Living and a Difference in the Second Half of Life. New York, NY: Workman Publishing Company.

Alderman, Tracy Anne. (1992). Self-monitoring: A new paradigm. Examining motivations for and origins of self-monitoring. California School of Professional Psychology - San Diego, CA. 9307892.

Covey, Steven. (2004). Seven Habits of Highly Effective People. New York, NY: Free Press.

Erikson, Erik. (1964). Insight and Responsibility. New York, NY: Norton.

Fraser, George. (2007). Click: Ten Truths for Building Extraordinary Relationships. New York, NY: McGraw-Hill.

Jones, Del. (Posted 6/7/2006 12:06 AM ET). Not all successful CEOs are extroverts. *USA Today,*
http://usatoday30.usatoday.com/money/companies/management/2006-06-06-shy-ceo-usat_x.htm

Levitt, T. (1990). Marketing myopia. In B. M. Enis, K. K. Cox, and M. P Mokwa (Eds.), *Marketing classics: A Selection of Influential Articles.* Upper Saddle River, NJ: Prentice Hall.

Maas, James. (1998). Power Sleep. New York, NY: Villard Books.

McKeown, Greg. (Posted 8/8/2012 10:00 AM ET). The disciplined pursuit of less. *Harvard Business Review HBR Blog Network,*
http://blogs.hbr.org/cs/2012/08/the_disciplined_pursuit_of_less.html

APPENDIX A - LIST OF EXERCISES AND WORKSHEETS

Blooper	Exercises/Worksheets	Page #
Having No Brand at All	• My Brand Objective	17
	• Create a Personal Brand Statement	18
Dancing the Night away	• Networker or Net Player?	26
Being Less Than Authentic	• My Two Faces	32
	• My Iceberg	36
The Chameleon	• Flexible, Political or Chameleon?	42
Foot in Mouth Syndrome	• Name it! Own it! Reframe it! Move Forward!	46
Wallowing in the Dead Zone	• Lessons Learned	50
Head in Sand Syndrome	• Total Recall – Two Views of Reality	55
Ignoring the Elephant in the Room	• My Elevator Speech	62
Misleading Packaging	• Make-over Survey	67
Ignoring your Target Market	• Target Market Analysis	73
Letting your Brand Become Rusty	• What has my Brand Done for me Lately?	78
Ignoring your Cyber Brand	• Social Media Game Plan	86
Flying Solo	• My Brand Publicists	93
	• The Power of Alliances - Two Degrees of Separation	94
Time Mismanagement	• How I Currently Spend my Time	100
	• How I Should be Spending my Time	101
Spreading your Brand Like Butter	• Analyzing my Strengths	107
Ignoring your Competition	• Analyzing my Competition	112
Thinking you are too Old to Brand	• Tough Love Conversation	123
	• Reinvention Plan	123
Thinking you are too Young to Brand	• Timeline of Accomplishments	132
	• Me in Five Years	133
Getting Lost Behind Someone Else's Brand	• Coming out from the Shadows	138
Neglecting to Leave a Brand Legacy	• My Brand Legacy	142

About the Author: Charmon Parker Williams, Ph.D. is an industrial/organizational psychologist who has had an extensive career working with global companies designing and leading organizational effectiveness strategies. She has a notable track record in Organizational Development, Leadership Assessment and Development, Diversity and Inclusion, Strategic Planning for Non-Profits, and Group Facilitation. Her accomplishments transcend a variety of industries in the private, non-profit, and public sectors.

Currently, Dr. Williams is the president of Parker Williams Consulting and has presented on personal branding and other career development approaches both nationally and internationally as well as coached professionals, executives, and entrepreneurs on individual branding strategies. She has been a contributing writer for a number of industry related publications and has been cited in the Wall Street Journal.

info@personal-branding-bloopers-blunders-boo-boos.com

Exploring Judaism:

A Reconstructionist Approach

Exploring

A Reconstructionist

Rebecca T. Alpert • Jacob J. Staub

EXPANDED AND UPDATED

THE RECONSTRUCTIONIST PRESS   *Elkins Park, PA*

Judaism:

Approach

Library of Congress Number: 00-190796

International Standard Book Number:
0-935457-50-X

Published by
The Reconstructionist Press
7804 Montgomery Avenue, Suite 9
Elkins Park, Pennsylvania 19027

Printed in the United States of America

Composition by Duke & Company
Typefaces: Text, Berkeley Old Style; Display, ITC Isbell.
Book and cover design by Adrianne Onderdonk Dudden

In honor of
Miriam and W. Maxwell Passerman
whose grant has made possible
the publication of the first edition
of this introduction to
Reconstructionist Judaism.
And in honor of
David and Miriam Brous,
Jerome and Linda Golden,
Fred and Linda Greenberg,
Don and Betsy Landis,
Bernie and Elaine Roberts,
Miriam Roland, and
Aaron and Marjorie Ziegelman
whose grants have made
the publication of subsequent reprints
of Exploring Judaism *possible.*

For our beloved teacher

Rabbi Ira Eisenstein

whose work we are honored to carry on

Contents

Acknowledgments

We began the acknowledgments of the first edition of *Exploring Judaism* in April 1985 with the following thought: "Writing a book is often pictured as a solitary enterprise. In fact, the opposite was true for us. This book is an exercise in collaboration. We begin by acknowledging each other; it is no exaggeration to say that we found working together to be an amazing experience of discovering how easily two can speak with one voice."

We begin again by acknowledging each other; the fifteen years that have passed since our first collaborative experience have only deepened our mutual respect and admiration.

This second edition came about because we were compelled to acknowledge the growth and changes in the Reconstructionist movement since 1985. We are grateful to the many readers of the first edition who encouraged us to think about how to write about those changes. Mordechai Liebling and David Teutsch were instrumental in responding to this need and in getting us started, and we are grateful to them.

We are also profoundly grateful to David Teutsch and Richard Hirsh for their diligent and thoughtful editing of the whole manuscript, and to Jeffrey Schein, Mark Seal, and Mordechai Liebling for their comments on particular sections.

We could not have completed this work without the editorial

support of Alan LaPayover, Seth Goldstein, Moti Rieber, and Denise Samuel, and we thank them profusely. We are also grateful to Lani Moss for the skillful and supportive way she saw this project through to its completion.

We also acknowledge our partners and children, whose presence sustains us: Barbara, Leah, Andrew, and Hana Staub, Lynn and Avi Alpert, and Christie Balka. We owe a special debt of gratitude to Ira Eisenstein, who will always be a model and inspiration.

We close these acknowledgments as we did the ones in the first edition, with a caution to readers: "We have tried to present a Reconstructionist perspective that reasonably represents the various outlooks included today in the Reconstructionist movement. As we hope will remain clear throughout the chapters that follow, no one can speak for all Reconstructionists. This is a healthy consequence of the movement's ideology, which encourages individuals and communities to engage Jewish civilization in various aspects. Thus, we interacted not only with each other, but with the various voices in the movement. We tried to speak for ourselves and others as well. The results are not to be taken as the official viewpoint of the movement; ultimately, this book represents our views alone. We do hope, however, that it offers the reader a sense of the Reconstructionist perspective."

Rebecca T. Alpert
Jacob J. Staub

25 August 1999
13 Elul 5759

Preface

In recent years, the Reconstructionist movement has enjoyed un-precedented growth. The number of affiliated congregations and havurot quadrupled between 1980 and 2000 to more than 100, and the number of members of affiliated groups continues to grow be-tween 10% and 20% each year. The new groups include a generation of American Jews who had never before associated with the move-ment. The growth of the Reconstructionist Rabbinical College (RRC), founded in 1968, has provided North American Jews with a new generation of leaders who have a different concept of the rabbinate, the synagogue, and the meaning of Jewish life. As a consequence, the graduates of the RRC find themselves in great demand. The move-ment has pioneered in revitalizing Jewish communal and spiritual life in such matters as the development of birth rituals for girls, out-reach to intermarried couples, inclusion of lesbian and gay Jews, and the synthesis of contemporary and traditional forms of worship. Thousands of people across the North American continent who had been disillusioned with the Jewish community and alienated from the Jewish tradition are now active and committed Jews because of their involvement with Reconstructionism. Thus Reconstructionism has enabled Jews to find new ways to express what it means to be a Jew today.

Reconstructionism has become recognized by the organized

American Jewish community as a major Jewish movement. But many North American Jews have never heard the term, or are unclear about its meaning. This book seeks to remedy that circumstance.

What is a Reconstructionist? All those associated with the movement are accustomed to the question and to the frustration of not being able to answer it "on one foot," in a simple declarative sentence.

"Reconstructionist Jews are willing to question conventional answers and keep open minds. They believe that a Jew need not and ought not sacrifice intellectual integrity for the sake of his/ her Jewish identity."

"Reconstructionists are Jews who take the Jewish tradition seriously and live Jewish lives even though they don't believe in the divine, supernatural origin of the Torah."

"Reconstructionists believe that, just as Jewish civilization has adapted to new circumstances throughout Jewish history, so must it adapt to North American society at the beginning of the twenty-first century."

"Reconstructionists tend to conduct more intimate worship services in which everyone is involved, and the rabbi, in addition to leading, also encourages others to lead."

"One of the ways that Reconstructionists tend to express their Jewish commitments is through social and political action."

Though each of these statements is accurate, none is a fair and comprehensive one-sentence definition. We can find out more by asking a different question. A better question than "What is a Reconstructionist?" is "How do Reconstructionists approach living as Jews?" We ask this question because we assume that what matters about Judaism is how we live it every day. Being Jewish affects our total being—our thoughts and feelings, our behaviors and relationships, our stance in the world community. This book describes the Reconstructionist approach to being Jewish.

One does not become a Reconstructionist simply by joining a Reconstructionist synagogue or by paying dues to a national organization. Our name itself indicates *active participation* in a shared process. No mere passive adjective describing a "type" of Judaism, our name says that each of us engages in the reconstruction of Jewish life and tradition to integrate them with the particular path that each of us chooses. The Reconstructionist community is not a body of synagogues and rabbis that others merely support. It is rather a community in the full sense of the term, in which no one's duty may be done vicariously by others. It is a community of Jews who commit themselves to ongoing study, to discussion of issues, and to a life of intelligent decision-making.

Jews can and do take different approaches to Jewish life. To some extent, our differences may be understood by looking at the names we call ourselves. Clearly, those who approach Judaism as "traditionalist" or "conservative" are looking to preserve and express those values and behaviors which they see as *inherently meaningful* and *permanently present* in Judaism. Those who describe themselves as "reformers" emphasize making changes and adapting traditions to bring Judaism into consonance with the world in which we live.

Those who seek to reconstruct, on the other hand, approach the issue of Jewish life in a significantly different manner. The term "reconstruct" involves two clear assumptions. First, that each generation prior to our own played a role in constructing the Judaism which is now ours. Thus, traditional meanings have changed over time; they have not always been conserved in the past and certainly should not be seen as permanent today. Reconstructionists use the foundation and building blocks they have inherited from the past, reordering and adding to them so that they fit the needs, values, and tastes of this generation, without altering them in ways that would make them unrecognizable or sap their richness.

The second assumption is that the basic structures of Jewish life are in need of serious rethinking. These include such institutional structures as the Jewish community and the synagogue, with special reference to the quality of interpersonal relationships and value orientations that exist within them. Reconstructing also applies to the organized Jewish community as a whole, including the nature of diaspora Jewry's all-important relationship to the State of Israel and the centers of Jewish creativity there. It applies to the basic intellectual structures of Jewish life as well as to the social ones—to the way we think about God, to traditional religious language, to prayer, and to the role of the Jewish people in history.

How this approach has been used by Jews who call themselves Reconstructionists will be spelled out in the pages that follow. In a world changing ever more quickly, it becomes increasingly important to think through carefully how we will reconstruct Judaism in every generation. That will help us to fulfill our Jewish lives and pass on a thriving Jewish culture to our children. Thus, being a Reconstructionist means being actively involved in exploring one's Jewishness. We do this not only for ourselves. The approach that we take, which has made it possible for us to live meaningful lives as Jews today, provides an example to others. So many Jews who are dissatisfied with the Jewish institutions in which they were raised are at the same time searching for meaning, looking for a place to call home. A Reconstructionist community may in fact be such a place.

That place would not exist within Jewish life were it not for the teachings of one great man, Rabbi Mordecai M. Kaplan (1881–1983).

Kaplan proposed the term "reconstruction" for his vision of a contemporary Judaism and articulated a program for its implementation. It is Kaplan's conceptual framework that provides the blueprint for this volume.

Kaplan set the standard for us: to reconstruct. It is up to us to study the program he created for the reconstruction of Judaism in his generation, and then to build upon it for our own time. That is how we understand his mandate and legacy to us.

Fifteen years after first completing this project, we find ourselves astonished at the extensive response of the Reconstructionist movement to Kaplan's mandate to build upon his plan of reconstruction in each generation. What began as a simple effort to update this volume has resulted in significant revisions and additions that reflect our contemporary situation of growth and change.

This expanded and updated version takes us further in our Reconstructionist exploration of Judaism. Our description of Kaplan's vision in the first six chapters has changed very little. However, the second half of the book, chapters 7–12, which show how to put Kaplan's blueprint into practice, has been greatly expanded to reflect the richness of Reconstructionist life today.

We examine how the civilizational approach has produced a deep and varied spiritual life for Reconstructionists. We look at how our focus on community has compelled us to become more inclusive, particularly of groups of Jews who have been and still are marginalized in Jewish life. We close by examining the vitality of Reconstructionist institutions and the exponential growth of the Reconstructionist bookshelf.

Kaplan's mandate is where we begin again. But his legacy is about openness to change, and we look with pride at the ways we have honored that legacy in reconstructing Jewish life for another generation.

Exploring Judaism:

A Reconstructionist Approach

1
The Creation of an American Judaism

The Choice to Be Jewish

Jews have not always been able to *choose* whether or not to identify with the Jewish people. That choice has been available for just over two hundred years. Prior to the modern era, the Jewish community was granted complete jurisdiction over its members by outside governing authorities. For Jews, Jewish law was the only law. Jewish education was the only education available. The only social services were Jewish. Jews lived in a *kehillah*—an organic Jewish community from which the only exit was apostasy. Converting to Christianity or Islam was, for most Jews, an unimaginable option. The wide cultural gap between the Jews and their neighbors in most periods of Jewish history made social integration difficult. Moreover, Jews believed in the divine origin of the Torah and their election by God, just as Muslims and Christians made similar, competing claims.

Thus, while the vast majority of Jews alive today have the ability at any time to abandon all connections with the Jewish people and our tradition without adopting another religious affiliation, this revolutionary circumstance is relatively new. It is a consequence of one of the fundamental aspects of the modern nation-state, which extends the rights and responsibilities of citizenship to individuals, but not to groups. In the past, the Jewish community often had to strike a bargain with the ruling monarch—for example, promising a certain number of tax dollars in return for the right to live autonomously under Jewish law. The modern state, by contrast, normally does not tolerate autonomous subgroups, but rather demands the individual citizen's complete political allegiance.

To be sure, one can look back into Jewish history and see periods during which individual Jews asked daring questions and had a great deal of freedom. But those daring questions were about *how* to be part of the Jewish community. The radical break that occurred with the beginning of modernity has afforded Jews the choice of *whether* to remain in the Jewish community at all.

Such is the mixed blessing of the "emancipation" of the Jewish people, which commenced at the end of the eighteenth century.

While Jews rejoiced at the equal rights which they were accorded (believing naively that social and political integration would bring an end to anti-Semitism), many rabbis anxiously lamented the new freedom of the individual Jew, who was now at liberty to ignore rabbinic pronouncements.

But there is more. It was not only the political realities that changed. The prevailing worldview underwent a radical transformation as well. In the past, Jews had shared with Muslims and Christians common beliefs in God, in sacred scripture, in reward and punishment, and in life after death. They had differed on the details while agreeing on the principles. Now, the newly emancipated Jew entered societies in Western Europe and North America in which the prevailing thinking was influenced by humanism and by the scientific revolution. People cared more about human potentialities than about God's attributes; more about happiness in this life than about heavenly reward; more about investigating the causes of natural phenomena than about attributing them to God's will. Christian culture had already been adjusting to these questions for several centuries, since the Renaissance and the Protestant Reformation. By contrast, Jews were thrust out of their ghettoized existence abruptly, without time for Judaism to modernize. The initial impulse of many of them was to discard Judaism entirely.

Finally, Jews—especially in North America—were faced with a modern political ideology that beckoned all citizens to become one nation under God, to abandon their foreign baggage and embrace fully a new, unprecedented society in which everyone was equal. In this context, Jewish commitments seemed not only obstructively separatist but antiquated as well. It was an integrated person indeed who could fully embrace the universal human family without abandoning Jewish allegiances.

Much of the history of Judaism in the modern era can be seen as a struggle between opposing forces. On the one hand, social, political, and ideological forces have drawn Jews away from Judaism, while on the other, committed Jews have devoted themselves to the task of persuading other Jews to remain Jewish. Out of our European heritage came Reform, Conservative, Orthodox, Zionist, Yiddishist, and other ethnic/cultural and philosophical approaches to the challenge, all of which have been transplanted in one way or another to the Western hemisphere.

Perhaps the only truly indigenous American attempt to respond to the problem of modernity for American Jewry is the approach of Mordecai Kaplan. How Kaplan came to focus on an American response to the modern challenge becomes clear when we look at his life in the context of American and Jewish history.

The Life and Thought of Mordecai M. Kaplan

Kaplan was born in Lithuania in 1881. At the age of nine he came to America when his father, an Orthodox rabbi, was called to these shores to become the assistant to Rabbi Jacob Joseph, who was serving at the time as "Chief Rabbi of New York." This attempt by East-ern European Jews to set up a community cohesive enough to have a chief rabbi indicates that there were Jews who wished to establish the traditional Jewish communal structure in America, so that Jewish identity would not be eroded by modernity. But the vast majority of Jews saw America as a place where they could shed much of their Jewishness.

In his youth, Kaplan was sheltered from Jews who rejected Juda-ism altogether. He was influenced, however, by new approaches to the Jewish tradition. He was exposed at an early age to people like Arnold Ehrlich, a scholar of the Bible who asked radical questions about divine authorship. He was sent to study at the fledgling Jewish Theological Seminary of America. Unlike the traditional yeshiva, which sought to strengthen Jewish separation, the Seminary was organized to "Americanize" Eastern European Jews while immersing them in Jewish study.

Kaplan also attended Columbia University, becoming exposed to the teachings of modern American thought. He studied philos-ophy, sociology, and anthropology, and began to develop a broad view of human culture and the place of religion within it.

Although these new ideas challenged the traditional Jewish world-view, for Kaplan they also provided the rationale for remaining Jewish. He applied the theories he learned to describing how Judaism could function in the modern world. Kaplan took it as his challenge to prove that being Jewish is an exemplary way of being human, and that Judaism should be understood in light of the latest theories and knowledge of human culture. For Kaplan, bringing contemporary insights to the understanding of Judaism results in living a rich life as an American *and* as a Jew, without the need to forsake either cul-ture for the other.

Kaplan spent many years working out his theories. Although he

maintained an ongoing position as a faculty member and adminis-
trator at the Jewish Theological Seminary until his retirement in 1963,
that institution did not provide a setting where Kaplan's program for
Judaism could be carried out. He needed to find a community of
Jews who were interested in working with him on the experiment
in Jewish living. A founder in 1912 of the Orthodox Young Israel
movement, and in 1913, along with Solomon Schechter, of the Conservative United Synagogue, he found neither fully responsive to the
American Jewish challenge.

In 1922, Kaplan, together with several followers from his former
Orthodox congregation, founded the Society for the Advancement
of Judaism (SAJ), a synagogue in New York City. With the establishment of the SAJ, Kaplan was free to propound his ideas and discuss them with a group of people open to his views. Because of his
experiences at the SAJ, he was able to write and bring his ideas to a
wider audience. In 1934, at age 53, Kaplan published his first major
work, *Judaism as a Civilization: Toward a Reconstruction of American
Jewish Life,* which is considered his magnum opus. Many other works
followed. With the founding of the Jewish Reconstructionist Foundation in 1940, Kaplan achieved an international platform that stood
unequivocally for the approach he advocated.

His many books, the magazine he published—the *SAJ Review,*
later renamed the *Reconstructionist*—his daring liturgical innovations,
his involvement in restructuring Jewish communal and educational
institutions, and his activism on behalf of women's religious equality
were his main contributions to Jewish thought and to the debate on
why and how to be a Jew in modern America.

Kaplan drew his followers from the ever-expanding population
of the SAJ and from the many people around the country who heard
him lecture and teach. But it was as a teacher of rabbis at the Jewish
Theological Seminary that his reputation was established. While

many of his students did not identify as his disciples, they neverthe-less were influenced by him in subtle and profound ways, so that it is not an exaggeration to state that Kaplan transformed the nature of American Judaism in the 1930s and 1940s.

Some of the rabbis he trained became ardent followers of Kaplan. They urged him to spread his message, and to start a movement in Jewish life with institutions to promote his ideas. The leader among them was Rabbi Ira Eisenstein, who also married Kaplan's eldest daughter, Judith. It was Eisenstein who formally assumed the leader-ship of the Reconstructionist movement. He wrote books that inter-preted Kaplan's teachings and became the editor of the *Reconstructionist* magazine. He also was primarily responsible for leading the key insti-tutions of Reconstructionist life—the Jewish Reconstructionist Feder-ation (the organization of congregations and havurot) and the Recon-structionist Rabbinical College, which he founded in 1968.

As the institutions of Reconstructionism have grown and devel-oped, Kaplan's program remains at the core of Reconstructionism. For several decades, the Reconstructionist movement was based pri-marily on his teachings. Today, however, the majority of Reconstruc-tionists are no longer drawn from those devoted to Kaplan and the *specific* formulations of his ideas. Kaplan's teachings are viewed not as the end of the story, but as the beginning. The Jewish Reconstruc-tionist Federation, the Reconstructionist Rabbinical College, and the Reconstructionist Rabbinical Association are all growing and thriv-ing, and people are drawn to an ever-expanding Reconstructionist movement.

Kaplan set the agenda, pinpointing those areas of Jewish life that need reconstruction if we are to meet the challenge of remaining Jewish in the modern world. But if we are to remain true to Kaplan's teachings, we must take cognizance of the fact that the world in which he lived and wrote was vastly different from our own.

Kaplan's life was very much influenced by the burgeoning wisdom available from the social sciences. Those new understandings of human life, which Kaplan unreservedly accepted, led him to various conclusions about what it might mean to be Jewish. Today we draw on a much wider range of academic disciplines. Indeed, even the discipline of sociology, on which he relied, has developed in unanticipated ways. At the same time, we are more willing to question the authority and objectivity of social scientific research.

Kaplan's thinking assumed that the values embodied in American society—values like liberty and democracy—are the culmination of the progress of human civilization. Today, we tend to be less certain that all aspects of American society are the ideals toward which every civilization ought to aspire, and we tend to put increased emphasis on non-American aspects of the Jewish tradition. Thus, our sense of the proper balance between the two is different from his. In Kaplan's day, the predominant worldview exalted the impersonal approach of the scientist and assumed that rational beings would use their minds together to create a better world. Today, living after Auschwitz and faced with the continuing danger of nuclear and ecological disasters, some of us question more vigorously the extent of our capabilities to bring about a better world by using politics and technology to achieve the good and the true. We no longer view science and technology uncritically; we use them while recognizing them as tools to be regarded cautiously.

Kaplan lived in an era when nationalism was perceived to be a force for good. Today, some of us question the power of nation-states to do more than war against one another.

In Kaplan's generation, intellectuals were involved in a debate about theism and atheism. Today, post-modernism has replaced empiricism as the frame of reference, so that most thoughtful Jews do not struggle with the question, "Does God exist?" but rather with the question, "How can we be certain about values like truth, goodness, or beauty in a fragmented world?"

Finally, we live today in a global village in which East and West are no longer so separate. Whereas Kaplan was working in Western categories, Jews today also must respond creatively to the challenge of Eastern religions. There is a new focus on the cultivation of inwardness and spirituality.

The task undertaken below is to describe Kaplan's program for reconstructing American Judaism, to look at that program through contemporary eyes, and to validate, augment, or reconstruct elements which need to be presented today in a different light. In order to be faithful Reconstructionists, we must build our reconstruction of Judaism on our own worldview, with Kaplan's thinking as our cornerstone and our challenge. Thus this book should chart a way of being Jewish that meets decisively the challenge of living as a Jew today.

2
An Evolving Religious Civilization

Searching for a Definition

What modernity gave to the individual Jew in terms of rights and identity, it took away from the Jews as a group. No longer would the community, the *kehillah,* function as an all-embracing Jewish society that provided for the individual's social, religious, economic, and political needs. With the disappearance of the *kehillah,* the community lost much of its ability to preserve group identity. The resulting benefits were enormous, both to Jews *as individuals,* and to general society in terms of the contributions of individual Jews. One need only mention Freud and Einstein in this context to highlight the point. But the loss to the Jews *as a group* was enormous as well, for they no longer possessed an encompassing sense of identity.

Many Jews welcomed the option and rejected identification with the group entirely. But for most, Jewish group identity was still a crucial matter. Attempts were made to redefine Jewish group identity in new terms.

Some sought to define being Jewish as membership in a religion. This brought Judaism into line with Christianity and made it understandable to those with whom the Jews were now permitted to associate. This definition worked not only for Reform Jews but for the more traditional Jews in Western Europe as well.

Others, chiefly in Eastern Europe, were influenced by modern nationalism and sought to describe being Jewish as being part of a nationality. They urged Jews to seek a territory in which to live together so that their nation could be like all other nations. This solution to the question of Jewish identity is most often associated with Zionism and the establishment of the State of Israel. But there were also groups of Jews who wished to set up Jewish collectivities in the other lands in which Jews lived.

Still others, influenced by theories about ethnic origins, defined Jewishness as a factor of ethnic identity. They linked Jews by physical characteristics and traits. This definition of Jewry was imposed externally as often as it was self-defined. It could be negative ("Jews are rich and have large noses"), positive ("Jewish men are intelligent and make good husbands"), or neutral ("Jews like to eat lox and bagels").

Of course, each of those definitions of being Jewish has *some* truth to it. There are Jews for whom being Jewish involves religious faith alone, or Israeli citizenship alone, or pride in one's ancestry alone. What was missing in Kaplan's time was a definition of Judaism broad enough to include *all* of these subgroups, so that Jewish nationalists, Jewish social activists, and Jewish worshippers could articulate the nature of their unity. It was the genius of Mordecai Kaplan to capture this sense of Jewish collectivity. He defined Judaism in a way that combined all of these discrete elements for the first time.

Peoplehood

Kaplan began by observing that the Jews are a people. As a people, Jews are interconnected through a common history, experience, and destiny; they are linked together as a group by their shared past, their mutual concern in the present, and their shared future destiny.

Individuals may choose diverse ways to link themselves to the Jewish people, but it is *belonging* to that people that makes us all Jews. This definition of Jews as a people does not only link us to our ancestors. It also illustrates that we are but one among the many peoples of the world, an integral part of the human family. While other interpretations of Judaism have sought to describe us as a people *apart,* Kaplan's definition suggests that we should see ourselves as related to other peoples and similar to them.

By redefining Jewishness in terms of belonging rather than believing, Kaplan sought to recapture some of the flavor of Jewish living prior to the modern era. Before the political emancipation of the Jews, a Jewish person acquired Jewish identity by virtue of membership in the community and not just because of theological or political or liturgical commitments. One came to one's Jewishness because one was raised in the Jewish community and culture. Members of the community, like an extended family, diverged widely in their philosophical, devotional, and even ritual commitments, but as they fought with one another, their Jewishness was not at issue.

The Problems of Belonging

For Kaplan himself, and for his initial audience of first-generation American Jews, this sense of belonging still came naturally. They were in direct touch with parents who had lived in the shtetls (Jewish villages) of Eastern Europe. They spoke Yiddish and had been raised in places like the Lower East Side of New York. Their task was to Americanize—to shed the trappings of Jewish belonging. Many were on the verge of cutting all ties to the Jewish tradition. Thus they were interested in Kaplan's argument that they could *belong* to the Jewish people without necessarily believing or behaving in the traditional manner of their forebears.

Jews today often do not see themselves as part of the Jewish community and do not always experience a sense of identification with the Jewish people as a whole. Today, a sense of belonging primarily to the Jewish people is anything but natural. We no longer live in Jewish communities. Our friends, neighbors, and colleagues are not necessarily Jewish, and if they are, their Jewishness is often incidental to our relationship with them. Many of us don't know how to sing the songs of Shabbat, for example, and even those of us who do know them often cannot sing them comfortably at a Friday evening dinner or a Saturday lunch.

Moreover, we have lost our ancestors' sense of oneness with the past. They interpreted the events in their lives as an integral part of a cosmic and providential drama. They had been exiled for their sins, and they awaited messianic redemption in their belief that God would not abandon them. They believed that their souls had been present at Sinai for the giving of the Torah because they belonged to a community whose reason for being was that very event.

We, by contrast, have lost that sense of active memory. Most of us understand the experiences of our ancestors in their historical context. It is often difficult for us to imagine that they really believed that God was an active force in their lives and the life of the Jewish people.

Kaplan suggested that an empathic understanding of our past would make it more meaningful in the present. Much of the effort of Reconstructionists is devoted to regaining a oneness with the past, even as we maintain an awareness of the importance of the present. This quest for belonging will be elaborated below, when we describe the Reconstructionist approach to ritual, to historical awareness, and to a contemporary community.

Judaism as a Civilization

Once belonging is established as the essential part of Jewish group self-definition, we must begin to discover the basic characteristics of the group to which we belong. What is Judaism? Kaplan supplied that definition too. Judaism is not merely a religion, a nationality, or an ethnicity. Kaplan defined Judaism as the *evolving religious civilization of the Jewish people.* Each of the key words in this definition will be discussed separately to show its full breadth and depth.

Like peoplehood, *civilization* implies a totality. Civilization encompasses all of the elements of group life: art, culture, philosophy, language, law, ethics, celebrations, patterns of eating and dressing, and sancta (holy things, times, events, and places). Every group that has ever functioned has included these elements in its group life. Being Jewish, by Kaplan's definition, is in some ways like being Greek, Irish, or Native American. One belongs to a group and participates in the life of that group as one's primary way of being in the world. As will be discussed later, one can live in more than one civilization at a time.

Because of the nature of contemporary society, our lives are fragmented into many pieces. Family, work, and leisure activities fall into separate compartments. In the process, we lose the sense that our lives are unified wholes. A civilizational definition of Judaism can be of assistance in regaining our self-integration. As individuals, we may need to pursue paths that emphasize different parts of ourselves. If we are an organic part of Jewish civilization, however, we can begin to see ourselves as elements in a greater scheme of things and thus achieve a greater sense of wholeness.

Viewing Judaism as a civilization also enables us to appreciate those elements of Judaism often taken for granted or forgotten. The Jewish arts—music, literature, dance, drama, sculpture, storytelling, and photography—take on new importance when looking at the totality of Jewish civilization. Kaplan urged that we emphasize these underdeveloped elements. They are the natural expressions of a living civilization and have been ignored for too long. The recent burgeoning of Jewish crafts and art is a welcome revitalization of Jewish civilization.

Finally, the civilizational view leads us to appreciate that each of us has something to contribute to Jewish life, no matter what our talents or interests. Jewish creativity arises in many areas: the arts, cooking, writing, teaching, building, settling arguments, choosing values, parenting, social action, playing, dreaming. All of these activities—and more—can be cultivated as part of the civilization of the Jewish people; one's Jewishness need not be measured primarily by synagogue attendance or eating habits.

A Religious Civilization

No two civilizations are identical. Some seem to produce great architects; others, intricate systems of social organization. When Kaplan defined Judaism as a civilization, he did not intend to imply that Judaism is substantially identical to all other civilizations. For him, the primary identifying feature of Jewish civilization lies in its religious aspects.

What do we mean by religion? Religion is the search to discover what is ultimately meaningful in life and to find ways of expressing the resulting visions of the ultimate in behaviors and ideas.

Taking his cue from the studies of social scientists, Kaplan understood religion as a group phenomenon rather than as an individual one. Kaplan did not agree with Alfred North Whitehead, who defined religion as what a person does with solitude. Although every individual arrives at his or her own religious vision and finds those elements in religious behavior that enhance his or her own life, this search always takes place within the context of a group.

Every group expresses its vision of the ultimate through statements of faith and ritual actions, through sacred stories and traditional customs. Words, narratives, and patterns of behavior all derive their sanctity from their personal connection with an ultimate source of wisdom and power. And members of the group unconsciously interpret the meaning of their lives through the narratives, values, and symbols that they have internalized.

In theistic religions, that source of wisdom is called God, and in traditional forms of Judaism, God reveals divine wisdom in the Torah. Thus, all aspects of a Jew's life can be sanctified because they can be viewed in terms of their divine source and connection. One recites a blessing of gratitude for each kind of food one eats. When one treats one's customers in accordance with the *mitzvot* (commandments), one is a partner with God in the redemption of the universe. When one reads the newspaper, it is with the implicit understanding that current events have a greater meaning and purpose—even if that purpose eludes us. In sum, a religion is the aspect of a culture with which we structure reality, separating the significant from the insignificant, interpreting the apparently random events of our lives in a meaningful and orderly way.

Of course, the traditional Jew believes that all of the commandments, articles of faith, and rituals are literally God-given. Taking his cue from modern historians and social scientists, Kaplan understood that *every people* makes such a claim for the religious aspect of its civilization. For most of us, it is more accurate and more meaningful to understand the religion of the Jewish people as the expression of our highest values and most profound wisdom, without claiming that our religion is exactly identical with the will and wisdom of a perfect God. In other words, what a generation hears God say tells us at least as much about the problems and values of that generation as about God. As social situations and moral values change, so do human interpretations of God and the regulations of halakhah (Jewish law).

One of the distinctive characteristics of Jewish civilization is the way in which religion is infused in elements of culture—food, clothing, language, literature, law—which are not usually associated with Western definitions of religion. In Christianity there is a clear distinction between the sacred and profane aspects of one's life. That tendency is even more pronounced in America, where the separation of religion and secular life, of church and state, is elevated to a constitutional principle. Jewish civilization, by contrast, is a religious civilization—its language is a sacred one, its meals have ultimate significance, and there is not a similar distinction between synagogue and marketplace.

Furthermore, the great ideas that Judaism has contributed to human understanding have been expressed in religious terms. The social concepts and moral values that have shaped much of Western civilization are suggested in the Ten Commandments and made explicit in the great religious literature of the Jewish people—the Bible, the Talmud, the collections of Midrash, the Siddur. Religion was not divorced from life in the daily activities of the Jewish people. Perhaps the chief impact of these ideas, which have so greatly influenced Western civilization for several thousand years, lies in the way they bring religious values to daily living.

For most Jews today, even if religion is central to their Jewish perspective, it is not all-encompassing. This is the case because of the role of religion in contemporary society, where religion is commonly restricted to those aspects of life that are synagogue/church-related and that involve an explicit profession of faith in God. More than ever before, today one can live a Jewish life and not perceive it as "religious" in any way. One can decide to participate in and observe Jewish customs and rites without attaching ultimate meanings to them. For example, it is possible to keep a kosher home not because "God said so," but rather for the purpose of maintaining a link to the Jewish collectivity, or because one's family did, or because one wants any Jew to be comfortable eating in one's home, or because one finds *kashrut* aesthetic—without ever having a sense of *kashrut* as a religious observance. One can be fluent in Hebrew and use it daily as a teacher, interpreter, or flight attendant for El Al Airlines, without attaching any explicitly religious meaning to the language. Without examining the religious significance of the holiday, one can light Hanukah candles every year as a way to express one's Jewish identity, while most of America expresses its Christian identity.

Many people would be tempted to dismiss such secularization of Jewish custom as inappropriate and inauthentic. Certainly, the traditionalists among us affirm unremittingly that Jewish civilization must remain as halakhically and supernaturally oriented as it was in the past. Reconstructionists, by contrast, believe that our civilization must be reconstructed to adapt to the unprecedented circumstances of our era. At a time when traditional beliefs about God and miracles and providence are called into question, it is legitimate to be a cultural Jew who both identifies with Jewish civilization and remains uncomfortable with its inherited religious strand. The secular Jews who express their Jewishness by writing Yiddish stories, eating latkes, making *aliyah* to live on a secular kibbutz where Jewish tradition is disregarded, doing Israeli dancing, or making an annual contribution to Jewish philanthropic organizations, should not be excluded from Jewish life because they refuse to see themselves as religious.

Reconstructionists would argue nonetheless that Jews who disavow the central religious aspect of Jewish civilization are not only ignoring the ways in which Jewish cultural forms subliminally transmit values and condition one's sense of life's meaning; they are also missing out on the most enriching and profound parts of the tradition they inherit. It is true that the religious insights of our ancestors are phrased in supernaturalistic terms and images that often no longer speak to us. But when the traditional rationales for beliefs and practices lose their meaning, Jews can and should revalue them to express our own most exalted values—thus continuing the evolution of Judaism. This will be discussed at greater length below when we address ritual observance directly. Nevertheless, defining Judaism as a "religious civilization," rather than as a "religion," leaves room for secularist perspectives without mistaking the vital role that religion has played and continues to play in the lives of Jews.

The Evolution of Jewish Civilization

The last element of the definition suggests that Judaism is an *evolving* civilization. At first glance this appears obvious. Don't all civilizations evolve, change, and grow? From the vantage point of the historian, this clearly is the case. From the perspective of traditional Judaism, however, the idea that Judaism is evolving presents serious problems. Rabbinic Judaism was founded on the supposition of the fundamental immutability of the Torah, God's word. True, we have had scholars in every generation to interpret Torah, but only to extract Torah's *unchanging* meaning as it applies to the *changed* social situation of each generation. Furthermore, from the viewpoint of traditional Judaism, the latitude of interpretation as well as the ability of the interpreters grows weaker in time as we move further and further away from the event at Sinai.

In our definition of Judaism as evolving, Reconstructionists take fundamental issue with this perspective. For us, Judaism has been created by Jews over the course of our history. Judaism necessarily has evolved because all of human culture evolves and adapts to changing historical circumstances. It is inaccurate to claim that the rituals and beliefs of contemporary Orthodox Jews date back to Sinai. In every era, our ancestors interacted with neighboring cultures and reinterpreted laws in accordance with the needs and values of the times. The creation story in Genesis resembles Babylonian stories from the same period; the Ten Commandments, Hittite treaties; the Pesah Seder, a Roman feast; the dress of Hasidim, the garb of eighteenth-century Polish nobles. Slavery was prohibited rather late in Jewish history, and the bar mitzvah ceremony introduced even later.

The term "evolution" is sometimes understood as implying that Jewish civilization has progressed steadily from the time of our "primitive" ancestors to our own era, in which our understanding of nature is more accurate than ever before and our ethical sensibilities are more elevated than ever before. Such views are a form of modernistic triumphalism.

That is *not* the intention of our use of the term "evolution." In the evolution of species, one form survives because it is better adapted to new environmental conditions. It is not superior except with reference to the current conditions in which it lives. Similarly, we advocate an evolution of Jewish civilization which continually adapts to the ever-changing conditions with which Jews are confronted. Our position does not require a belief that, in all or even most respects, contemporary Jews know more or are more ethical than previous generations of Jews. To be sure, on some issues—for example, the equality of women and men or the abolition of slavery—we believe that our ethical values transcend those of our ancestors. Our historical perspective, however, cautions us against making such claims too often and too confidently—for we are as much the products of our times as our ancestors were the products of theirs.

Thus, we do not claim that we understand God better than the prophet Isaiah or that our sense of justice transcends that of Joseph Karo, the author of the *Shulḥan Arukh* (a code of Jewish law). Rather, we think that because our environment is different from our ancestors', we must transform their beliefs and practices into a contemporary idiom. When those beliefs and practices are transformed in this way, they can function for us as they did for earlier generations. Thus, Reconstructionists are involved in a sensitive balancing act, in which we seek to reinterpret the past in a contemporary form without discarding the treasury of wisdom embedded in Jewish civilization.

Once we recognize the evolution that Jewish civilization has undergone over three thousand years, we can begin to sense its power and resiliency. Jews have been able to live among so many different peoples with different cultures because of the ability of the Jewish people to take elements from the outside culture and adapt them for our purposes, making them Jewish.

The development of the holiday of Hanukah illustrates this idea. Originally a commemoration of a historical event (probably a victory in a Jewish civil war), Hanukah took on different meanings in different eras. It attached itself to the time of the winter solstice where, like Christmas, it replaced a pagan festival which brought light to the dark winter. Its original significance was de-emphasized by later tradition, which did not glorify human victory in war, and its celebration was commemorated by a special *haftarah* (prophetic reading) from the Book of Zechariah which states, "not by might, nor by power, but by my spirit, says the Lord of Hosts." In modern times, Hanukah was revived both by Zionists, who wanted to glorify Jewish efforts in military endeavors, and by Jews integrated into Christian society, who needed a counterpart to Christmas.

Conscious Changes

All of our holidays, practices, and even beliefs have evolved, and they must continue to evolve if Judaism is to stay vital in today's world. While it has always been the case that Judaism has undergone adaptation, this generally has not been a self-conscious process. Jews for much of our history believed that innovations actually were more accurate understandings of the original unchanging, divinely revealed Torah. What is fundamentally different now is that we are conscious of the changes. Today we must live and work with the awareness that we ourselves can and do make changes.

In essence, this is the challenge of our time. In many ways, our self-consciousness makes the inevitable changes more difficult, but not less inevitable. Kaplan recognized the nature of this radical difference brought about by modernity, and challenged us in turn to face it. When we accept the definition of Judaism as an evolving religious civilization, we begin to come to terms with the enormity of the task of renewing Judaism for our time. In a world that is changing ever more quickly, we too must change more quickly to keep up.

If we accept the fact that Judaism evolves—and that change is essential to Jewish life—we might be led to the extreme position that nothing in Judaism has remained constant, or that change is the only constant factor. This would be an erroneous assumption. From the Reconstructionist perspective, what is constant in Judaism is the Jewish people and its devotion to the highest ideals of its religious civilization. The Jewish people who share in this devotion should determine in any given era what Judaism will be like. Of course, we must continue to be deeply immersed in the worlds of our ancestors as well as in our own world; thus, Judaism at any given time becomes a blend of our inheritance, of our own experiences, and of our vision of the future.

This outlook presumes a tremendous amount of faith in the ability of the Jewish people to survive and sustain itself. It also places a great responsibility on the individual Jew to be part of this process of continuing Jewish survival. We do not believe that the survival of the Jewish people is an end in itself. When Kaplan defined Judaism as the religion of ethical nationhood, he sought to express our conviction that Jewish civilization is a means to greater ends—the fulfillment of the individual, the responsibility of individuals to treat others as reflections of the divine image, and the responsibility of each community to seek global justice and peace among all communities. To be true to our heritage, we need to do more than emphasize Jewish survival; we must also make the Jewish civilization function in the service of these transcendent ends. That is why the tradition cannot be left to speak in archaic, irrelevant idioms, and that is why we cannot shirk the responsibility to become part of the process of the evolution of the Jewish people.

Despite those around us who study rates of Jewish births and intermarriage and make dire predictions, despite the difficult and tenuous condition of Jews in the State of Israel and elsewhere, Reconstructionists today maintain an optimistic view concerning the future survival of the Jewish people. While sharing others' concern about "Jewish continuity," we are also inspired by the thousands of previously unaffiliated Jews who are joining our congregations and havurot each year, and by the surveys that show that most Reconstructionists are more committed to Judaism and more ritually observant than were their parents. We believe that Kaplan's definition of Judaism is fundamentally sound, as long as the Jewish people maintains its will to survive.

The question that remains to be addressed is how we, the Jewish people, should go about reconstructing a Judaism for our day that will make us want to perpetuate ourselves—that will make us feel that we are passing a good heritage to the next generation.

3
God

Although religion is paramount in the Reconstructionist definition of Jewish civilization, conspicuously absent from our definition of Judaism is any mention of God. This is no accident. Reconstructionists believe that *the Jewish people* is the constant that runs through all the various stages in the evolution of Jewish civilization. Jewish conceptions of God have changed over the course of our historical odyssey. Even the claim that God is One has acquired different meanings: the midrashic writer's *Shekhinah* (divine presence) weeping in exile, the medieval philosopher's unchanging One, and the kabbalist's *sefirot* (divine emanations) provide little basis for the claim of theological uniformity. To *define* Jews in terms of their beliefs about God is thus impossible, unless we choose to distort the reality of the Jewish experience.

Though precise definitions of God are not Jewish touchstones, it is nevertheless the case that Jewish people have always believed in God and that this belief has been central to living a meaningful Jewish life. Today, developing a vocabulary of faith is an important part of our self-understanding as Jews.

Kaplan's Belief

Mordecai Kaplan had a distinctive and controversial concept of God.

Although not all Reconstructionists share Kaplan's theology, an understanding of it may be helpful in challenging us to discover what God means to each of us.

Kaplan himself was raised to be a believing Jew. In the world in which he lived, God's presence gave meaning to the Jew's life. God was perceived as Creator of the universe, Revealer of the Torah, and Arbiter of the destiny of the Jewish people. God commanded Jews to behave in certain ways; without God's command, those rituals and behaviors would have been meaningless to them. God set the destiny of the Jewish people; without that role in the world, being Jewish would have lost its meaning. In ways that are incomprehensible to many of us today, God's assistance was sought at every turn, and changes of fortune were attributed to God's will. One spent hours of one's day in prayerful conversation with God and in the study of texts believed to be of divine authorship. Truly, Jews could thereby perceive the whole world as divinely inhabited.

Yet as a young man, Kaplan began to doubt the efficacy of this traditional worldview for his life. Like so many other people, he could not believe the literal truth of the claims of the Jewish tradition. He began to doubt, for example, that God literally spoke to human beings and that those words were recorded in our sacred texts. He could not believe that the destinies of human beings are determined by an Almighty Person who is conscious of and concerned with our every human thought and action. He became skeptical of the prospect that God rewards and punishes us both in this life and, after death, in the World to Come. Unwilling to accept the explanation that biblical language and anthropomorphism could be dealt with as metaphor alone, Kaplan sought other answers couched in the language and thinking of his day.

Influenced by religious naturalism, Kaplan began thinking of God less as a Person who controls the world from above and more as a Force or Process within the universe. In one significant way, this perception of God was true to the Jewish tradition. As early as the rabbinic period, Jews began to interpret biblical descriptions metaphorically. Yet, denying God as a Person who directs the affairs of the world, and particularly who acts in relation to the Jewish people, was a radical departure from the main currents of the tradition.

Despite claims to the contrary, Kaplan never denied the existence of God. Rather, he rejected the belief that God is a Person—a Being with thoughts and feelings like those of humans, who is aware of and concerned with the everyday affairs of the world. He found this traditional supernaturalistic concept impossible to believe, and he sought to reconstruct the Jewish concept of God precisely so that educated, modern-minded Jews would *not* abandon their belief in God. He thus described God in categories that did not require him to forsake his intellect.

Functional Reinterpretation

To understand Kaplan's discussion of God, we need to understand the method he used to reinterpret the tradition. He did not believe that a contemporary Jew is *absolutely* free to attribute new meanings to traditional concepts and rituals. Rather, he argued that it is our task to understand and empathize with the components of our traditions, so that we can determine how beliefs functioned for our ancestors in their own terms. Once that is accomplished, authentic reinterpretation would express in our terms the functional equivalents of what Jews in the past had expressed in their own idioms. For example, if the retelling of the Exodus story at the Pesaḥ Seder served as a device to liberate Jews and to have them confront the meaning of freedom, then it is authentic for us today to discuss the meaning of freedom at the Seder.

In the case of God-belief, Kaplan asserted that traditional conceptions of God had served Jews in the past by guiding them to salvation. By salvation, he meant those things for which people ultimately search: to find holiness, meaning, and peace in life; to bring about the betterment of the world.

In the traditional conception, God's Torah guides the individual to sought-after goals in this world and the next. Through God's redemption of the people Israel, the world will become a better place.

In Kaplan's functional reinterpretation, God becomes "the Power that makes for salvation." Kaplan identified God with the powers that help people find salvation. He emphasized the ways that God should *function* in people's lives. His main goal was to foster Judaism as the vehicle through which Jewish people work to achieve the goal of salvation.

Transnaturalism

Kaplan believed that the divine works through nature and human beings. He neither identified God with things in the world (natural) nor did he consider God to be beyond or detached from the world (supernatural). Therefore, Kaplan's theology came to be called "transnatural."

In this view, there is more to the universe than the sum of its parts. In the organic interrelationship of all of its processes, there are divine powers that truly exist apart from the empirically verifiable phenomena of nature. They are manifest, for example, in human self-consciousness. It takes faith in God to believe that the world is structured in a way that gives significance to the human quest for salvation. A transnaturalist, however, believes that God works *through* us rather than *upon* us. Thus, our sense of responsibility to bring divinity into the world is sustained by the faith that there is a power at the source of human endeavors.

In more recent years, one of Kaplan's students, Rabbi Harold Schulweis, has developed a new means of expressing transnaturalistic belief that he calls "predicate theology." In grammatical terms, he suggests that we refer to God not as subject, but as predicate. This linguistic change liberates us to think about God in new ways. Using Schulweis's terminology, we would say that it is more important, for example, to believe that justice, kindness, and compassion are godly, than that God is a Person possessing the attributes of justice, kindness, and compassion. This is another way of expressing the importance of human responsibility to bring *godliness* into the world. This does not necessarily involve changing the traditional language of prayer, but rather the way we understand that language. For example, we refer in our prayers to God as the One who frees the captive. We express our hope in this way that the divine forces that create freedom —on both the political and personal levels—will be effective. We also affirm our commitment to making those forces manifest—both through political action and through our will to thrive and transcend our limitations. We believe that these forces are manifestations of the godliness that pervades creation.

This type of belief is not all that different from the conception of God held by such medieval philosophers as Maimonides, who is recognized universally as one of the greatest Jewish authorities. Maimonides developed a theory of negative attributes because he understood that God cannot be described as subject. He conceived of God as immaterial, unchanging, and unaware of the details of this world. He believed that our knowledge of God could be derived only from our understanding of the divine laws that inhere in the universe. The Reconstructionist conception of God is thus not as radically discontinuous with the past as it might first appear.

A transnaturalistic faith also answers one of the most troubling questions human beings have ever asked: If God is the force behind everything and controls all events, why do the innocent suffer? Another of Kaplan's students, Rabbi Harold Kushner, has given a contemporary transnaturalist's response to this question in his popular work, *When Bad Things Happen to Good People*. The answer is that the question itself is based on a faulty assumption. God is neither all-powerful nor present everywhere. Rather, as the nineteenth-century Hasidic master Rabbi Menahem Mendel of Kotsk teaches, "God dwells where we let God in." God is only manifest in the world where and when we ourselves approach salvation. God is not a Person who rewards and punishes us like a parent.

The innocent may suffer because we have not worked hard enough to end the suffering of the earth's creatures, or because random things occur over which neither we nor God have any control. Some ills—like war and famine—are subject to our redeeming efforts. Others—like critical illness and natural disasters—can at best be ameliorated. When we can assist those in need or comfort those in pain, God is working through us. When we cannot, it may be said that we experience God's presence in our sorrow.

Questioning Transnaturalism

Some may wonder if transnaturalists aren't just pretending—that they don't really believe that God exists and only choose to call human activities "godly." After so many centuries in which God was conceived supernaturally, it does sometimes seem that a God without supernaturalism is no God at all. What good is God if God neither intervenes in human history to reward, punish, and effect God's purposes, nor abides in a celestial realm, listening attentively to prayers? If God does not perform miracles, why pray for recovery when you are sick?

If God does not command us, why should we perform ritual acts at all? Actually, transnaturalists have good reasons to retain a faith in God, to perform rituals, and to pray.

It does require an act of faith to be a Reconstructionist. No one can demonstrate scientifically or prove rationally that there are divine forces that make for salvation. When a dictator is deposed, when a poet composes a verse, when a human relationship flourishes, when a person achieves a liberating insight—all these phenomena could be explained merely in terms of natural causes and effects. Belief in the existence of a transnatural God, however, enables us to derive strength because we view such occurrences in a larger context. They are the accomplishment of divine ends—bringing love, justice, and beauty into the world. Only a person who devotes a great deal of *kavanah* (intention) and energy to living in harmony with the divine presence in the universe can know from experience how very real God is, conceived transnaturally.

Critics of transnaturalism have suggested that this approach to God is cold and impersonal; that in explaining God in this manner, God is reduced to a concept and that this process undermines the awe and mystery present in the traditional Jewish view of God. But what could be more awe-inspiring than the feeling we have when we sense ourselves to be the conduit of a power working in the universe to make it a better place to live? Or when we perceive the power working through nature which enables trees to grow or flowers to bloom? And what could be more mysterious than the way in which those processes unfold themselves? Transnaturalism doesn't reduce God to a concept; it provides human beings with language that speaks of God as present in the world, rather than hovering over it. Transnaturalism allows us truly to see ourselves as partners in creation.

Moreover, there is ample opportunity for a believer in a transnatural God to cultivate a spiritual practice that makes God present in all aspects of life. As we describe in chapter 7, some Reconstructionists choose to engage in a discipline of regular *tefilah* and/or meditation, both in and out of the synagogue, that yields an ongoing awareness of and appreciation for the sacred nature of all existence. They speak literally when they say, on Shabbat morning, "*Nishmat kol ḥai tevarekh et shimkha*—the soul of every living thing shall bless your name." They experience *ahavat olam*—perpetual divine love—about which we sing on Friday evenings. Belief in a transnatural God rules out appeals to God the Person to answer prayers and to intervene supernaturally in human affairs. It in no way precludes the believer from experiencing the presence of God permeating all aspects of our lives.

Uncommanded *Mitzvot*

Transnaturalism rejects the belief that the words of the Torah come from divine revelation at Sinai or that the *mitzvot* are each divinely ordained commandments. From a transnaturalist viewpoint, God is not an omnipotent commander who rewards and punishes. What then is the rationale for obeying Jewish laws? What does it mean, for example, to address God as the one who commands us to light Shabbat candles? In what sense are we commanded?

The answer to this question is found in our initial definition of what it means to see oneself as part of the Jewish people. We behave as Jews because we value our connections to Jewish people, past and present. Jewish rituals have a sacred history that reflect inherited wisdom as well as group renewal. They should not be discarded casually. Otherwise, each generation could begin anew rather than reconstruct.

We often choose to retain the traditional forms of Jewish practice, even when we no longer mean what our ancestors meant when they spoke those words or performed those actions. We do so because such rituals both enrich us and sustain us—leading to our salvation in terms of our own values. Sanctified by the intentionality of our ancestors, the ritual forms themselves are permeated with a sacred aura that is ideally suited to help us deepen our connections to the divine presence.

Thus, when we light the Shabbat candles, we do more than mark the beginning of a day of rest devoted to our ultimate values. The flickering candles themselves possess a power to transform us because of the *kavanot* (meanings) that past generations attributed to those candles: for example, the identification of that light with the *Shekhinah* (divine presence) or the experience of receiving a *neshamah yeterah*—an additional soul that enables the Jew to reach greater spiritual heights on Shabbat.

Meanings give birth to new meanings. The sense of being commanded comes to us through traditional forms that give us a clearer vision of the divine imperatives in our own era. For example, the Shabbat candles remind us that fire is both life-giving and destructive, and that the messianic hope of Shabbat depends on our ability to harness our technology for constructive purposes. If God is not the commander of these acts, God nonetheless is reflected through them.

Worship

If God does not hear and answer prayer, how and why do Reconstructionists worship? This question, often asked about prayer, is based on a mistaken assumption. It is not the case that the primary purpose of prayer in Judaism is to petition God to grant one's pleas. The Hebrew verb "to pray" (*lehitpallel*) is in a grammatically reflexive form, which usually indicates an action which one performs by and for oneself. Accordingly, most rationales given for prayer throughout Jewish history have asserted that praying improves the moral and spiritual character of the one who prays.

Thus Reconstructionists are acting traditionally when we express gratitude, humility, or wonder in prayer, even as we see the words of the liturgy as metaphors which evoke the highest aspirations of the Jewish people. A goal of prayer is to develop those qualities by tapping into the divine power that enables us to become more ap-preciative and humble. Prayer always has functioned to make us aware of the divine presence, and so it continues to function. We seek to unite ourselves with the transnatural One that works within us. A list of the ways in which prayer works in Reconstructionist contexts is included below in chapter 7.

Myth and Metaphor

Many Reconstructionists have difficulty accepting Kaplan's approach to God in all of its facets, and it is not necessary to do so to identify with the Reconstructionist movement. Reconstructionist congrega-tions—and the Reconstructionist Rabbinical College—include many spiritually-oriented Jews who find Kaplan's identification of God as *Process* alienating. When they *daven* at worship services, and when they attempt to pursue lives of sanctification, they experience God as a *Being* with whom they can, in some sense, converse, and from whom they can derive strength and fortitude. That understanding can fit into Reconstructionist thought as long as it does not include affirmation of Torah-from-Sinai and direct supernatural intervention in our individual lives.

Though there is much debate among Reconstructionists about the language and imagery of prayer, the debate is *not* about super-naturalism. It is rather about the way prayer can and should func-tion to express mythically what is beyond exact description.

All Reconstructionists would agree, for example, that though we refer to God as the Healer of the sick, we should not accept our ancestors' conception of God as supernaturally intervening to perform miraculous cures. Yet after the physician has administered the prescribed treatment, there is an unpredictable variable, so that not all patients respond identically. The energy of the struggle for life rises and subsides in ways that cannot be measured. Kaplan would have described that struggle in terms of impersonal life forces; other Reconstructionists choose to describe it in terms of a personal God who transcends nature. Both would agree that God does not consciously and intentionally intervene to suspend the laws of nature in order to reward and punish. The debate, then, is *not* about supernatural intervention. It is, rather, about whether God, who is beyond accurate description, should be described metaphorically as Person.

Kaplan and earlier generations of his disciples cared most of all about intellectual integrity, and they fought the battle on the issue of the words of our prayers: We should not, they argued, ever say what we do not mean. A new generation shares that commitment but is often more inclined to use traditional formulations because of their mythic and poetic power to move us—even though we don't understand those phrases in terms of the supernatural idiom of our ancestors. The natural world, after all, includes not only those phenomena that scientists can measure, but also the often complex workings of the human psyche. It is therefore possible for a naturalistic Jew to affirm the value and centrality of mystical consciousness, and the power and importance of prayerful intentionality.

Chosenness and Vocation

Not all of Jewish doctrine about God is so easily assimilated to a Reconstructionist world view. If we cannot say that God chose the

Jewish people, why do we consider ourselves chosen? How can we bless God for having "separated us from all other peoples of the earth, and not cast our lot with theirs"?

Kaplan's response was that we should not do so, and the liturgy of the Reconstructionist movement does not include references to the chosenness of Israel. As a result, Reconstructionists have changed the words of some of the most central and best loved prayers: the *Kiddush* (the sanctification over wine) recited on Shabbat and holiday evenings, the blessing said when called to the Torah, the *Havdalah* prayer recited at the close of Shabbat, and the *Alenu* prayer, with which every worship service is brought to a close. A more complete description of the approach of Reconstructionist prayer books can be found below in chapter 10.

In place of chosenness, the editors of the Reconstructionist prayer books substituted the concept of vocation. Instead of regarding the Jews as "chosen from among all peoples," we understand ourselves —and all peoples—as being "called to do God's work." That is to say, we follow a specific path to salvation through the preservation and development of our inherited traditions. Other peoples follow their own paths; ours is not necessarily superior to theirs, nor can we be certain that, on any particular issue, it is divinely grounded.

In this context, the traditional belief that there is a *brit*, a covenant, between God and Israel, is usefully revalued. Reconstructionists do not accept literally that the Torah includes the unchanging and ever-lasting terms of the Jewish people's responsibilities to God. We can speak, however, of an evolving Jewish understanding of covenant— a holy relationship grounded in mutual trust and respect, modified from the hierarchical biblical relationship between God and Israel —and about the responsibilities of Jews to behave, ethically and ritually, as if they were covenanted to do so. We can also speak of a multi-covenant theology, through which we recognize that other peoples have developed their own distinctive covenantal approaches to human responsibility.

As with other liturgical changes, Reconstructionists continue to debate whether these particular emendations are necessary. The debate should not, however, be misunderstood. The question is *not* whether Reconstructionists should return to a blanket claim of superiority for the Jewish tradition. It is rather about mythic and metaphorical language in the liturgy and whether it is possible to reinterpret without changing the words.

Why did chosenness require special attention when so much else in the prayerbook was left alone, to be understood metaphorically? The motivation for these liturgical changes was ethical. Kaplan and his disciples were concerned that a sense of chosenness might degenerate too easily into chauvinism, self-righteousness, and unfounded claims of ethnic superiority. They believed that the ultimate salvation of the Jewish people is interdependent with the salvation of all peoples, and they thus were concerned that Jews not insulate themselves from their neighbors.

Clearly, the Jewish belief that we are the chosen people has been central to the identities of countless generations of Jews. We have believed that the Torah is a gift from God, and that God chose us from among all the peoples because we were willing to enter into a covenant, agreeing to live according to the divine commandments. Thus, the notion of chosenness has functioned in the past to validate and give meaning to the Jewish way of life. To be sure, we were never supposed to believe that *Jews* were superior, only that our Torah is the true and only complete reflection of the divine will. Later, when Jews were subjected to persecution and to Christian missionizing in the rabbinic and medieval periods, the belief in the exclusive value of the Torah gave our ancestors the strength to resist apostasy and despair.

Given the circumstances of liberal North American Jews—who

neither wish to live separately from their non-Jewish neighbors, nor believe that *any* religious tradition is divinely revealed in a literal sense—our task is to discover the functional equivalent of the chosen people doctrine. How can we express the unique value of Judaism so that Jews will be moved to greater Jewish commitment, without simultaneously implying that one religion is inherently better than another? Clearly, the Reconstructionist does not want to resort to God the Chooser for validation; all persons and peoples manifest the divine when they actualize their "salvation," and the expression of their insights and images is conditioned by their respective civilizations. But if Judaism is not superior, some will ask, then why should a Jew remain Jewish?

Reconstructionists answer this question, first, by referring to the richness of the Jewish heritage. So many Jews are virtually ignorant of the depths of Jewish spirituality, the beauty of Jewish poetry, the sensibility of Jewish ethics and law, the pathos of the Jewish experience. When Jews come to know and live these traditions and thereby enrich their lives, this is the basis for a far more important and authentic claim than one that is based on retention of a sense of superiority.

Jews live Jewish lives because they want to feel at home, to see and experience the world with the insights of a Jewish outlook. Some also want to claim that their way is better than all others, but Reconstructionists think that it is possible for a healthy individual to retain a good self-image without simultaneously denigrating the worth of others. Similarly, it is better for Jews to retain a healthy respect for other traditions—and to interact with them and their adherents—even as we take pride and derive meaning from our own heritage. It is possible and desirable to be "centered" without claiming to be the center of the universe. Only when all peoples learn this lesson will we achieve the equivalent of the messianic era.

4
The Past Has a Vote, Not a Veto

Kaplan's views on chosenness stand out in contrast to his attempts to reconstruct most other elements of Jewish life. He rarely felt strongly that a concept was so unamenable to reconstruction that it had to be altered radically. For the most part, radical alteration was not the desirable reconstruction that Kaplan sought or envisioned. In fact, Kaplan personally remained a traditionally observant Jew throughout his lifetime.

The criterion by which Jewish life was to be reconstructed can be described by Kaplan's epigram, "The past has a vote, not a veto." Understanding what Kaplan meant by that phrase is the first step in developing the model for the reconstruction of Jewish life that must be pursued in every generation if Jewish civilization is to continue to thrive.

The Authority of the Past

"The past has a vote, not a veto." That is the answer to the question: What is the authority of the past? Preceding generations attributed the authority of the tradition to divine revelation. The Written and Oral Torah were seen as the record of God's will as it was revealed to Moses and Israel at Mount Sinai. Thus, the very notion of innovation was discouraged. Ancient and medieval innovators claimed—and believed—that they were but recovering and restoring the original meaning of the Sinaitic revelation. As the Jewish people adapted to new, changing circumstances and Jewish civilization evolved, our ancestors engaged in what Kaplan called "transvaluation"—claiming ancient authority for new insights.

Today, our awareness of historical forces is radically discontinuous with the ahistorical consciousness of our ancestors. To claim that Judaism is an evolving civilization is to acknowledge that people and traditions change in response to historical circumstances. We innovate consciously today with the awareness that we ourselves are shaped by our milieu, just as our ancestors were shaped by theirs. We engage in conscious "revaluation," in Kaplan's terms, rather than in our ancestors' "transvaluation."

But Reconstructionists are not dispassionate historians who claim objectivity. While we attempt to understand the experience at Sinai, for example, by striving to recover the social, political, cultural, and psychological forces that shaped Moses and the Israelites, we do not claim that the divine voice they heard was the projection of their primitive imagination. We acknowledge the existence of God and thus the reality of divine-human encounter. What we deny is that the records of such revelatory encounters are transcripts of God's speech. God, it will be recalled, is discovered quite naturally by humans who seek God. Thus, the content of a revelation is the record of a particular human quest and discovery; the evolution of Jewish civilization is the natural progression of successive generations of Jewish people who have sought and found God in their own terms.

Seen in this light, the value of the past is considerable. The Jewish tradition is a record of the insights of prophets and sages through the generations. Neither human nature nor the nature of the divine has changed over the millennia; only the concepts and idioms through which Jews understand the world have evolved. Thus, we strive to translate the insights we have inherited from the Jewish past into our own terms. We thereby revalue inherited beliefs and practices so that we can enrich our lives through them. Reconstructionists who observe Shabbat and the holiday cycle of the Jewish year, for example, do so in order to immerse themselves in the sacred forms and calendrical rhythms with which our ancestors shaped their world. There is more to the Jewish outlook than a series of propositions to be judged true or false. Judaism is a civilization that communicates and acculturates in many nonverbal ways.

When Past and Present Conflict

The process of revaluation is no simple task. For all the brilliance and depth of insight of our ancestors, their values are often not applicable today in a straightforward way. They are occasionally even repugnant from our perspective. Kaplan insisted that we preserve and observe Jewish customs and values as long as they continue to serve as vehicles towards salvation—the enhancement of the meaning and purposefulness of our existence.

When a particular Jewish value or custom is found wanting in this respect, it is our obligation as Jews to find a means to reconstruct it—to adopt innovative practices or find new meanings in old ones. That the past has a vote means that we must struggle to hear the voices of our ancestors. What did this custom or that idea mean to them? How did they see the presence of God in it? How can we retain or regain its importance in our own lives? That the past does not have a veto means that we must work to hear our own voices as distinct from theirs. What might this custom or that idea mean to us today? As participants in a secular civilization, how can we incorporate our values into our lives as Jews?

It is clear that our ties to our Jewish past and our sense of the secular present often pull us in opposite directions. Reconstructionists seek to find ways to merge those two sensibilities while remaining faithful to both of them. Kaplan's statement that the past does not have a veto implies that tradition is susceptible to adaptation. Innovation need not entail the destruction of tradition; on the contrary, change is an important part of keeping tradition alive, as it has been throughout Jewish history. As the world changes faster, Judaism must be reconstructed ever more quickly if its wisdom is to continue to guide us.

Post-halakhic Judaism

By contemporary definitions, one cannot define Reconstructionism as a halakhic form of Judaism. If halakhah were defined as the Jewish process of transmitting tradition and practice, then we certainly could see ourselves within the framework of halakhah. Unfortunately, today the term has taken on the meaning of a rigid body of law, changeable only under rarefied circumstances. In past generations and other eras of Jewish life, halakhah functioned as we think it should today: though in theory it was seen as immutable law, in fact it served as a body of tradition that could adapt to the needs of the Jewish people throughout the ages.

We also question the effectiveness of the halakhic method itself for dealing with contemporary concerns. In traditional Judaism as well as contemporary Orthodox and Conservative Judaism, only rabbinic scholars who are experts in the history and development of halakhah are empowered to make halakhic decisions. The halakhic method presumes that all questions are answerable with reference to legal precedent. It ignores the possibility that new issues, while they may be guided by old values, must be discussed with reference to the world in which we now live.

Furthermore, Jewish teachings no longer function for us as law, nor can they be expected to do so. For law to function, it must have an organized structure to create and adjudicate it. There must be sanctions against anyone who disobeys. Nowhere in the world does Jewish law now function in that way. In tightly-woven Orthodox communities, the members choose *voluntarily* to place themselves "under the yoke of the law" and can choose to leave at any time. Even in Israel, where Jewish law governs issues of personal status, the law can be circumvented. Therefore, thinking of halakhah as binding law is misleading in today's world.

Finally, this change in social circumstances is not accidental. It reflects a basic value of Western democracy—that individuals ought to make religious choices autonomously. Our ancestors believed that the ideal Jew was one who subordinated independent judgment and instead behaved in accordance with the will of God. By contrast, we believe that moral and spiritual faculties are actualized best when the individual makes conscious choices. Thus, even if there were an opportunity to return to an authoritarian community in which the traditional *mitzvot* were enforced coercively, we would not choose to do so.

The individual's choices, however, can and should not be made alone. Our ethical values and ritual propensities are shaped by the culture and community in which we live. Living a Jewish life, according to the Reconstructionist understanding, means belonging to the Jewish people as a whole and to a particular community of Jews, through which our views of life are shaped. Thus, while Reconstructionist communities are neither authoritarian nor coercive, they aspire to influence the individual's ethical and ritual choices—through study of Jewish sources, through the sharing of values and experiences, and through the impact of the climate of communal opinion on the individual. Some groups even hold community *kallot* (study week-ends) in which recommendations about ethical or ritual practice are developed for members. Many members of Reconstructionist communities, for example, have not considered observance of Shabbat as a possibility before they joined; when they become acquainted with Jews for whom Shabbat is a key practice, they often decide to explore Shabbat observance for themselves. No one forces them. They are not judged negatively for what they do or don't observe. Nevertheless, their perceptions, and hence their choices, are affected by their participation in the community.

The Reconstructionist movement strongly advocates that Reconstructionist groups consider collectively questions of ethical and ritual behavior, but Reconstructionism ultimately is an *approach* to Judaism. We learn and appreciate what the tradition has to say, we come to a spectrum of options that reflects that understanding, and the organizations of the movement may even issue a set of guidelines. But ultimately we believe that in all cases, be they questions of ritual or principle, individuals must decide for themselves about the proper Jewish way to proceed in a given situation. While we may share certain values and life situations, no two sets of circumstances are identical. We hope that the Reconstructionist process works to help people find the right answers for themselves, but we can only assist in helping individuals to ask the right questions so that their choices are made in an informed way within a Jewish context.

To be true to ourselves we must understand the differences in perception between us and those who have gone before, while retaining a reverence for the traditions they fashioned. If we can juxtapose those things, we ensure that the past will have a vote, but not a veto. It is important to describe some practical examples of how this principle works. How might a Reconstructionist approach a matter of ritual or ethical difficulty?

Ethical Dilemmas

What then would be the process of ethical decision making? To begin with, we would examine our own intellectual, emotional, and moral preconceptions, so that we can be honest about our own viewpoints. Otherwise, we will be forever trying to force the tradition to agree with us, or looking only for ways in which it does. This is unconscious transvaluation—looking to the past for justification of the way we wish to behave—rather than the desired conscious revaluation.

Second, we would do a thorough search of Jewish law and teachings to ascertain whether or not there are halakhic positions on the issue, how they were derived, and upon what Jewish values they were based. Obviously, this part demands a great deal of knowledge about the sources and how to use them.

We then would compare those two conclusions. If they are consonant, we might want to stop the process there. If they are dissonant, we probably would examine things further. We might ask ourselves on which values we base our intuitive responses. Are they Jewish values? Are there Jewish values that suggest a different conclusion from that derived from the halakhic process? This last set of questions is at the core of revaluation.

Abortion

As an example, let us look at the issues raised by abortion. Rachel Cohen, who is pregnant with her second child, undergoes amniocentesis and discovers that she is carrying a Tay-Sachs child. Both she and her husband David wish her to have an abortion. They are aware that aborting a fetus with a congenital illness could send the wrong message to society; one that suggests that the lives of people with disabilities are worth less than other lives. Nonetheless, they do not think that they have the emotional or financial resources to go through with the pregnancy. And they don't want this unborn child to experience a difficult life and an early death.

With the assistance of a rabbi, the Cohens study the halakhic position: this is not grounds for an abortion. Based on the argument of the sanctity of life, all lives are of equal value. Abortion of a potential life cannot be sanctioned under these circumstances. The only universally recognized halakhic warrant for abortion is if the mother's life itself is in danger.

The couple is deeply distraught. Not only must they consider doing something very difficult, but they must do so knowing it contravenes halakhah. Then the Cohens begin the process of revaluation. Are there other possibilities within the Jewish value system that might provide a different outlook?

For example, they consider the value of *shelom bayit,* concord in the household. What does it mean in this situation? Would it be possible for the Cohens to live with the tension created by the birth of this child? What would the effects be on their marriage? On the sibling? What kind of financial and emotional strains would occur? There is precedent in Jewish tradition for permitting abortion when the health of the mother, mental or physical, is seriously in question. There is also precedent for abortion when a nursing sibling would be deprived of adequate nourishment because of the pregnancy. The principle of *shelom bayit* might be extended to cover these and other possibilities, such as the feelings of the father and his ability to handle the situation, or the capacity of the marriage to tolerate the stress.

The Cohens might even want to take the process a step further, bringing their decision to a congregational support group whose members would help the Cohens to find a meaningful ritual to support them in their decision—a ceremony after the abortion, or a special welcoming ceremony, if they decided to go through with the difficult birth. These are some of the possibilities opened up by the process of revaluation.

An exploration of this case would lead the Cohens to consider the ramifications of their actions and to understand them in terms of a larger value system. It would provide them with the kind of communal support necessary to carry through a decision such as this. It would also grant them the dignity of knowing that the decision is theirs to make, and that they would receive communal support regardless of what they decided.

Traditional Jewish values like *shelom bayit* were used through the ages by halakhic authorities to justify decisions they made in other areas, but not to provide support for abortion. In the case under discussion, this is a competing value to be overruled by the (nearly) absolute value of the sanctity of human life. In halakhic communities today, it is left to rabbinic authorities to determine whether newly emerging circumstances (in this case, our ability to test for the Tay-Sachs gene *in utero*) should lead to a departure from halakhic precedents. The Reconstructionist approach promotes the right and the value of individual Jews to take part in that decision-making process and affirms that this is valuable. Our approach recognizes and affirms their responsibility to decide, and it provides them with the resources to negotiate such a decision with the help of the Jewish heritage.

Ritual Decisions

Does this process work for ritual decisions as well? What about the case of Miriam Feinberg, who is getting more involved in Jewish life but for whom *kashrut* (Jewish dietary observance) is difficult? She would begin by examining all the feelings she has about *kashrut*. Let us assume Miriam initially sees little value in *kashrut*. She was not raised in a kosher home and has never observed *kashrut* as an adult. She can't imagine why one would go to the expense of buying kosher meat or two sets of dishes; she can't figure out why certain products aren't kosher; she has no desire to give up eating or cooking some of her favorite foods. Nevertheless, as the result of her participation in a Reconstructionist community in which *kashrut*—in various forms —is an important practice for many members, she becomes curious.

The Reconstructionist approach would suggest that Miriam familiarize herself with the halakhah about *kashrut*—preferably with a group of people in a Reconstructionist context who are struggling with the same issue. Some of them may have been raised in kosher homes and have negative associations with *kashrut* related to their experiences of halakhic coercion, with which they want to come to terms. Others, also raised in kosher homes, may be comfortable with *kashrut* as a nostalgic connection to their parents and grandparents, but they have ethical objections to the way that animals are treated by the kosher food industry. Others may come from liberal backgrounds, where they may have been raised to regard *kashrut* as an antiquated practice that is inappropriate for contemporary Jews. For them, *kashrut* represents a repudiation of their own personal Jewish history with which they have only positive associations, unrelated to dietary restriction.

Since the intuitions of the members of the group are in conflict with traditional observances, a process of revaluation is in order. That revaluation, in the case of a ritual practice, has two components —one intellectual and the other experiential. First, the group would want to seek out new meanings for the observance of *kashrut*. A list might include: making our homes more Jewish, allowing anyone to eat in our homes, getting in touch with Jewish tradition, making eating something we do with more attention, becoming aware of *tza'ar ba'alei ḥayyim* (the traditional concern with the pain of living creatures), and supporting the kosher food industry so that Jews who choose to keep kosher can do so. They would then want to experiment with keeping kosher, perhaps cooking kosher meals together or eating out in a restaurant and ordering only "kosher" items, or learning how to make their dishes and utensils kosher, or buying a kosher cookbook and making special meals.

Members of the group might find that they differ over which meanings enhance their personal practice, depending on individual perspectives, circumstances, and background. The *experience* of keeping kosher itself is likely to affect each member's views of the practice in unanticipated ways. The meaning and significance of a ritual observance cannot always be reduced to a clearly articulated value. Rituals have subliminal power that condition one's outlook, so that sometimes the original reason for taking on a practice proves not to be the most important one. This is part of what we mean when we say that Judaism is a *civilization,* and that Jews who immerse themselves in that civilization are transformed by it.

Eventually, some members of the group might choose to keep some portion of the traditions of *kashrut,* as opposed to attempting to take on all of them. They might, for example, become vegetarians or observe an eco-*kashrut,* in which they choose to eat foods based upon their impact on the environment; both of these are completely compatible with traditional *kashrut.* They might eat only kosher foods but not have special dishes, keep kosher only in the home, choose specific foods from which to refrain, or buy only kosher meat. Their initial choices will not be irrevocable; their *kashrut* practice is likely to continue to change as part of the dynamic processes of their lives. For some, *kashrut* may become a central component of their Jewish identities, sanctifying their tables and leading to a greater appreciation of their blessings. Others may find that, for a variety of reasons, *kashrut* never resonates with any power. Still others may decide to adopt a form of *"kashrut"* that is unrelated to traditional observance. For all of them, engaging in this experiment with the experience of traditional *kashrut* will have enriched their appreciation of the Jewish heritage.

In addition, the group might decide that, apart from variations in personal observance of *kashrut,* the synagogue ought to serve as a repository for more traditional practice, and that *kashrut* should be observed in the communal kitchen. In point of fact, all Reconstructionist groups that own their own kitchens have decided to keep them kosher. They take the category of *kashrut* seriously and formulate a communal *kashrut* policy. But how then can members with non-kosher homes be included in communal celebrations? The process for making such collective decisions is discussed in chapter 7.

Should we be concerned that the dietary practices of Jews vary so widely, and that some may even use the term *"kashrut"* to refer to totally unprecedented eating practices? Is this not a prescription for chaos that reduces the likelihood of Jewish survival and renaissance? Reconstructionists respond in two ways.

First, the variation in Jewish practice is a fact of Jewish life at the beginning of the twenty-first century. It is not caused by the Reconstructionist or any other liberal Jewish approach. It is the consequence of the political and social emancipation of the Jewish people. Rather than agonize over the facts, Reconstructionists choose instead to *attract* Jews to join meaningful communities in which they may choose to become more engaged with the Jewish heritage.

Second, a close study of Jewish history reveals the evolving nature of Jewish civilization. Most (if not all) Jewish beliefs and practices that are today regarded as "traditional" began as unprecedented innovations, resisted by the traditional authorities of the time. Many innovations through the ages did not survive, and it is therefore impossible to predict what will one day become traditional. Thus, while some of us may find this uncertainty unnerving, we can never know which of today's experiments will eventually be adopted by large numbers of Jews and thus become "Jewish" and traditional. It is clear, however, that if our past teaches us anything, it is that Jewish civilization will continue to flourish only as long as it continues to evolve.

When last surveyed, 35% of Reconstructionists asserted that they observe *kashrut,* and that they are more ritually observant than their parents were. According to the Reconstructionist program, this is information to applaud. The fact that a significant percentage of Reconstructionists are choosing to keep kosher is evidence that a democratic, non-coercive process is effective. We seek to create communities in which members come to lead ever more intensive and meaningful Jewish lives—lives that are enriched by study, ethical practice, and ritual observance. We do not, however, expect each Jew to find the identical path to this goal. The goal is engagement, involvement, and enrichment. It is not uniform belief or practice.

It is healthy for the Jewish people to revalue: to look for meanings beneath the surface of extant rituals; to look for new rituals that better express old meanings. This process will keep Judaism a vibrant and living tradition within which there are and will continue to be many forms of self-expression.

5
Living in Two Civilizations

The insights for reconstructing traditional Jewish concepts of God, Torah, and Israel grew out of the political emancipation of contemporary Jews, our exposure to Western intellectual disciplines, and our social integration as responsible citizens of the Western democracies. In this chapter, we shall present the Reconstructionist view of democracy and of the appropriate attitudes that Jews might take towards the larger, secular society.

The Open Society

Many people have postulated that Judaism can only survive in a hostile environment—that anti-Semitism is the main reason that Jews have remained Jewish in the modern era. If the democracies of Western Europe and North America had lived up to the original promise of emancipation, they claim, then it would have only been a matter of time before all Jews yielded to the enticements of assimilation. They point, on the one hand, to the hopes of assimilated Western European Jews before the rise of Nazism and to the progressive assimilation of American Jews; and, on the other hand, to the renaissance of Jewish identification after the Holocaust and again after the dramatic Israeli victory in the 1967 Six Day War. They regard the openness of democratic societies as a threat to Jewish survival, and, consciously or unconsciously, their program for Jewish survival depends upon convincing Jews to retain a certain degree of distrust for and alienation from non-Jewish culture and people. In its extreme form, this sort of outlook becomes the basis for the embattled mentality of many contemporary Jews, who bemoan the progressive integration of Jews into North American society even as they support the attempts of Jewish organizations to eliminate the very discrimination against Jews that, according to this view, prevents their full integration.

Reconstructionists disagree with this negative understanding of the place of Jews in secular society. We believe that Judaism can survive and prosper in an environment that is supportive of or indifferent to Jewish interests. We are not unaware of the problems caused when Jews live in an open society. We believe, however, that it is self-deceptive and self-defeating for North American Jews to regard that open environment as hostile even as most Jews enjoy unprecedented prosperity. After all, most of us do not contemplate abandoning our current comfort to move to Israel, nor are we anxious to retreat into a segregated Jewish community. Moreover, as increasing numbers of Jews raised in assimilated homes seek ways to increase and intensify their Jewish identification, we believe that it is possible for the Jewish community to flourish in an open environment that offers Jews other options. We need not rely on anti-Semites; we can instead affect our own fate by reconstructing Judaism into a form that Jews will choose to embrace.

The Promise of America

Long before American Jews had successfully ascended the social, economic, educational, and political rungs of society, Mordecai Kaplan recognized the promise of North American democracy for Jews. As the great immigration of Eastern European Jews was ending in the 1920s and American Jews were struggling for acceptance in the 1930s and 1940s, Kaplan declared that such democratic values as freedom, tolerance, equality, universal enfranchisement, and individual opportunity represented the most elevated form of political life yet developed by a society. While others, then as now, regarded the successful integration of Jews into democratic society as a mixed blessing—regretting the loss of Yiddish, the abandonment of traditional practice, and the replacement of Jewish learning by secular study—Kaplan saw an opportunity to integrate democratic values into a reconstructed Jewish civilization.

He called his program "living in two civilizations." Whereas in the past Jews had lived in segregated, autonomous Jewish communities and thus had been able to live completely in a single Jewish civilization, there was no denying that Jews who now found themselves in democratic societies lived primarily in a secular civilization —governed by American legislatures and courts, speaking English, working in secular environments with non-Jews, being educated in public schools, embracing American music, and structuring their lives according to American values. Had we *also* been *required* to abandon our Jewish identities, then we would have faced a critical threat to Jewish survival. In fact, however, the most wonderful aspect of democratic America is its pluralism. Church and state are separate. White Anglo-Saxon founders accepted (however reluctantly) waves of immigration by diverse ethnic, racial, and religious groups. The Constitution protects their right to be different. This is, as Kaplan foresaw, truly a fertile environment in which Judaism can flourish in a new, democratic way.

For this new kind of civilization to thrive, however, Jews have to learn how to live in two civilizations. They live, of necessity, primarily in an American civilization. But because of the separation between church and state and because of America's tolerance of diverse cultural expression, they can also live in a Jewish civilization—worshiping and studying together, forming Jewish political and social organizations, providing Jewish social services and developing an American Jewish way of life parallel to the distinctive ways of life of other racial or ethnic groups. Rejecting the melting pot metaphor long before it fell out of fashion, Kaplan argued that American civilization is incomplete; it cannot fill all of the needs of its citizens precisely because it has no established religion and expects its citizens to develop their own means of religious and ethnic expression. Its genius is that it is an umbrella civilization—structured to unify its diverse elements without forcibly homogenizing them.

Kaplan called upon Jews to embrace the open society—not only because its structural pluralism does not require the abandonment of Judaism, but also because American ideals at their best coincide with Jewish ideals as they ought to be developed and reconstructed. Jews have much to learn from America. Traditional Judaism contained elements of democratic values, but those elements were only imperfectly formed. For example, Jewish law respects the rights of the individual; medieval Jewish communities developed a variety of modes of representative government; and traditional Jewish authority had not been centralized for a millennium, so that the customs and legal interpretations of one segment of Jewry were respected by other segments that followed different customs and interpretations.

Kaplan boldly sought to develop these democratic aspects of pre-modern Judaism into a full-blown democratic Jewish civilization. Halakhic authority, which had ceased to function, would be reconstructed by involving *all* Jews. He envisioned an organic Jewish *kehillah* that Jews would choose freely to join. Moreover, he believed it is in the best interest of Jews to contribute to a pluralistic America in which all groups unite in common civic values such as equality, tolerance, freedom, and pluralism.

Being Jewish and American

Thus in the Reconstructionist framework, it is not necessary to choose between one's Jewish and American identities. One can—indeed, one must—live in two civilizations. When the two civilizations are in harmony, this is both simple and effective. Just as we find meaning and value in celebrating Sukkot as Jews, so too we can find meaning and value in celebrating Thanksgiving as Americans. These two holidays have a similar meaning and purpose (giving thanks for abundance, reminding us of our obligation to care for those less fortunate) and have certain parallel observances (centered around the family meal in the sukkah or in the home). It might be argued that there is little need for celebrating both. Why bother to express oneself in two different idioms?

Living in two civilizations means seeing this redundancy as an advantage. One experience can illuminate the other. Seeing the similarities reminds us of the comfort of living as both Jews and Americans. It enables us to remain in contact with the world outside as well as with our deeply meaningful past. It gives us a language to share our celebration of Judaism with those who are not Jewish. Furthermore, Thanksgiving and Sukkot remind us of our history and its lessons. We celebrate and question values developed by our ancestors—American and Jewish—out of their separate experiences, while affirming our attachment to both.

It is also the case that there are elements in each civilization that are not paralleled in the other. The Jewish civilization, for example, has placed little emphasis on athletics. Yet sports can provide catharsis, stimulation, and greater mental and physical health to participants and observers alike. Similarly, the American civilization has little to offer in terms of life-cycle rituals—weddings, funerals, births, or even divorces—that are necessary to bring meaning to crucial events in life.

Furthermore, an American Jew can be heir to Jewish traditions that yield insights into divine aspects of the universe, provide enlightening struggles with complex ethical dilemmas, and give a multifaceted system of ritual and devotional practices that can sanctify life and make connections between people. In its depth and richness, the Jewish tradition offers models of behavior and realms of discourse that are not available in contemporary secular culture. On the other hand, North American culture has much to offer—not only in terms of material prosperity and professional opportunity, but also in its literature, art, and cinema; in its respect for individual autonomy and liberty; and in its cosmopolitan amalgamation of diverse cultures.

More challenging are the situations in which living in two civilizations brings about conflict. Committed Jews in North America are faced with choices at every turn. Little League games conflict with religious school classes, golf tournaments with Shabbat services, and opera performances with Jewish lecture series. Parents must choose between paying Jewish day school tuition or saving for college tuition. With a limited amount of time and energy, membership on the Jewish community center board and participation in a political campaign may be mutually exclusive commitments.

Reconstructionists tend to welcome these choices as evidence of the rich opportunities available to us in North America. We do not seek to retreat into a parochial world, nor do we think that Jews ought to feel guilty for their desire to be full participants in the secular culture. Rather, we believe that Jewish civilization offers Jews a different kind of social, cultural, and spiritual enrichment that is not available elsewhere. When attending a Jewish lecture or concert offers that enrichment, Jews will choose to participate. They will do so not out of guilt or nostalgia, but out of excitement and satisfaction.

Education

The question of education in the context of two civilizations also creates a conflict. The first generation of Reconstructionists opposed the establishment of Jewish day schools in their belief that Jews should be in the vanguard of the continuing struggle to keep America true to its democratic, pluralistic ideals. All American children, they thought, should be educated together in shared American civic values. Jewish identity could be nurtured adequately in supplementary afternoon and weekend schools, and primarily in the acculturating experiences of the Jewish home and community.

With hindsight, we now can see that this hope has not been realized. The progressive Americanization of Jews has made it unrealistic to rely exclusively upon Jewish families in which parents are often in need of Jewish education themselves. Nor can we depend upon supplementary religious schools faced with children tired after a day at school and resentful of time taken away from competing extracurricular activities. That is why we have rethought the value of Jewish day schools.

The Reconstructionist response has been multifaceted. We have emphasized family programming such as the *shabbaton* (Shabbat retreat) and the Shabbat Seder (a Friday night meal and ritual including the whole family). We have also long advocated summer camping. These programs expose young Jews to an authentic, all-embracing Jewish experience they can then replicate on their own. The programs also involve parents, who can then learn together with their children. We have developed the havurah—a small group of people who celebrate, study, worship, and take on social justice projects together—as a way of re-creating in a contemporary setting the warmth and activities of a traditional community. We have affirmed the importance of continuing adult education in recognition that training that ends with bar/bat mitzvah or even confirmation leaves Jews with the impression that Judaism is only for children or adolescents. Judaizing one's life is an ongoing process. Our educators have been at the forefront of curricular and pedagogic innovations, adapting models from the general culture to the needs of the Jewish school.

Day schools also do not accomplish our goal of living in two civilizations. Minimally, they will have to avoid inculcating in their students a sense that Jews are and ought to be separate from their non-Jewish neighbors. Logically, that attitude eventuates either in *aliyah* (when Jews decide that Israel provides the only complete Jewish environment), or more frequently, in Jews who pursue their educations and professions in American society but who feel, in their heart of hearts, that their successful integration is a betrayal of their Jewish identity—what sociologist Charles Liebman has called "the ambivalent American Jew." Reconstructionists have articulated a unique vision of a day school that has yet to be implemented: a school in which American children from a variety of religious, racial, and ethnic groups would study together for half the day and then separate for the other half while they studied their own distinctive heritage, language, and history. Such a model would be grounded on the ideal that unity in diversity is the most exalted ethical path.

Social Action

Because of our embrace of the open society, Reconstructionists have viewed involvement in American social and political issues as integral to a vibrant and meaningful American Judaism. Just as we seek to democratize the Jewish community, so also do we recognize the need to bring the insights of the Jewish tradition to bear upon the issues that American society confronts.

It is well known that Jews in America have always been social activists. Before World War II, Jews were active in the labor and socialist movements. In the 1960s, Jews were prominent in the civil rights, anti-Vietnam War, feminist, and gay liberation movements. More recently, the environmental and anti-genocide movements have been important to Jews. Our behavior in recent elections continues to show that we do not vote primarily our pocketbooks—that we display an extraordinary degree of concern for social, economic, and racial justice.

As Reconstructionists, we are concerned with building upon this phenomenon. It is not enough for American Jews to be socially concerned. If we are to pursue integrated lives in two civilizations, we should bring traditional Jewish values to our social concerns. The Jewish values of *tzedakah* and *gemilut hasadim,* for example, are not identical to Christian charity or social democratic welfare. The Jewish approach to the rights and responsibilities of individuals and societies is a largely untapped source of insights into contemporary questions about the social allocation of resources. These are visible in the resolutions of the Jewish Reconstructionist Federation and the Reconstructionist Rabbinical Association, as well as in the editorials and articles in the *Reconstructionist.* The Reconstructionist Rabbinical College's Center for Jewish Ethics is publishing a series of study guides that help people to gain access to Jewish sources as they develop their positions on social and personal ethics. Over the years, the RRC has housed such organizations as the Shalom Center and *Shomrei Adamah,* interdenominational Jewish centers devoted to peace and environmental issues.

Of course, not every traditional Jewish value is acceptable to contemporary American Jews. We have much to gain by incorporating new ideals into the Jewish civilization—for example, the equal role of women, the rights of gay men and lesbians, or support for people with disabilities. Nor does the Jewish tradition ever speak in an unambiguous voice. The various embodiments of that tradition over the course of three thousand years of evolution allow for divergent interpretations. Israeli West Bank settlers and Peace Now activists alike make the claim that they are authentically Jewish. Committed American Jews can be found on both sides of the debate about capital punishment. We do not maintain that authentic Jews must adopt one political view to the exclusion of all others. Rather, we suggest that both the Jewish community and American society have much to gain when committed Jews study their tradition in order to apply its insights to contemporary issues.

Jews and Christians in America

With the continuing presence in the U.S. of a vocal religious right that supports visible expressions of Christianity in schools and other public places, more Jews have begun to feel uneasy, revising their view that America is a secular and hospitable society. Focused on the fact that most Americans are Christian, some Jews now assume that Christianity is the true religion of America, and that Jews are therefore, at the least, peripheral.

As Reconstructionists, we have no quarrel with the right and responsibility of other Americans to introduce their own religiously derived values and perspectives into public-policy debates. It is precisely such behavior that we advocate for Jews as part of the pluralistic model for unity in diversity.

Yet, bringing religious perspectives into the public arena must not conflict with the right of religious groups to be different. When religious groups seek to pass legislation concerning matters about which we lack a consensus, then influence becomes control, and the rights of the minority are undermined or denied. The attempt to legislate religious perspectives, and to claim a consensus where one does not exist, is destructive to the values of pluralism and mutual respect.

It is urgent that we initiate and support intergroup dialogue as a way to build bridges of understanding between Jews and other groups who share these concerns. We continue in our common efforts with like-minded Christians who also advocate separation of church and state and who share our dedication to preserving a pluralistic society where the right to be different is respected. It is precisely through open communication and political action that we can overcome threats to the American values we hold to be precious.

Changing Jewish Views of America's Promise

Over the last few decades, the idealistic view of American democracy has come under assault from a variety of perspectives. In the 1960s, the civil rights movement and resistance to the Vietnam War made Americans more aware of the existence of poverty, racial injustice, and American militarism—problems which continue to this day. It thus became more difficult to maintain an unambiguous patriotism that views America as an unsullied beacon of freedom. Many question Kaplan's enthusiastic embrace of American culture in light of the failure of Western democracies to prevent and to adequately combat the Holocaust, in light of the environmental hazards to which modern science and technology have led, and in light of the growing recognition that life in secular, prosperous America fails to meet adequately many of our spiritual needs.

In the 1930s, Kaplan was engaged in an attempt to convince recently arrived Jews that in adopting American values, they need not abandon their Jewish heritage. Thus, he stressed the coincidence of American and Jewish values. Today, now that we have Americanized, it is clear that the values and worldview of the two civilizations are not and cannot be identical. To be sure, they are complementary —it is possible for a committed Jew to be integrated into American life. Where the burden once was to become more American, living in two civilizations now requires Jews to work at becoming more Jewish.

As we continue to develop Jewish traditions in ways that speak to contemporary people living in two civilizations, a certain amount of caution is required. We do not want to reduce Judaism to those parts that can be seamlessly reconstructed to agree with contemporary values. Jewish traditions should rather be regarded as needed correctives to the materialism, competition, rootlessness, and alienation that accompany contemporary secular culture. As we can be enriched as Jews through our immersion in contemporary culture, even more can we as Americans enrich our lives by turning to the treasures of Judaism and to the wealth of contemporary Jewish creativity both in Israel and around the world. Living in two civilizations should be understood clearly as a delicate balance in which we give and take from two competing but compatible systems without subordinating one to the other.

Reconstructionism around the World

The Reconstructionist focus on living in two civilizations was created out of the experience of Jews living in the United States. Nonetheless, the model may be (and has been) used for Jews living in other countries and cultures. The influence of Reconstructionist thought has been felt especially in Canada, where there are active Reconstructionist groups in Montreal, Toronto, and Ottawa. The goal of living comfortably in a society that allows Jews the freedom to participate and yet remain apart applies to the Canadian scene, in some ways even more than to the United States.

Reconstructionism's influence has also been felt in the Carib-bean. In Curaçao, two congregations, one Reform and one traditional, were united into one Reconstructionist group following a Kaplanian model. The Jewish Reconstructionist Federation is a member of the World Union for Progressive Judaism (WUPJ), and through WUPJ auspices, Reconstructionist rabbis have served communities in France, Belgium, Holland, Germany, Austria, South Africa, and the former Soviet Union. The "two civilizations" problem is relevant in every secular nation.

Above all, Reconstructionists have been involved in creating alternative forms of religious expression in Israel. The issue of living in multiple civilizations exists for the Israeli population as well. They must understand the varied Jewish cultures with which they live, as well as the Western and Near Eastern settings that influence their lives and fates. There is a congregation in Jerusalem, *Mevakshei Derekh* (Seekers of a Way), that was founded on Kaplanian principles.

In Israel, Jews can explore "living in two civilizations" in a unique fashion. Since Judaism serves as the dominant influence there, Israeli Jews must meet the challenges of being in power, of granting other minorities the rights to explore their own civilizations, and of avoiding the creation of a state interpretation of Judaism that stifles other interpretations and new ideas.

Moreover, it is in Israel that the challenge of integrating the tra-ditional aspects of Judaism with contemporary values is most pressing. However one defines the Jewishness of the Israeli state, the challenge of applying tradition to a contemporary society remains an ongoing task. The activities and philosophy of Reconstructionism in Israel are described in the next chapter.

6
Zion as a Spiritual Center

The Reconstructionist understanding of the civilizational character of Judaism predictably has led us to Zionist conclusions from the very outset. If Judaism is recognized as the civilization of the Jewish people, then there is no denying the particular attachment of our people to the Land of Israel—the site of our origins and genesis, and the focus of our hopes and ideals through the millennia. Kaplan and his associates were supporters of the Zionist cause decades before American Jewry reached its current consensus. They worked for Zionism while other Jews declared that America was their Zion, denied that Israel could emerge before the coming of the Messiah, or worried that Jews would be accused of being disloyal if they allied themselves with another nation.

While he articulated the possibilities for modern Jews who live in two civilizations, Kaplan was aware that Jewish civilization could flourish completely only in a society in which it is primary. He was convinced that Zionist efforts to reestablish a Jewish presence in the land of Israel were central to the Jewish future.

Spiritual Zionism

In the first part of the twentieth century, before the establishment of the State of Israel, the Zionist movement was divided. Political Zionists emphasized the need for a Jewish state to which Jews could go to escape anti-Semitic discrimination. A Jewish state could normalize the status of the Jewish people by making us like all other peoples. Spiritual or cultural Zionists, by contrast, emphasized the need for a return to the Land so that Jewish culture could flourish in a Jewish environment, and so that the values of our tradition could develop in a healthy, modern setting. It was with the latter, the spiritual Zionist camp, that Kaplan was associated. Its foremost spokesperson, Ahad Ha'am, was one of Kaplan's most significant teachers.

Ahad Ha'am rejected the stifling atmosphere of Russia, where he lived. He dreamed of a society in the land then known as Palestine where Jews could use the Hebrew language to express the nuances of their insights, where the Jewish heritage could be studied through the prism of the modern outlook, where legal restraints would not limit careers or education, and where a new society could develop naturally out of the collective experiences of Jews in their own land. Its culture would be authentically loyal to its heritage, yet thoroughly contemporary in applying that heritage to a modern society. Its cultural renaissance could be a beacon radiating Jewish renewal to communities across the globe, and the foundations it laid would ensure that Judaism would make an invigorated transition to the modern era.

Deeply influenced by the vision of Ahad Ha'am, Kaplan was outspoken in his support for the Jewish upbuilding of Palestine. The dream began to take shape as Hebrew became a spoken language again, reborn after two thousand years of use only for study and prayer. Scholars began to study biblical history. The Hebrew University became a center for the study of Judaica. Folk music and dance were created, incorporating biblical themes. Agricultural settlements and trade unions were founded on the basis of the conscious adaptation of prophetic and rabbinic ideals to the economy of a modern society.

Other Jewish Centers

Kaplan differed from cultural Zionism, however, in one significant respect. While he agreed with Ahad Ha'am that Israeli culture would be the center of the Jewish renaissance, he believed that Jewish centers in the Diaspora should influence that center as well as be influenced by it. Each Jewish community had developed its own customs and viewpoints through interdependent connections with others over the last two thousand years. So, too, could the interaction of American Jewry, with its distinctive environment, enrich Jewish civilization as a whole. He rejected the political Zionists' *shelilat hagolah* (the negation of the Diaspora), affirming that Israel was not the only site in which Judaism could flourish.

Kaplan understood that, for American Jews, America is home, and that its Jewish renaissance ought thus to occur in the context of life in two civilizations. While others implored Western Jews to make *aliyah* for the sake of Jewish survival, Kaplan's position remained that Jews who do not face persecution will opt for life in Israel only when it offers them a credible promise of a fulfilling Jewish life. His focus remained, therefore, on the need for Israel to develop a reconstructed *Jewish* culture and ethos.

What Is a Jewish State?

Despite the reticence of most committed Western Jews to make *aliyah,* Israel remains central to our loyalty and self-definition. In supporting Israel, we do more than contribute to the security and welfare of our fellow Jews. We also affirm our vigilance against the machinations of anti-Semites. And we pledge our solidarity to the Zionist political programs that are based upon taking our fate into our own hands. Moreover, long after the "miracle" of statehood and the War of Independence, we are still thrilled to think that biblical archaeology can be the passion of a nation, that a modern university would devote its computer facilities to the accessioning of rabbinic responsa, that *Adon Olam* can top the music charts on the radio. Furthermore, we have come to depend on the resources of Israeli scholars and educators for our own Jewish enrichment.

In the first years of the state, many Israelis were content to claim that theirs was the only Jewish community capable of surviving and worthy of surviving. In those years, Reconstructionists articulated the hope that productive relationships might be established between Israeli and other Jewish cultural centers. Today, Israelis see more clearly that Israelis are Jews too, and that all Jews share a common fate and hope. The current debate in Israel is rather about what it means to be a Jewish state.

Competing Visions

That debate can be summarized with reference to two issues. First, the original Zionist program was, to a certain extent, utopian and even messianic. By returning to the Jewish soil after languishing on alien turf, the Jewish spirit would be revived. The society to be formed would be based on such ancient biblical ideals as justice and true community, and thus the normalization of the Jewish people in its own land would serve the community of nations as a model to be emulated. Israelis would teach others how to drain swamps and make deserts bloom, how to form a prosperous and democratic society out of diverse population groups.

The utopia envisioned by pre-state Zionists has been modified by reality. The problems Israel faces are staggering—hostile neighbors and increasingly angry Israeli Arabs, terrorism, enormous defense budgets, cultural conflicts between Ashkenazim and Sephardim and between Orthodox and non-Orthodox Jews, and the relentless temptations of popular Western culture. In place of the original vision, we now witness the growth of a new Israeli messianism—one that rejects the Israeli founders' dream as "Western" and seeks to replace it with a fundamentalist Orthodox vision of Israel as the instrument of the divine will. The Jewish people, it claims, were given title to the Land by God in biblical times, and it is therefore unconditionally ours. Our victories are divinely willed, and our enemies are God's enemies. If Palestinian claims stand in the way of our possession of God's gift, then we may disregard their rights for the sake of heaven.

Reconstructionists, for all of our devotion to Israel, stand adamantly opposed to this fundamentalist, pseudo-messianic revival. We believe that the reestablishment of the State of Israel resulted not from the supernatural intervention of God into history, but rather from the tireless and idealistic efforts of Zionist pioneers. We remain committed to a vision of an Israeli society that, applying ancient Jewish values to new circumstances, treats all of its citizens justly and seeks peace with its neighbors whenever possible. We turn to Kaplan's formulation of Judaism as a religion of ethical nationhood as we support those Israelis who are devoted to these traditional Jewish values that have preserved us through the centuries.

Responsibility to Non-Jews

The second area of debate concerns the responsibility that Jews—in Israel and elsewhere—bear to non-Jews. The founders of the Israeli state were committed to the establishment of a society that would differ from others in its approach to international relations. Israel would, of course, develop the capacity to defend efficiently the lives and safety of its citizens. Its wars, however, would only be wars of defense, its military campaigns designed thoughtfully to minimize unnecessary civilian casualties, and its readiness to negotiate for peace constant, even in the face of relentlessly hostile neighbors.

Even before 1948, some Zionist factions attacked this commitment, believing it to be based on an unrealistic view of the world. Jews had always been prey to their enemies, and the primary contribution of an independent Jewish state would be its ability, at long last, to fight those enemies on equal terms. This view has been reinforced continually—by the Holocaust, by the silence of Western nations in the weeks preceding the Six Day War, by the aid and comfort that Palestinian terrorists found for many years in the capitals of the civilized world, and now, by the pressures exerted on Israel to make peace with the Palestinians. All such events are taken to confirm the view that the Jews have no reliable friends and that our exclusive responsibility is to strengthen our capacity to foil the designs of our foes.

Most Reconstructionists take their stand with the vision of the Israeli founders and with the signers of the Oslo accords and proponents of peace. The long-term viability of the Jewish state depends, we believe, on its loyalty to traditional ethical principles. The lesson of the Holocaust is not only that we must be vigilant in our own defense, but also that we must oppose injustice and cruelty no matter who is the victim. It is through a religion of ethical nationhood that the State of Israel and Jewish civilization as a whole will weather the challenges ahead. Judaism must stand for an enriching and ennobling way of life if it is to be worth defending indefinitely. A program advocating survival for its own sake preserves the shell while allowing our precious core to slip away. Israel can demand support both from Jews and from nations only as a democratic state that is simultaneously a loyal ally and a strong upholder of the highest ideals. While we recognize that there are many ways to pursue peace, we stand with those Israelis who believe that though peace is a gamble, it is a risk worth taking, because the alternative is far more dangerous.

Religion in Israel

The Labor Zionist program was formed by pioneering activists who rebelled against the Orthodoxy of their Eastern European origins. Thus, they formulated a secular model for the Israeli state that spurned not only Orthodox religion but all Jewish religion. The 2000-year history of the Jewish people in the Diaspora initially was ignored, and Judaism as religion was abandoned to the Orthodox rabbinate.

As a result, the quality of Jewish life in Israel has suffered. Israelis have long defined themselves either as *dati'im* (Orthodox) or *ḥiloni'im* (secular), with little room for a non-Orthodox, liberal religious expression. The complexity of Israeli coalition politics has exacerbated this problem because it has allowed Orthodox political parties to bargain for power beyond their numbers and to acquire substantial financial resources. They have used that power and those resources to thwart attempts to develop non-Orthodox religious alternatives.

It is ironic that the diversity of Jewish religious alternatives has been so limited in the Jewish state. Israelis are often prevented by state law and coalition agreements, for example, from using public transportation or attending concerts on Shabbat or acting in other ways that offend Orthodox sensibilities. They are restrained by those same regulations from developing alternate forms of Shabbat observance that would violate the halakhah of the Orthodox. Orthodox synagogues, *yeshivot,* and school systems routinely receive financial support from the government. Non-Orthodox synagogues most commonly are left to their own devices. The message is clear: The only legitimate form of Judaism in Israel is Orthodox Judaism. The Orthodox rabbinate remains adamant in its opposition to any kind of recognition for other religious alternatives. Faced with that circumstance, many Israelis have chosen not to define themselves as religious.

This explains why the only non-Orthodox alternatives in Israel are foreign imports—Reform, Conservative, and Progressive alternatives that are supported from abroad. The Jerusalem congregation *Mevakshei Derekh* (Seekers of a Way), founded on Kaplanian principles, had to meet in a high school for two decades before the municipality could be prodded into granting it a parcel of land on which to build. In contrast to Orthodox synagogues, most of the funds for construction of a synagogue-center have had to be raised privately. It is primarily Western immigrants, aware that there are meaningful religious alternatives to Orthodoxy, who are the mainstay of these small movements.

But the potential is there. Israelis, no less than other Jews across the globe, confront the challenges of modernity. They, too, are in need of the spiritual treasures of our traditions as they deal with neighbors and cope with the stresses of contemporary life. Secular Israeli society itself provides them with what diaspora Jews lack: a schooling in Jewish history and Israeli culture; new folkways dealing with Shabbat and the holidays; and an effortless immersion in Jewish language, landscape, and lore. But Israel has insufficient opportunities for spiritual exploration and for plumbing our tradition for fresh ideas about how to confront personal and national moral questions. Israelis who are uncomfortable with Orthodoxy need new Israeli forms of religious life.

In recent years, there has been encouraging movement in this direction among "secular" Israelis. Groups of non-Orthodox people who want to study traditional Jewish texts and to celebrate Shabbat and holidays are beginning to spring up across the land. In response, the Reconstructionist movement offers classes and seeds havurot, offering Israelis our perspectives and experiences about how Jewish traditions can be reconstructed to address contemporary spiritual concerns. We are not, however, interested in transplanting to Israeli soil our North American cultural forms. Israelis themselves will have the responsibility of determining the indigenous structure, shape, and name of any new movement that emerges. Reconstructionists are interested in sharing our perspectives and in learning what we can from the viewpoint of Israelis, whose circumstances are so different from our own.

Reconstructionists tend to feel a close kinship with those Israelis —the noted novelist Amos Oz, for example—who are moving towards a reclamation of Judaism as a *religion* of ethical nationhood, towards a revival of Jewish religious life in a liberal, egalitarian, naturalistic way. It is not for us to prescribe the forms that an indigenous and liberal Israeli Judaism should take. We maintain our solidarity, however, with those struggling for a pluralistic Jewish society in which religious options are not constrained by the dictates of the Orthodox rabbinate. Pluralism is as crucial in Israel as it is in America or Europe.

Criticism of Israeli Policies

For many years, awestruck by the monumental achievement of the builders of the Jewish state, diaspora Jews idealized the state and believed it could do no wrong. As the new state struggled to build a viable economy and to overcome international hostility, Jews around the world believed that their role was to serve as Israel's unconditional defenders. No one could understand the meaning of Israel as well as Jews; only we understood that the existence of the State of Israel needed no justification.

Since the 1967 war, however, Jewish communities have debated the appropriateness of Jewish criticism of Israeli policies, especially when that criticism intensified after the 1982 war in Lebanon and the outbreak of the intifada. Jewish critics may have noble intentions but should be wary lest loving criticisms become ammunition in the hands of those who wish to delegitimize the State of Israel.

Reconstructionist Jews are sensitive to these concerns; those Jews who issue public statements must weigh their positive effects against their potential dangers. We do not believe, however, especially after an elected Israeli government signed the Oslo accords and committed itself to peace, that the solidarity of the Jewish people requires that we mute our criticisms in fear of what non-Jews will say. The issues that are debated, often vociferously, within Israeli society—the fate of the Jewish settlements of the West Bank, Orthodox hegemony, Ashkenazi-Sephardi relations, questions of Jewish identity, the status of Israeli Arabs—are too important to the fate of all Jews to be left to Israelis alone. It is therefore our view that non-Israeli Jews must insist that their voices be included in those debates, at least by supporting those voices in Israel with whom we agree. Just as Israel's victories since 1948 have given us newfound pride, so can its moral character diminish or reinvigorate our moral self-understanding.

Zionists Can Live in the Diaspora

Israelis are less likely today than ever before to insist that Jews in the Diaspora must make *aliyah* to be truly loyal to the Jewish state. One still hears the claim, however, that Jewish life in North America, for example, is doomed to failure—because of the inevitability of anti-Semitism and/or because of the irreversibility of progressive assimilation. The common Israeli reading of history is that all previous golden ages of Jewish life in the Diaspora have ended tragically, and that diaspora Jews who ignore this long series of precedents are self-deluding.

Reconstructionists reject the claim that living in Israel is the only possible way to ensure Jewish survival. We are firmly convinced of the need for the Jewish state—both as a haven for the oppressed and as the optimal site of Jewish cultural and spiritual renewal in our time. As Jewish civilization has been enriched by the diversity of Jewish communities in the past, so today do both Israeli and diaspora Jews have much to gain by developing in independent but interrelated ways.

We do not regard the State of Israel as the complete realization of the age-old Jewish ideal of Zion. Israeli Jews, no less than diaspora Jews, are struggling with the meaningful adaptation of Jewish traditions in a new era. They, like us, are fallible. They are locked into a particular socio-political circumstance that requires them to be relentlessly vigilant against military attack and limits their interaction with the non-Jewish world.

North American Jews live in very different circumstances that, for the foreseeable future, will allow us the unprecedented opportunity to develop as Jews while being intimately connected with non-Jews in an open, pluralistic setting. While the future cannot be foretold, we certainly hope that both Jewish experiments will continue to flourish, contributing new chapters to Jewish history and supporting each other.

Indeed, the common *assumption* that Israeli and North American Jews are, or ought to be, the same can itself lead to and exacerbate misunderstandings and ill will. After more than a half-century, the two groups have very different outlooks that have been conditioned by their circumstances.

In North America, one *chooses* to affirm a Jewish identity and is compelled to justify that choice by articulating the value of being Jewish—because of Jewish ethical or social justice teachings, because of the spiritual enrichment derived from Jewish practice, because of the contributions that Jews can make to pluralism and intergroup understanding. And those values are articulated in ways that make sense in the larger non-Jewish culture of which we are a part, and by which our security is not threatened.

In Israel, Judaism isn't a conscious choice. Jews speak Hebrew, live according to the Jewish calendar, walk on ground that everywhere reflects Jewish history, and adapt for better or worse to the challenges created by living among other Jews whose ways of life differ from their own. An exorbitant percentage of people's salaries is deducted from their paychecks to pay taxes to support the Jewish state. One breathes "Jewish" air naturally and thus has no need to reflect upon *why* one does so. Israeli Jews are threatened not by assimilation but by terrorist bombs and neighbors with missiles and armies.

No wonder Israeli Jews cannot comprehend how North American Jews can claim to be Jewishly equal to them. We don't speak Hebrew or pay taxes or serve annually for a month in reserve units of the Israel Defense Forces. No wonder our understandings of the value of Judaism sound to them as if they are borrowed from non-Jewish sources. On the other hand, no wonder Israelis appear to North American Jews as uninterested in making Judaism meaningful and as obsessed with security. Each group is adapting Judaism, of course, to its specific circumstances. Attempts to judge either group exclusively by the other's criteria are ill-conceived.

For all the differences and misunderstandings between North American and Israeli Jews, it turns out that we share more in common than we thought. Both communities share a concern with Jewish continuity. Israeli Jews may not be concerned with intermarriage and assimilation, but they are concerned with whether the next generation will be *Jewish,* in any meaningful religious sense of the term. Many non-Orthodox Israeli Jews are now interested in progressive religious practices and interpretations that have developed in North America.

The challenge before North American Zionists is thus neither to convince our most committed people that a full Jewish life is possible only in Israel, nor to sound the trumpets of doom about our future. It is rather to develop creative programs that bring us in closer touch with Israelis. Our philanthropic generosity is an important indication of our commitment that needs to be broadened. Subsidized summer programs for teens and adults, educational tours, work-study programs that bring diaspora Jews into close touch with Israelis, opportunities for study institutes, organized programs facilitating sabbatical exchanges with Israelis—all of these ideas and others should be given priority by the North American Jewish community. Their success cannot be measured by the number of participants persuaded by them to make *aliyah,* but rather in the enrichment they provide for the quality of our Jewish lives. Closer links between Israeli and diaspora Jews can enrich and strengthen both.

In the end, both the land of Israel and its people will remain central to the consciousness of committed Jews everywhere. Our fate is linked inextricably to theirs, and we look to them for leadership. Reconstructionists, however, maintain that, in addition to basking in the rays that come forth from Jerusalem, diaspora Jews must also generate light, for our own illumination and that of Israelis as well. Only in a partnership that acknowledges and values our differences can we fulfill the destiny of the Jewish people.

7
Living as a Reconstructionist

What do the lives of Reconstructionist Jews look like? How are all of the theories articulated in the preceding chapters manifested concretely in the life of an individual?

The underlying principle on which all of Reconstructionist life is based is that Judaism is a religious civilization that provides us with a rich, meaningful, and elevated path—a path studded with sacred moments. All of these treasures—the accumulation of experiences, values, and insights of generations past and present—can best be accessed as we become immersed in the rituals, ethical behavior, texts, and customs to which we are heir. And Reconstructionists do that in a community composed of people committed to addressing together the challenge of making the Jewish heritage speak to the contemporary Jew. Judaism is no mere set of principles or values. It is a way of life, and it is by living this life that one can enter that world.

Reconstructionists seek to be shaped by the Jewish heritage, but we do not wish to return to the past. Many traditional practices do not "work" in our lives today without modification, and often, many traditional values conflict with our current ethical intuitions. We do not surrender unconditionally to the imperatives of our ancestors, but as much as possible, we do want to be shaped by our encounters with them, in the context of contemporary Jewish communities.

Moreover, Reconstructionists, like all people, connect to our traditions in a *variety* of ways. Recent studies suggest that there are different "spiritual types." Not everyone is religious in the same way. Some people find prayer and ritual to be natural avenues of spiritual connection. Some people find holiness in analysis and study. Some experience God most readily in social action or in interpersonal relationships. Others find transcendence in observing the natural world or experiencing the creative process. There is even a spiritual type who best connects to God and religious life through iconoclasm—remaining true to God by smashing the idols of religious hypocrisy. It is therefore wrongheaded to expect everyone to be Jewish in the same way. No individual is purely one of these "types," but each of us has greater propensities in some directions than in others. Viewing Judaism as a religious civilization that encompasses all of these paths, Reconstructionists affirm the validity of each of them and seek to encourage one another as we each find our own way.

Study

Talmud Torah, the study of our sacred inherited texts, is an activity that has tended to mark the lives of Reconstructionists since the movement's beginnings. Many Reconstructionist havurot function primarily as study groups. Adult education is a central component of our synagogues. *Divrei Torah* (Torah commentaries), sometimes prepared by members, sometimes by the rabbi, are more common on Shabbat morning than sermons, and they are often followed by lively group discussion. One of the defining features of a Reconstructionist community is that the lives of its members include lifelong Jewish learning.

The genesis of the centrality of Torah study for Reconstructionists lies in an understanding of Judaism as an ever-evolving religious civilization that is best lived in participatory decision-making communities. Thus, a Reconstructionist is not likely to accept a Jewish teaching or perform a ritual without also learning where that teaching or ritual originated and how it and its meanings have changed through the centuries. We study texts not because they are inherently authoritative. We study with an openness that includes a healthy skepticism. We want to learn from the teachings and customs of our ancestors, but we don't assume that they are always correct. We measure them against contemporary values and insights, and we are not afraid to criticize them. The Torah we study includes not only ancient texts but contemporary ones as well. And we struggle with Torah together, in groups in which the value of a person's opinions is not determined only by his or her Jewish erudition. We learn Torah from one another, from the various areas of expertise that each of us brings to the discussion, and from our life experiences.

The study of sacred texts is not an intellectual process alone. Real *talmud Torah* involves the growth of the individual as a whole person, an experience of fellowship and community, and the opportunity for spiritual experience. When we learn, we need to involve our whole beings. We must use the experience as an opportunity for growth and change. The information we acquire in study is only the beginning of learning. True learning takes place when we are able to use what we know in our lives. What we learn, especially in a Reconstructionist framework, should help us make decisions about the kind of people we want to be in the world and about the values that undergird the way we live our lives. A standard method of Jewish study is in *ḥevruta,* with a learning partner. Studying the texts that we have looked at in partnership with others inevitably leads to new interpretations and to spiritual growth.

It is noteworthy that many Reconstructionists would tell you that they prefer to study rather than to pray. We do not contrast study and prayer. We rather affirm that study is a form of prayer, an activity that, for some, focuses us on our ultimate beliefs and values as effectively as singing or chanting the words of the prayer book. When sparks of Torah are generated in our discussions, our hearts are moved.

Prayer

Given the notoriety Reconstructionists have acquired because we do not believe in a God who intervenes supernaturally in our lives, the extent of our prayer lives raises questions. While some Reconstructionists do regard study as their preferred form of prayer, we *also* pray in the conventional sense of that term: awakening with the prayer *Modeh Ani* (I acknowledge You) in the morning, donning *tallit* (prayer shawl) and sometimes *tefillin* (phylacteries) to recite the morning prayers, reciting *berakhot* (blessings) and chanting *pesukim* (Biblical verses) as we make our way through the day, reciting *Birkat Hamazon* after meals, meditating. Why do Reconstructionists pray? Here are some reasons:

- *Spiritual Discipline.* Most of us go through the day without consciously experiencing God's presence. Prayer helps to develop and maintain a spiritual sense. Focusing regularly on our sacred encounters helps us to notice them as they occur.

- *Meditation.* Most of us live at a very rapid pace. We welcome the opportunity to slow down and remember what has deeper meaning beyond our daily routines.

- *Group Connection.* If we are not careful, it is easy to become isolated. Even if we interact frequently with others, our daily lives rarely afford many opportunities to let our guard down and express what is really important to us. It is a real treat to be connected to a group, all of whose members are seeking together.

- *Celebration.* For many of us, few experiences transport us as powerfully as group singing. We may be grateful for a life passage, or for the blossoming of flowers in spring, but without our prayer communities, we might never sing about it.

- *Group Support.* Life is unfortunately filled with disappointment, illness, and tragedy. Social scientists now tell us what we already knew: that recovery from family discord, depression, and even physical illness is enhanced when we experience the support of a caring group. Praying for a sick person is efficacious even if you don't believe that God intercedes supernaturally. Our prayers do have power.

- *Rededication to Principles.* It is very easy to lose perspective, to miss the forest for the trees, to get so wound up in a situation that we lose sight of who we are and what we stand for. Praying draws us out of ourselves and helps to restore the larger picture.

- *Acknowledgment of Need.* Most of us are raised to think that we have control of our lives, and that therefore we are responsible for what happens to us—good and bad. In truth, we have far less control than we think, and it is good to acknowledge our vulnerability. Prayer allows us to admit that we need help when we are frightened, overwhelmed, or desperate. Removing our defenses can move us to the honest self-awareness we require to get past our personal obstacles.

- *Building Community.* Communal worship services have an additional function for Reconstructionists, who are most interested in building a sense of Jewish community. The words and melodies of the liturgy allow us both to express our common aspirations, hopes, and frustrations, and to share in an aesthetically satisfying Jewish activity. When we use the words of past generations to express our contemporary concerns, we develop an empathy with the insights and concerns of our ancestors, as well as a bond with all Jews living today.

Tikkun Olam

Reconstructionists seek to live in two civilizations—the North American and the Jewish. As described above in chapter 5, this has led the movement to place social action (*tikkun olam*—repair of injustice in the world) high on its agenda. It is not only as individuals but also as Jews working together in our communities that Reconstructionists seek to improve the world. *Tikkun olam* committees have promoted a wide range of such projects: internal programming to educate members about how to live in environmentally sound ways, political lobbying and demonstrating to protest genocide or welfare cutbacks, volunteering in inner city soup kitchens, turning synagogues into homeless shelters, declaring sanctuary for illegal immigrants fleeing political oppression, escorting women into clinics past violent anti-abortion protestors. Pre-b'nai mitzvah classes and youth group programs have *tikkun olam* components that emphasize the centrality of this work for Jewish living.

It is not assumed that all members of a given congregation will agree on every issue, but it is also not required that everyone agree before a sub-group can work on an issue that is dear to the hearts of its members. Indeed, it is not unheard of that a single community might spawn two groups, each working on opposite sides of an issue. The goal here is not to promote political uniformity. It is rather that Jews find ways to integrate their commitments so that their social action work can become an aspect of their *Jewish* identities.

Many Reconstructionists have their most profound experiences of God through *tikkun olam*: working together, fighting injustice, acting to help others. It is not out of charity that they ally themselves with those who are oppressed or less fortunate, but rather out of the teaching that all human beings are worthy of respect and opportunity. If that is true, then injustice and discrimination deprive people of their birthright, and *tikkun olam* may be the most concrete and palpable way to make God's Presence manifest in our world.

Finding Spirituality in Relationships

Human beings are created in the image of God, as we are told in the first chapter of the Book of Genesis. Therefore, it is in relationships with other people that we can have an immediate experience of divinity. This happens most effortlessly, in the best of circumstances, in the unconditional love we receive from our parents and give to our children, affording us an intuition about the nurturing power of the universe. In relationship with a lover, we get a glimpse of what it might mean to lose our attachment to ego, to see through the apparent separateness of created things to their underlying Unity. We learn the meaning of faith and trust from our devotion to our closest friends. As the philosopher Martin Buber taught, we meet God when we remain truly open to the other.

Reading the biblical descriptions of God, and many of their subsequent interpretations through the generations, however, does make one wonder. God is portrayed as impatient as well as long-suffering, as punishing as well as forgiving, the Source of fear as well as of love. Reconstructionists view the image of God as Almighty Monarch as a reflection of social and cultural norms that were prevalent in the past but that no longer speak to us. In focusing on the rabbinic teaching that we are *partners* with God in the work of creation, we cultivate an awareness of God as the source of strength, courage, generosity of spirit, and inspiration. We can best cultivate our awareness of God by how we act with other people and are treated by them.

Furthermore, we need not wait to find God-revealing relationships. Part of the challenge of cultivating a spiritual life in secular society is that it is difficult to speak about moments of transcendence, even to our closest friends. We don't have the vocabulary, or we are afraid they'll think we are religious fanatics. To address this challenge, Reconstructionists have begun to encourage spiritual *ḥevruta*—a relationship in which two peers meet regularly, often weekly, to listen to each other's spiritual experiences.

God in Nature

Ask a group of Reconstructionists to describe the moments in their lives when they have felt most powerfully the Presence of God, and a significant percentage will describe experiences of nature. A sunrise, hiking in the mountains, the blossoming of flowers—these are experiences that have the potential to evoke a sense of wonder that connects us to a palpable power in the universe.

Part of Kaplan's vision of God was transnatural—a power that works through nature. It is in the natural world that we can best glimpse that power. Being in nature arouses our senses: the scent of pine trees, the sound of birds in a forest, the cool breeze on our skin as we walk through the woods, the spray of the ocean against the crystal blue sky. Being in touch with these phenomena touches us, literally, at the deepest part of our being, reminding us of the Power in the world that is beyond expression in words.

The unity and interconnectedness of the cosmos are easily experienced through a daily walk or jog in the park or woods. But we may also bring this awareness to our prayer lives. Seeing God's presence in the natural order, Reconstructionists may then tap this source of inspiration to gain insight into the words of prayers and psalms and the significance of rituals. We notice our breath when we recite *Nishmat Kol Ḥai* (The Breath of All Life). We step out of doors to gaze at the sunset as we welcome the Sabbath Bride in chanting *Lekhah Dodi*. The ritual mnemonics of traditional practices serves more effectively as reminders when we have already traveled to spiritual places to which they are pointing.

Creativity and the Arts

Each civilization produces its own forms of art, which express most articulately the way that reality is structured in that culture. Judaism is no different. Over the thousands of years of the evolution of Jewish civilization, artists have written poetry and music (sacred and secular), designed synagogues and ritual objects, crafted clothing and stories, composed folk dance, and illuminated manuscripts. Jewish art plays an important role in the spiritual lives of Reconstructionists in several different ways.

First, Reconstructionists have sought to recover and reclaim the artistic creations of the Jewish past. There is no better example of this phenomenon than the work of Dr. Judith Kaplan Eisenstein, Kaplan's daughter. A pioneer who was one of the first Jewish musicologists, she published manuscripts of classical Jewish music and brought that music into the synagogue service—both to beautify the service and to add a significant dimension to the community's Jewish acculturation. There is more to the liturgy, for example, than the meaning of its words. Hearing it sung as Jews in the Italian Renaissance heard it deeply enriches the experience. Similarly, the medieval illuminations of the Bible or Haggadah add a visual overlay to the meaning of their words.

Second, Reconstructionists seek to recognize and honor the work of Jewish artists today as significant expressions of Jewish life, even though most of their work may not be created explicitly with the Jewish community in mind. Saul Bellow. Yehudah Amichai. Marge Piercy. Elizabeth Swados. Leonard Bernstein. Tony Kushner. Wendy Wasserstein. Adrienne Rich. Marc Chagall. The ongoing development of Jewish civilization is by no means confined to the books and commentaries of rabbis.

Third, Reconstructionist communities are enhanced immeasurably by the creative work of their members—their songs and poems, the Torah-scroll covers they embroider and the skits they compose and perform on Purim. The ongoing reconstruction of Jewish civilization must include contemporary expressions of Jewish experience if traditions are to be re-phrased in the idioms of our day. For this, the creative work of community members often is a fertile resource.

Fourth, the Source from which prophecy and mystical visions once arose is, one suspects, the same Source from which contemporary creative expressions arise. As the poets of ancient Israel were regarded as prophetic messengers of God's Word, so do we become elevated—and provoked—by the creations of the artists among us. The rabbis declared that the era of prophecy had ended, in order to close off competing claims of authority. Reconstructionists do not share that concern. We rather seek to foster an ongoing process of revelation.

Embodied Spirituality

In biblical times, the soul was seen as a fine material substance located *in* the body. Ever since, Jews have developed the belief in a pure, immaterial soul struggling to free itself from the lowly body mired in this crass, material world. In modern times, we have proudly contrasted Judaism's affirmation of the pleasures of this world with the otherworldly emphasis of Christianity, but modern Jewish movements have continued to focus more on the mind and spirit rather than the body. Under feminist influence, many Reconstructionists are now reclaiming the body as a spiritual instrument.

At the simplest level, care of the soul depends on care of the body. What we eat, how much we sleep, and our level of physical stress all influence profoundly the health of our spirit. Taking time to breathe, to taste our food, to sense as well as to observe our environment, for example, leads to a greater sense of wholeness and well being.

Beyond that, it is not only with words and thoughts that we can pray, if prayer means experiencing the Presence of God. We can do so by singing and swaying, as is done traditionally in Jewish worship. And we can do so by moving our bodies, by smelling and tasting and touching, by worshipping with our whole physical being.

Religious Iconoclasm

"Religious" is a word that is often associated with "pious" and "deferential." "Irreligious" has come to be synonymous with "irreverent." Such associations are not indigenously Jewish, and they do not work well as a way of understanding all forms of Reconstructionist religiosity.

At its mythic origins, Judaism is portrayed by the Aggadah (rabbinic homilies) as beginning when the Patriarch Abraham smashes his father's idols. He cuts through the conventional beliefs of his native culture one by one until he realizes that the unseen God is beyond all else. Abraham and Moses are both portrayed in the Torah itself as questioning God's own (destructive) judgments. The Jewish stance of religious engagement by questioning conventional pieties is also well expressed in Maimonides' accusation of idolatry against anyone who believes that God literally speaks or acts in this world, no matter how pious the believer. The iconoclast clearly has deep roots as a Jewish spiritual type.

A Reconstructionist Jew, by definition, is someone who *questions:* Who actually wrote this or that section of the Bible? Does a particular teaching reflect values that we would still call divine? Why should a given ritual practice be observed? All Reconstructionists ask these questions. Some, however, focus on questioning as the religious activity about which they are most passionate. They seek God through intellectual skepticism. They do so not because of ideological differences with others who move past the questioning to embrace texts and traditions fervently. The different approaches may be better understood as manifestations of different spiritual types.

The many Reconstructionists who pray by studying, and who often relate to religious beliefs and practices by debunking them, may appear to be an historical anomaly. Depending on the decade, the religious respectability of this type of questioning fluctuates. For much of the twentieth century, when reason was preeminent, the religious authenticity of dispassionate Torah study was rarely questioned. By the turn of the millennium, however, the cultural climate shifted so that emotional expression is almost an assumed requirement for spirituality.

Cultural trends aside, however, there is much to be learned from the iconoclast. If Judaism is the ever-evolving religious civilization of the Jewish people, then *all* of our beliefs, practices, and values are historically conditioned creations of human beings, and hence less than absolutely true or valid. With Abraham and Maimonides, some people remain true to God by never forgetting that fact, never willingly suspending their disbelief. They find holiness in the very questioning of everything others hold sacred.

The iconoclast does not, it should be emphasized, abandon the community and its pursuits. In Reconstructionist settings, people with this skeptical bent are often the most faithful of participants at services and Torah study classes, often the most active of community leaders. They engage Torah and God by taking traditional practices and teachings seriously enough to argue *against* them. They do not walk away.

In Reconstructionist settings, such Jewish iconoclasts are welcomed not only because of a commitment to pluralism and diversity. Their contributions to the collective communal quest for holiness are critical because they make us examine more closely all of our practices and values. In what ways does our pursuit of spiritual experience anesthetize us to the pain we ought to feel about the injustice in the world? How do our ritual practices create undesirable separations from non-Jews? Do our particular beliefs about God challenge us, or do they make it easy for us to avoid necessary change? When does our devotion to social justice enable us to ignore the way we are mistreating one another? These are examples of iconoclastic questions by which we all ought to be regularly challenged, even when they are upsetting and provocative. They might be said to be the questions of the Living God.

No matter how individual Reconstructionists experience spirituality—through writing a poem, observing the stars, praying, dancing, reading a text, working for social justice, or arguing—all of us seek to live in Jewish time, according to its calendrical rhythms. Presented with ethical dilemmas, we turn, in community, to the study of our sacred texts in order to engage in intergenerational dialogue with the wisdom of those who have come before us. We recite traditional blessings that open us up to daily wonders that we might otherwise overlook, and we pray the words of the Siddur to structure our experiences of God. Most of all, because we are committed to community, we find the Presence of God in one another, in our mutual support and caring, in the sparks of insight generated in our Torah study, in the way our voices join in prayer and celebration, and in the ways that we work for *tikkun olam* (to make this world a better place).

The Spirituality of Shabbat

Jewish time is lived, first and foremost, from Shabbat to Shabbat. The Shabbat was a radical innovation in ancient Israel, a declaration that we can be freed from the inexorable march of time, freed from the lunar and solar calendar, freed from social and economic inequities, free to stop, to relax, to relinquish our obsessions, to admit that life goes on even if we are not minding the store or ploughing the field. Implicitly embedded in the observance of Shabbat, therefore, is an approach to life that reflects many central Jewish values.

The ancient Israelites who celebrated Shabbat could not have known how important it would be for those of us who live in the twenty-first century. What an idea! That there is the beat of another drummer, so soft that it is all but inaudible in the din of our daily lives, yet so powerful that if we align ourselves with its rhythm, our entire lives can be sanctified by it.

In an age of twenty-four-hour supermarkets, of a global village in which events transpire even when we are asleep and we awaken already in need of catching up, there is no greater gift than Shabbat. Shabbat means no work. Budgeted, inviolable time to sit at leisure with family and friends. Time for a nap, for a walk without a destination. Communities of individuals who stop together to pray and study and sing and eat.

Enticing, but easier said than done. Those of us who have lived in Israel may yearn for a society in which everything closes down by mid-afternoon Friday, enabling us to shop and cook and breathe deeply in preparation. Traditionally, you don't rush home from a busy day to Shabbat. You start preparing on Wednesday or Thursday, cleaning the house and quieting the mind so that when you light the Shabbat candles, you are truly prepared to welcome the Sabbath Queen.

Few of us are so lucky. Our "villages" do not close down on Jewish time. Moreover, the idyllic image of Shabbat rests on the assumption that someone stays at home to make Shabbat for the rest of us. Even if we manage to leave work a bit early on Friday afternoon so that we arrive home by sunset, it is unlikely that our day will have been spent cultivating a consciousness of Shabbat or that the table will have been set for our arrival.

In addition, many of us have never experienced a *full* day of Shabbat. Without that experience, the twenty-five hours may appear onerous with all of its traditional prohibitions. Shabbat may be inviting, but *how* do we learn to rest? What is attractive about doing nothing?

Reconstructionists address this as an incremental challenge. Observing *part* of Shabbat is worthwhile in itself. There are many points of entry. Resting on Shabbat is *not* doing nothing. In the silence, as we cover our eyes to bless the Shabbat candles, there is a window of connection—with our loved ones (whether they are still with us or not), with the Source of Creation. Or sharing a cup of *kiddush* wine around the table, we are reminded of what is most important in our lives. In lingering after the meal to sing, the stress of the week's work abates, and we remember why life is worth living. When joining in community to sing and chant the Shabbat *tefillot* (prayers) and discuss the Torah portion, we find ourselves transported to a sacred realm. We do not frown upon such nontraditional modes of Shabbat rest as gardening or going to a museum. We do not demand of ourselves and one another that Shabbat observance be all or nothing. But as we deepen our experience of rest and renewal, each in our own way and at our own pace, the *Havdalah* ceremony on Saturday evening becomes a powerful punctuation of our week, serving to distinguish between sacred and profane time.

The Rhythm of the Calendar

As we move through the seasons of the Jewish year, our lives can take on the resonance of its cycles. Too often, Jews move briskly into the celebration of a holiday, forgetting the attendant preparation that can deepen their experience. Reconstructionists seek to remedy that situation, opening up ever expanding experiences of sacred Jewish time.

It is in the lull of August that the month of Elul comes, initiating the period of *teshuvah* (return) and *ḥeshbon hanefesh* (self-examination) that precedes the High Holy Days. It is in this period that Jews traditionally take stock of the year gone by, working to repair relationships and noting the direction of their own lives. The shofar is to be blown each morning, awakening us to the challenge. *Seliḥot* (prayers for forgiveness) are recited throughout the month, and the period culminates in the *Seliḥot* service on the Saturday evening preceding Rosh Hashanah. Those who involve themselves in this process may become more acclimated to the teaching that *teshuvah* is an ongoing enterprise, even for the most righteous, and that Jewish living includes a serious ethical and introspective component, a discipline to be cultivated year-round.

Rosh Hashanah begins the *Aseret Yemei Teshuvah* (Ten Days of Return) that end with Yom Kippur. Reconstructionists join together to reflect on the year gone by and the year ahead, experiencing the power of a *community* of individuals turning inward in solidarity. The High Holy Day *nusah* (prayer melody) and the sounding of the shofar move us subliminally to awaken to the divine call. The themes of the *Mahzor* (High Holy Day prayer book)—including images of a world in which God's Presence is manifest, of every one of us "remembered" by God, of the hope for a messianic future—are transformative even though we don't literally believe that God sets our fates in the Book of Life. They set before us a perennial image of the better world towards which we strive. As we fast on Yom Kippur, confronting our imperfection and mortality, we seek to connect to the Source of All and to feel the forgiveness that can be so elusive as we judge others and ourselves.

Building a sukkah immediately following this introspective period challenges us emotionally and spiritually as Jews have been challenged for millennia. Sukkot is a holiday of joyous celebration, of decorations, of *lulav* and *etrog* (the four species) and meals out in nature, culminating in the dancing on Simhat Torah. How do you move so rapidly from the solemnity of atonement to the harvest of the full moon? We interpret, as generations before have interpreted: that the cleansing of *teshuvah* allows us to experience anew the wonders of nature; that facing our mortality heightens our appreciation of our blessings, which are as fragile as the sukkah. The specific interpretation is less important than the way in which our following the cycles of Jewish time engages us with the infinite meanings of Jewish symbols.

In this way, Reconstructionists shape their lives. In the dead of winter, we light the Hanukah candles against the darkness. We celebrate Tu Bishvat, the new year of trees, eating an assortment of fruit that reminds us of the centrality of the land of Israel and its seasons.

A month later, we simultaneously embrace the silliness of Purim while struggling with a heroine who is a beauty queen and the bloody denouement of the Megillah.

Reconstructionists may get cranky in the weeks preceding Pesah as we groan about the way we are oppressed by the formidable task of ridding our homes of *hametz* (leaven). But in our exhaustion, we find ourselves identifying with our slave ancestors. Through the process of cleaning, we confront the ways in which we are still oppressed by our psyches and by society. And then, at the Seder table, as we recline, we experience freedom palpably, renewing our commitment to the God of liberation and the imperative to fight injustice everywhere. Indeed, the Passover Seder is paradigmatic of the way that the celebration of Jewish ritual in Jewish time enables us to relive the timeless, mythic truths embedded in our traditions—not merely as historical commemorations, but also as sacred narratives that shape us as we experience them.

And from the celebration of the Exodus, we count seven weeks to Sinai, to the revelation of the Torah on Shavuot. As we count, some of us follow the 50 stages of spiritual ascent enumerated by Jewish mystics. And all of us experience the emotional turbulence, directly following Pesah, of the week that includes *Yom Hashoah* (Holocaust Remembrance Day), *Yom Hazikaron* (Israeli Memorial Day), and *Yom Ha'atzma'ut* (Israeli Independence Day). The transforming power of Jewish history has recent as well as ancient layers.

The weeks of *Sefirah* (Counting) provide an opportunity to prepare ourselves once again to receive the Torah—by studying, by attending to the ways in which we are and are not open to the sacred and miraculous dimensions of Reality. Traditional rabbinic interpretations teach that only the *aleph* (a silent letter) of *Anokhi* (the first word of the first of the Ten Commandments) was actually revealed; that each person at Sinai heard something unique and appropriate

to her or his state of mind; that the souls of all subsequent generations were present at Sinai. If we had been present at Sinai, we might
ask, what would we have seen and heard? Taking the seven-week
trek through the wilderness between Pesah and Shavuot, we prepare
ourselves for the Torah study of the all-night *Tikkun Leil Shavuot,*
when we seek to stand at Sinai again.

As with Shabbat, this requires effort for most of us, who come
to the Jewish calendar as strangers. We are well educated, confident,
and competent in most aspects of our lives, but when we celebrate
Jewish ritual and study Jewish texts, we often begin as novices. The
thickness of Jewish culture can be off-putting when it is unfamiliar.
There is so very much to learn.

This is a challenge that all Jewish communities face in our day.
Reconstructionists address the challenge by acknowledging it and
by honoring our diversity. Each of us, in our communities, starts in
a different place and moves at a different pace in different directions.
Some of us eagerly embrace traditional practices. Some of us study
the origins and development of our customs without embracing them.
Some of us invest our energies in creating new rituals and ceremonies
that mark the sacred moments of the year. All of us are committed
to living in twenty-first-century Jewish communities in which members continue to learn, support one another in our diversity, and celebrate the *different* ways that Jewish civilization evolves through us.

Ethics

Torah lishma (the study of Torah "for its own sake") is a central Jewish
value. It is better to study, we are taught, without an ulterior motive
like earning a living or self-aggrandizement. Reconstructionists enthusiastically affirm this value. Immersion in the study of sacred inherited texts, and in discussions of their contemporary meaning, is

both effective and traditional as a way of accessing the wisdom and holiness to which Jews are heir. Reconstructionists *also* believe, however, that such study conditions and influences the values we pursue in our lives.

From the earliest teaching and writing of Rabbi Kaplan, Reconstructionists have been committed to the idea that the value of religious belief and practice can be measured by its fruits. How does a particular conception of or belief in God lead a believer to act in the world? What is the ethical impact of a particular religious practice? Kaplan, whose books include one with the title *The Religion of Ethical Nationhood,* was very clear. The raison d'être of the Jewish community must be measured by the way in which the lives of Jewish people become infused with the most exalted Jewish values.

How does this work? Not through pious pronouncements from the pulpit about ethical obligations, demanding that members be honest in their work lives or faithful in their relationships. These have no compelling power in North America, where no Jew is *forced* to join a synagogue, and so no rabbinic exhortation has commanding authority. Rather, the Reconstructionist approach is based on the belief that values are acquired through acculturation—when individuals are members of communities that play central roles in their lives, that embody the values that are to be conveyed, and that encourage members to study Jewish texts together as they explore what is right and wrong in specific circumstances.

Thus, the Reconstructionist Rabbinical College's Center for Jewish Ethics publishes materials for people interested in studying classical Jewish texts on the Ethics of Speech or Biomedical Ethics or Sexual Ethics, for example, in order to learn what Jews in the past have taught. Studying the voices of the past allows us to deepen and refine our questions, to benefit from the wisdom and insights of our ancestors, and to confront together the ways in which we do and don't share our ancestors' values. Above all, such study gives Jews access to sources from which they are otherwise cut off. Group discussions promote a climate in communities in which people become aware of the possibilities for guidance when they confront difficult and painful choices. What do I owe the business associate who is acting unscrupulously? How do I confront the community member who is acting hurtfully to me? Can a known philanderer serve on the synagogue board? When is it acceptable to direct the hospital staff not to resuscitate my parent? Jewish sources have much to say on all of these matters.

Reconstructionists believe that the very future of Jewish communities depends on our members' belief that our traditions can offer serious guidance for our ethical dilemmas. If the Jewish community is *only* an institution where I can belong, celebrate, and worship, but it is *not* the place to which I turn when I have excruciating choices to make, then it is really a leisure-time social club that I choose to attend when it is convenient. Jewish civilization will flourish if and only if Jewish people find it an invaluable and essential source of wisdom and direction.

But if Reconstructionists don't view texts and traditions as authoritative, how can we be guided by them? Through the working of community. Reconstructionist communities seek to counter the cultural bias in North America that places a supreme value on individualism, personal autonomy, and privacy. It is not the case that a person's ethical behavior is nobody else's business. If Judaism is a civilization, then how you conduct your business, how you treat or mistreat other people, and how much or little you contribute your time and money to community building and social action *matter as much* as how much you pray.

In these and other areas of personal and social ethics, Reconstructionist communities set standards by which members can measure themselves. And the standards are established not on high, but by community members who discuss traditional teachings and then decide how to live their lives. People do the right thing not because they are commanded to do so, but rather because they are influenced by and feel responsible to other members of the community.

Communities are able to set standards when they also function as support systems. Parents struggling with adolescents, children of aging parents, people undergoing divorce, members in need of legal advice, individuals seeking friends with whom to celebrate Shabbat and holidays, sick people in need of company or transportation—in these and countless other ways, Reconstructionists seek to support one another within a *Jewish* communal context. There is more to Jewish civilization than study and prayer. And it is only when Jews extend themselves to and are assisted by fellow members in *various* aspects of their lives that the power of community becomes fully manifest.

The connection between theology and ethics also figures in the Reconstructionist equation. If God is portrayed exclusively with masculine imagery, for example, it is inevitable that this will affect the different ways that the believer values, and therefore treats, men and women. If God is believed to be dictatorial, or quick to anger, then that will have implications for those who believe that we are created in God's image. Every aspect of a Reconstructionist community—its liturgy, its school curricula, its by-laws and operating procedures—is subject to Rabbi Kaplan's pragmatic touchstone: How does it promote ethical values?

Kashrut and Eco-*Kashrut*

Jews in the modern era have often marked their break with tradition by abandoning the practice of *kashrut*. Once halakhah is no longer accepted literally as God's commandments and people begin to sift through which parts of our heritage are and are not worth preserving, there is perhaps no more primal and dramatic way to break with the past than to eat *treif* (non-kosher food). It is therefore remarkable that Reconstructionists—Jews who do not accept the divinely commanded origin of the *mitzvot*—keep kosher in such great numbers.

It is remarkable, but not surprising. If you believe that Judaism is a civilization, then the way you eat is a central component of your life as a Jew. We eat all the time, so *how* we eat necessarily conditions our values and perspectives.

To be sure, not all of the practices that Reconstructionists call "kosher" would be affirmed by halakhic Jews. As discussed above in chapter 4, the *ways* that Reconstructionists keep kosher vary widely. For many, vegetarianism is the way they practice *kashrut*. Some eat only meat that is kosher, and others refrain from eating non-kosher animals but eat meat that has not been slaughtered ritually. Some eat only food that is *certified* as kosher, and others make their own decisions by checking ingredients on labels.

Most feel strongly that, no matter what their home practice is, they respect others' differing approaches and do not allow *kashrut* to be a barrier to eating with others. This is because for Reconstructionists, keeping kosher is not about *obeying* a divine commandment, but is rather a means of sanctifying their lives—a value that must be balanced with other values, such as creating community. Thus, while individuals have limits about what they will and won't eat, they make every effort to shape their eating habits in ways that affirm the value of diversity.

In recent years, the increasingly popular Reconstructionist observance of *kashrut* has often incorporated vegetarianism and eating in ecologically responsible ways. Until recently, many modern Jews explained their observance of *kashrut* as a way of promoting good health. Today, many Reconstructionists feel commanded by the imperative to eat in ways that neither destroy the earth nor contribute to world hunger. They are vegetarians, or eat very little meat, because of a concern about the amount of grain required to produce meat, as well as a concern about the way that animals are treated in preparation for slaughter. And those who eat meat make choices about the kind of meat they eat, refraining from the meat of larger mammals and eating only food that has been raised in an ecologically concerned way. Many avoid food products that are produced and/or preserved with chemicals that damage eco-systems. Some also consider avoiding the use of paper and plastic products as part of keeping kosher.

What all Reconstructionist *communities* share in common is a respect for *kashrut* and thus a commitment to a kosher communal kitchen in which all members can eat. That generally means that dairy food with kosher ingredients prepared by members even in non-kosher homes is welcomed. Dietary laws are not used as exclusionary devices.

In the Reconstructionist observance of *kashrut,* we care not only about *what* we eat but *how* we eat. We seek to cultivate an awareness of our blessings, utilizing *berakhot* (traditional blessings) that sanctify the meal and slow us down to appreciate our bounty and notice its tastes and textures. We recite the *Birkat Hamazon* after the meal to express our thanks, and there are many different forms of these blessings that Reconstructionists have created to do so. Eating is a religious act, and it is also a political act, especially in today's consumer economy. We seek to take responsibility to distinguish between our wants and needs, to care about what is healthful for us as individuals and for the world as a whole.

As we do so, *kashrut* links us with our ancestors' transformation of the table into a sacred altar. Their blessings infuse our consciousness.

As we adopt their customs, we are linked to them, reminded of their values. And to their concerns, we add our own.

It is the rare individual whose Jewish life involves *only* prayer or ritual or study or ethical living or communal organizing or social action. There are very few "pure" spiritual types. The lives of Reconstructionist Jews are each deepened through involvement in many aspects of Jewish civilization. It is, however, in the definition of Judaism as a religious civilization that Reconstructionists come to see that communities are enriched by the diverse interests and commitments of their members, and that all manifestations of Jewish life have a legitimate place within a Jewish community.

8
Marking the Stages of Our Lives

If Jews today have to work to re-infuse the cycles of the Jewish week and Jewish year with sacred meaning, there is far less need to do so with regard to life's natural passages. To the contrary, we experience transitions—the birth of a child, the entry to adolescence, the sanctification of a relationship, death and mourning, and many others—as moments of heightened awareness in which we are most open to the mystery and sanctity of life, most in need of Jewish spiritual techniques and traditional practices to help us express our awe and fear, our joy and terror. And it is also at these times that we need and appreciate the support of our communities.

Accepting Jewish life-cycle rituals as we inherit them, however, is not sufficient for Reconstructionists. Minimally, traditional customs must be translated to express their meaning in a contemporary idiom and supplemented with music or reflections that add our voices to those of the past. Sometimes, rituals require a reconstruction that replaces outmoded or objectionable meanings with an expression of our values. One of those values is gender equality, but this is by no means the only change in life-cycle rituals that we have made. And Reconstructionists have been eager to develop rituals for life passages —retirement, leaving home for college, weaning, menopause—that were never marked in the lives of past generations. The transformative power of a life-cycle ritual derives not only from the sanctity that accrues from centuries of practice. It can be generated when we are supported at pivotal moments by a community that gathers to mark the occasion through the use of traditional Jewish language and contemporary expressions of the heart.

Bar and Bat Mitzvah

Since late medieval times, the Jewish community has celebrated the bar mitzvah ceremony when boys reached the age of thirteen. In traditional communities, in which boys were educated Jewishly as a matter of course, the thirteen-year-old would be called up to the Torah for his first *aliyah,* a right reserved for adult men. Boys did not learn Torah-reading and service leading for this moment, because these skills were a part of their education from early childhood. Becoming a bar mitzvah signified that the boy was now permitted to display these skills in public.

No corresponding recognition or public ceremony existed for girls. This was the case for two reasons. First, the bar mitzvah ceremony took place during the Torah service. Since it had become the tradition that women were not eligible to be called up to the Torah, the ceremony would not have made sense. Second, the fact that a girl reached adulthood had significance in terms of her marriageability and a small number of other commandments related to holiday and home observance—but *not* for any other new role she would play in the performance of *public* rituals.

Had traditional Jewish society been interested in valuing or publicly celebrating the woman's role, a ceremony might have been developed around a girl's transition to puberty. Without this interest, it is not surprising that no such public celebration developed. And if women, acting outside the public domain, developed private celebrations, that, too, is lost to us—the activities of women were not of interest to the men who kept public records for posterity.

For these reasons, Reconstructionists first instituted the now widely accepted ceremony of bat mitzvah. In Kaplan's era, bat mitzvah, which we take for granted, was unheard of. Long before, classical Reform Judaism had done away with the bar mitzvah ceremony. In Reform settings at that time, the Torah was not frequently read in public, and no one was called up to recite the Torah blessings. The traditionalists, on the other hand, had no notion that women's equality should be an issue within the context of Jewish life. In 1922, when Kaplan's eldest daughter Judith reached the age of twelve, it was decided that she would be called to the Torah during Shabbat services. The event went on with little fanfare, but it was indeed an historic occasion.

Kaplan created this event for his daughter because he was looking for ways to give the past a vote but not a veto. In this innovation, Kaplan retained the form and content of the traditional ceremony, simply broadening its meaning to include young women.

The same approach was later taken with regard to other inequities women faced in public Jewish ritual—being called to the Torah for an *aliyah,* being counted in a *minyan* (the ten who constitute a quorum for Jewish worship), and being counted as a witness for signing Jewish documents. These traditions are still meaningful, so there was no need to alter them radically; rather, there was a need to augment them by permitting women equal access to them, counting both women and men as part of the community that finds such actions meaningful. In Reconstructionist circles, women were taking this active role in ritual in the early 1950s, a generation before this became common elsewhere.

Today, thirteen-year-old girls and boys in Reconstructionist communities study together to become b'nai mitzvah, with no gender distinction. The issue that faces Reconstructionists along with all

Jews today is about how to make the ritual passage meaningful, more prominent than the party and the gifts. Reconstructionists do so in many ways: by involving pre-b'nai mitzvah in "mitzvah projects," in which their entrance into the community involves community and/ or social action work, in addition to the acquisition of synagogue skills; through family education programs that engage parents in learning and activities along with their child; by enlisting b'nai mitzvah to mentor younger children and to lead the community in the years *after* the big day; by addressing directly the issues raised by extravagant celebration and by applying Jewish values to them. For example, Reconstructionist congregations teach parents and children to give a percentage of gifts received to *tzedakah*.

While some have argued that thirteen is too young an age to mark a transition to Jewish "adulthood," there is nevertheless much wisdom in the traditional focus on the thirteenth birthday. Our teenagers may not be adults, but they are also no longer children, and the transition to adolescence is sufficiently turbulent and confusing to merit our communal attention.

Birth Rituals

Perhaps the most ancient of Jewish rituals is the *brit milah* (ritual circumcision) ceremony when a baby boy is eight days old. The Bible dates it back to the Patriarch Abraham, and Jews throughout the centuries have identified circumcision (*milah*) as the central mark of the *brit* (covenant). Since the nineteenth century, Jews have sought to balance the primal power of public circumcision with contemporary rationales, usually related to health, but as the medical establishment vacillates about whether circumcision is a recommended procedure, we find ourselves stripped of all pretense: The reason to have your baby son circumcised ritually is beyond all medical or ethical rationales. It is a visceral affirmation of Jewish identity and connection with generations, past and future.

In Reconstructionist homes, the *brit milah* ceremony includes the participation of both parents, and the traditional liturgy is often augmented by the parents' personal words, by explanations of the names being given to the boy, by blessings offered by family and friends. The parents are surrounded by the presence of loved ones. They receive much-needed affirmation of their wonder at the miracle of birth, and of their awe at the responsibility of parenting, including the sometimes frightening experience of being responsible for choosing to have their infant son ritually circumcised.

The larger challenge here is not only that there was no parallel covenant-entrance ceremony for baby girls. It is that male-authored Jewish liturgy suggests the subtle premise that women are not part of the covenant. In the Grace after Meals, for example, Jews for centuries have recited: *"al beritkha she-ḥatamta bivsarenu*—for Your covenant that you have marked in our flesh." Clearly, the implication is that women, whose flesh is not marked by *brit milah,* are not primary participants in the covenant. This is why the Reconstructionist text replaces this phrase with the inclusive *"al beritkha she-ḥatamta belibenu*—for Your covenant that you have marked in our hearts." The larger goal, therefore, of the creation of covenant ceremonies for baby girls is nothing less than to change this premise, thus including women and men as full members of the Jewish people.

Those ceremonies that have been created using Reconstructionist perspectives have paid a great deal of attention to the need to create *berakhot* (blessings) that reflect the understanding that women are part of the covenant of Israel. They have also sought symbolic acts to convey the power of circumcision—acts that express the deep psychological meaning of bringing a child into the world and into the Jewish community. Reconstructionist perspectives make us particularly attuned to the aesthetics of the ceremony. Seeing Judaism as a civilization reminds us of the need to engage the artistic and cultural dimensions as well. Two Reconstructionist ceremonies using these insights were among the first created by Jewish feminists. One was by the first rabbinical couple, another by a group of Reform and Reconstructionist woman rabbis.

The first ceremony, written in 1974 by Rabbis Sandy and Dennis Sasso, is called *Brit B'not Yisrael* (A Covenant for the Daughters of Israel). The following paragraph, to be recited by the parents, indicates its focus:

> We gather together on the Shabbat with family and friends to bring our daughter into the Covenant of the Jewish people. For millennia, the Shabbat has been a sign of covenantal commitment that has inspired generations of our people with the drive to creativity and the values of human dignity. Therefore, on this Shabbat we bring our daughter before this community that she may be linked with the Covenant of the people of Israel.

The nine woman rabbis who put together the second ceremony, *Brit Reḥitzah* (the Covenant of Washing) were searching for a symbol of covenant, and decided on washing the baby's feet, as they describe:

> The idea of water proved to be a compelling one. We wanted something ancient and Jewish, something without diversionary overtones, something physical and something meaningful vis-à-vis the event at hand: a welcoming into the covenant. We recalled that the Bible speaks of more than one covenant. In addition to the covenant with Abraham, which is the basis of the *brit milah,* a covenant is also made with Noah after the flood. Surely, we would want to welcome the baby girl into that covenant as well, a covenant that potentially involves all of humanity. With

Noah, we were once again drawn to water: the life-giving "Mayim Hayyim," that had threatened to destroy, but now preserved human life. Water. Washing. Welcoming. . . . Someone remembered that when Abraham was recovering from his circumcision, he was visited by three angels of the Lord who promised him that his seed would continue and that Sarah would have a son. Abraham greeted these strangers with the gracious Middle Eastern sign of hospitality—he gave them water to wash their feet. What better way, then, for us to welcome our new members into the family of people and the family of Jews? Foot washing is gentle, loving, and ancient. It is also tangible and earthy: there is touching and splashing and the cry of the baby when first shocked by the cold water. Through this act, we hoped to help create a meaningful and memorable rite of passage. The ritual grew, as you can see, organically and communally. The end product is not important. You may borrow it, adapt it, ignore it. What *is* important is that the process of creating Judaism is far from over. The committee hopes that others will continue the task. Judaism is too precious for us not to want it to grow.

Thus the form and content of the ceremony for welcoming baby girls into the world continues to develop dramatically, with various options offered to enable parents to involve themselves in this momentous event from the perspective of ritual.

Marriage and Commitment Rituals

Reconstructionists have elaborated on *kiddushin* (the Jewish wedding ceremony) in ways that heighten its significance, involve the couple in personalizing the ceremony, and address the problematic gender inequity in the traditional ritual.

The traditional ceremony is based on the halakhic view of marriage as a legal contract, in which the husband "acquires" a wife— by giving her a ring, making a legal declaration *("harei at"),* and having the transaction witnessed and recorded in the *ketubah* (marriage contract), which is then read out loud before the assembled community. At a Reconstructionist ceremony, the traditional forms are included—the *ḥuppah* (wedding canopy), the rings, the *ketubah,* the Seven Blessings chanted in traditional *nusaḥ* (liturgical melody), the broken glass—but everything is egalitarian. Rings are exchanged, vows are identical or equivalent, and Reconstructionist rabbis work with couples to write their own *ketubot* that articulate the goals they share for their relationship (such as sharing of household responsibilities, raising the children, or maintaining a high level of sensitivity to one another). The community assembles to witness and support the couple in their mutual commitment, and in that context, couples often write declarations of love or vows to each other.

In addition, the ceremony is often augmented with traditional customs that have been reconstructed. Bride or groom may visit the *mikveh* (ritual bath), not because of halakhic concerns about *tum'ah* (ritual impurity) but rather to immerse themselves physically by way of symbolically cleansing themselves before their rebirth into a new life together. There may be a *ḥasan's* and *kallah's tish* (groom's table and bride's table) in which men and women gather separately to sing and offer blessings prior to the *ketubah* signing. The *bedecken* (veiling) ceremony is no longer a last opportunity for the groom to inspect the bride but rather a precious moment preceding the ceremony in which the couple can connect, often after having been apart for the preceding days. In the evenings of the week following the wedding, the couple may celebrate *Sheva Berakhot* (The Seven Blessings) at festive meals hosted by family and friends. More and more, Reconstructionists are returning to traditional forms in order to celebrate, forms that were once abandoned because of their objectionable meanings but that have now been revalued.

And especially since the Jewish Reconstructionist Federation adopted a policy encouraging its affiliates to become *Kehillot Mekablot* (communities that welcome gay and lesbian Jews, see chapter 9), Reconstructionist communities have increasingly celebrated commitment ceremonies of same-sex couples. To celebrate the commitments of lesbian and gay couples as sacred, the symbols of the wedding ceremony are employed insofar as they are appropriate, and new traditions are created where they are needed and wanted. For example, gay and lesbian couples have chosen to rewrite several of the seven wedding blessings that refer specifically to "bride and groom." Of course, an individual rabbi's decision whether to perform a ceremony is a matter of conscience, and the decision about whether and how to become a welcoming community is decided by each congregation.

As Reconstructionist communities celebrate commitment ceremonies, they also seek to transcend centuries of prejudice as they call couples up for joint *aliyot* to mark other moments—*aufruf*, anniversaries, etc. It is a particular point of pride that we have led the greater Jewish community in integrating gay and lesbian Jews who choose to join and lead our congregations and havurot. Indeed, heterosexual couples may also choose in their own wedding ceremonies to acknowledge the barriers that remain for same-sex marriage in other parts of the Jewish community and in the secular world. For example, they may choose to take a drop of wine from the cup they drink under the *ḥuppah* to express the way that their own joy is diminished in the absence of true equality.

Reconstructionist affiliates also include significant numbers of intermarried couples and families because our communities have embraced nonjudgmentally those who are interested in creating

Jewish homes. While there is disagreement among our rabbis about whether they are comfortable officiating at wedding ceremonies of intermarried couples, there is no disagreement about whether to meet with them before and welcome them after the ceremony. Some Reconstructionist rabbis do officiate when the couple is committed to establishing an exclusively Jewish home and raising children as Jews. The Intermarriage Guidelines of the Reconstructionist Rabbinical Association urge those who do officiate not to employ the traditional symbols of the Jewish wedding ceremony, but rather to find other texts and symbols to sanctify the wedding. Reconstructionist rabbis don't co-officiate at weddings with non-Jewish clergy.

Jewish Divorce

Changing form and content has been necessary for Jewish divorce procedures. The essential problem here is that, traditionally, women are ineligible to initiate divorce proceedings. If a Jewish court cannot compel an unwilling husband to initiate a divorce, the woman cannot have another Jewish marriage. There are still cases today of *agunot*—women who find themselves barred from remarriage on this basis. The Reform movement avoids this problem by permitting remarriage without a Jewish divorce. The Orthodox and Conservative movements look for legal loopholes to enable women to be remarried. In Reconstructionist thinking, giving the past a vote but not a veto in this case means preserving the idea of Jewish divorce. Judaism seeks to mark and hallow each part of the life cycle. If a marriage is worth marking as a Jewish event, there ought to be a corresponding Jewish event to end a marriage. But if we believe in equality, women must be allowed to participate as equals or to initiate the proceedings when necessary.

In this case, raising the women's issue raised other questions and problems about the procedures entirely. Why should a man or a woman have to initiate divorce alone? If it is mutual decision, the procedure should be initiated by both parties. Just as in Reconstructionist weddings men and women give each other rings and pledge to be special for each other "according to the traditions of the people of Israel," so they should share as equals the responsibility for ending that status.

Reconstructionists have further been forced to question the text of the divorce document (*get*). Just as the *ketubah* (marriage document) has been reconstructed in content, though not in form, to illustrate the new relationship that has evolved in marriage, so the language of the *get* has been reconstructed to reflect the equality of the divorcing partners. In many cases, the scribe will be asked to write two documents, so that the man and woman truly divorce *one another.* In both marriage and divorce, the document form has been retained. Reconstructionists value having these written affirmations. They provide continuity with Jewish tradition while achieving intellectual honesty in content and acting as permanent records of the events.

The nature of the divorce ceremony is also in need of reconstruction. Unlike the wedding ceremony, in which the form itself carries deep meaning, the divorce proceeding was for many generations viewed exclusively as a legal procedure. Reconstructionists have perceived that, to achieve the level of meaning appropriate to divorce, a ceremony is needed that reflects the pain and sadness at divorce, the symbolic ending of a chapter in the life of the family, and the possibilities of new beginnings as well. To that end, the Reconstructionist Rabbinical Association has created new ceremonies for divorce proceedings.

Changing divorce procedures raises questions of the unity of the Jewish people, an issue of great importance to Reconstructionists. In making these changes, we realize that we are acting in ways that more traditional segments of the community consider illegitimate. To be sure, Reconstructionists do not permit someone to become involved in an egalitarian divorce without making that person aware that it would not be accepted by all segments of the Jewish community. Because the Orthodox recognize only divorces performed by Orthodox rabbis, however, there is no way to compromise concerning the form of the ceremony in order to achieve its universal acceptance.

Moreover, contemporary Jews continue to seek forms of Jewish expression that are meaningful and often find that traditional forms don't work. Thus, preserving ancient ways untouched may not be a sensible alternative. Innovation is not evidence that we are less sensitive to the need for unity; rather, it is evidence of our commitment to meeting the needs of contemporary Jews. This in turn makes us more passionate about the need for pluralism on the part of all Jews to be a cardinal principle of Jewish unity.

Death and Mourning

Reconstructionists also embrace traditional rituals to make our way through difficult times. When a loved one dies, we need a tried and tested path. For the most part, Jewish death and mourning practices provide ways to express pain and receive community support.

All too often, contemporary Western culture encourages us to avoid direct confrontation with the immediacy and reality of death. People now die in hospitals connected to machines, rather than at home in the arms of loved ones. The culture promotes a stoic etiquette that does not look kindly upon uninhibited public expressions of grief. Reconstructionists explore Jewish traditional practices as correctives to the assumptions of the general culture. We may tear our clothes or cut a ribbon at the start of the funeral as we declare that God is a Righteous Judge, and we may wear them through the mourning week of *shiva*. At the cemetery, pallbearers may carry the casket to the grave in full view of the mourners, and the mourners may shovel earth to cover the casket in the grave after it is lowered. Mourners may sit on low stools throughout *shiva* or desist from shaving or wearing makeup. These are not obligatory command-ments. They are some of the traditional customs we use today because they reflect an age-old wisdom about confronting and expressing our sorrow.

As with other life-cycle events, Reconstructionists tend to adopt ritual forms around death and mourning by expanding the circle of those who get involved. For example, Reconstructionist groups are forming *hevrah kaddisha* societies. These groups come together when someone dies to perform *taharah* (preparing the body for burial). They recite the prayers, and cleanse and clothe the body of the deceased with all the respect that our traditions demand. Perform-ing the ritual preparations themselves, rather than delegating the work to a funeral home, the participants come directly in touch with the sacred mysteries of life and death, engaging in holy work that deepens their own experience. And the mourners have the comfort of knowing that their friends and community care enough about them to perform these deeds of *hesed shel emet* (selfless love). Simi-larly, community members may take shifts for *shemirah*—sitting with the body until the funeral and reciting psalms or contemporary poetry so that the *met* (deceased) is never left alone. The experience of par-ticipation in such activities bonds community members together with a power, immediacy, and unity of purpose that is difficult to express.

At the funeral, mourners who so wish sometimes eulogize their loved one, although primary mourners may refrain from speaking so that they can experience their grief without distraction. Members of the community are sometimes invited to speak their hearts. It is nearly always the case that mourners reflect publicly on their loved one as part of the services that are conducted in their home throughout the week of *shiva*. Members of the community generally cook for the mourners—often in quantities that allow them not to worry about food preparation long after the week ends. People visit through the days of mourning, not only at service times. The community takes care of childcare and chauffeuring children and guests. The general effect is that, at the time of greatest pain and vulnerability, the mourners experience the comfort of belonging to a Jewish community.

Other Life-Cycle Passages

Not all transitional moments in our lives are acknowledged in the traditional Jewish ritual repertoire. Sometimes this is because rabbis in the past paid insufficient attention to the experiences of women. Sometimes it is due to the fact that our lives today are significantly different from those of our ancestors. As a result, the Creative Liturgy files at the Reconstructionist Rabbinical College, for example, are filled with prayers and ceremonies that mark such moments as when teenagers get their driver's licenses, when mothers wean their children, when a gay person chooses to come out, when adults make mid-life career shifts or retire, when young adults go off to college or older people move into graduated care facilities, when couples suffer a miscarriage, and countless others.

Even more frequently, people ask to be called up to the Torah on Shabbat morning for an *aliyah*, after which they receive a *Mi Sheberakh* (blessing) publicly acknowledging an event in their lives: expressing gratitude for a job promotion, for example, or sorrow over a friend's illness. Reconstructionists believe that groups of people who join together and support one another in restoring their souls and repairing the world can form holy communities. Such communities are built when the most meaningful experiences of our lives are shared in the context of our sacred symbols and the hallowed phrases of our liturgy, and when we share our skills and resources with one another as part of our communal responsibility.

9
Becoming an Inclusive Community

Belonging to the Jewish Community

In Reconstructionist circles, making our communities inclusive is one of our chief goals. We are acutely aware of the barriers that people encounter when they contemplate belonging to the Jewish community.

These barriers are often created by the fact that we live primarily in a secular society, so that Jewish customs remain unfamiliar. Many people trip first over the barrier of this lack of familiarity—"If I don't know how to read Hebrew and don't know what to do in a worship service," they ask, "how can I comfortably enter a synagogue and expect to have a meaningful, spiritual experience?"

In other cases, there are different sources of discomfort. Some people have yet to overcome emotionally difficult childhood memories —negative religious school experiences, family turmoil around bar or bat mitzvah ceremonies, conflicts with parents that were expressed as issues of Jewish observance even though their intrapsychic roots ran much more deeply. Others have invested time and energy in pursuing spiritual paths in non-Jewish contexts, and they are worried about how that fact will be treated by rabbis and others in the Jewish world. Others find certain Jewish communities off-putting because, without a spouse and children, they don't fit in, or because their economic circumstances make synagogue dues rates and unspoken dress codes prohibitive.

Not all of these barriers are justly blamed on the Jewish community. Reconstructionists believe nevertheless that it is the responsibility of Jewish communities to reach out and offer to assist people to overcome these barriers. Reconstructionist prayer books make it easy to follow and participate, even if you can't read Hebrew (see chapter 10). Our "Introduction to Judaism" outreach courses begin with an opportunity for participants to share. In safety, they discuss positive and negative feelings about Jewish and non-Jewish aspects of their journeys (see the Jewish, Alive and American program study guide described in "The Best Place to Begin" section of chapter 12 below). Our communities are well known for the warm welcome received by newcomers. Surveys of Reconstructionists cite this welcoming atmosphere as one of the main reasons they decide to join.

Another set of barriers derives from our inherited traditions themselves. Men made decisions. Women were not even counted, and their voices were neither heard in public nor recorded for posterity. Lesbian and gay Jews were completely invisible. Parents recited the Mourner's Kaddish over children who married non-Jews. Jews with disabilities were denied religious and ritual rights. The community prided itself on erecting barriers to prevent non-Jews from becoming Jews.

Thus, the Reconstructionist commitment to inclusivity is not only based on a desire to be warm and welcoming. It is deeply rooted in a commitment to democratic values and an understanding of the evolving nature of Jewish civilization. Rabbinic authorities, in the past and in our own day, have made different judgments, acting out of views formed in their particular social contexts. They were human judgments, not divine decrees. They were not made by people who cherished such values as gender equality, democratic decision making, or respect for those who were different from themselves, or who were aware of the complex nature of human sexuality. The community that Reconstructionists seek to create in our age is open, diverse, and welcoming.

Who Is a Jew?

Given the Reconstructionist emphasis on creating open, diverse, welcoming communities, why ask the question "Who Is a Jew?" at all? Because an essential task for every group is to define who belongs to it. Each community creates a system of meaning, with myths, symbols, and practices that embody its values. While Reconstructionists do not assert that the Jewish community is *superior* to others, we do affirm that communities are *unique and different* from one another. Meaning is created by differentiation, and communities of meaning create boundaries that define who is in and who is out.

Communities are also defined by *which* boundaries they create and *how* they create them. Boundaries can be maintained rigidly or flexibly. As Reconstructionists, we remain vigilant in examining when and how we erect boundaries in light of ever-evolving circumstances. That is why we attribute such importance to issues like patrilineal descent, intermarriage, and how to include Jews who have been excluded.

Given Judaism's long history and the countless migrations of the Jewish people, it is no wonder that our criteria for membership have fluctuated through the ages. At times, we have had very rigid boundaries, strictly limiting those people who could be defined as Jews by birth and conversion. At other times, we have been more fluid, creating categories for "fellow travelers" within the Jewish community.

For many centuries we had a very precise definition of who is a Jew. According to this definition, a person is Jewish if he or she is born of a Jewish mother or if he or she undergoes a process of conversion. This conversion process includes a lengthy period of studying Jewish culture, beliefs, and practices; ritual immersion for women and men; ritual circumcision for men; and examination by a *bet din* (Jewish court of three) that determines the candidate's commitment to living an observant Jewish life.

Today there are many people living Jewish lives who do not meet these criteria. Some were born to a Jewish father but not to a Jewish mother. Some are married to Jews and raise Jewish children, but have never converted. Others were converted to Judaism by rabbis who did not insist on *all* the halakhic criteria of conversion—for example, omitting ritual circumcision for adult males, not insisting that the convert lead a totally observant life, or accepting people for conversion for the sake of marriage. Still others have converted to Judaism in keeping with halakhah but are not recognized by the Orthodox because their conversions weren't witnessed by a *bet din* composed of Orthodox Jews. Some have had their Jewish identity questioned because they grew up in Ethiopia in a divergent Jewish tradition, or in the former Soviet Union where Jewish practices were prohibited, making their lineage difficult to trace.

Some rabbis in the Orthodox community have gone so far as to define these people out of the Jewish fold, requiring them to convert under Orthodox auspices if they wish to be recognized as Jews. Other rabbis, Reconstructionists among them, take a different approach. We respond by recognizing the need to broaden the definition of who is a Jew.

Including Jews by Choice:
Reconstructionist Conversion

Reconstructionists are committed to the ritual of conversion. We believe it is important for those not born of a Jewish parent who wish to belong to the Jewish community to undergo this symbolic rite of passage to establish their connection to the community, both personally and publicly.

While the Reconstructionist rabbi who instructs a prospective convert clearly differs from his/her Orthodox colleague in terms of the *content* of instruction, the *process* is essentially the same. We, too, insist on a significant period of study—but incorporate more than learning about how to be an observant Jew, though that is included, too. We want people who join us to feel a sense of belonging. Prospective converts to Judaism through the Reconstructionist method study history, observance, and beliefs, but they also learn to make choices. They are connected to the community through relationships with others who have chosen Judaism, and they are located in a Jewish community of which they can become a part after the conversion ceremony.

Reconstructionist Jews by choice go through a process that includes ritual immersion for men and women, circumcision for men (unless there is an extraordinary physical or emotional hazard), and a *bet din*—a discussion with three knowledgeable Jews (at least one of them a rabbi), who welcome the convert by engaging in a dialogue. Many Reconstructionist communities have added a public ceremony of welcome, sometimes held on Shavuot because of its connection to the biblical story of Ruth, the paradigmatic Jew by choice according to Jewish legend.

Rituals of Affirmation

There are many people today who were born Jews, and who remain Jewish in the technical halakhic sense, but whose religious odysseys have led them to serious participation in other religious communities. Sometimes they have maintained a Jewish identity throughout, but sometimes they have not. In situations in which a person has, at some point, divested himself or herself of Jewish identity and become involved with another religion, a re-affirmation of Jewish identity when the Jew returns to Judaism is sometimes useful to set all doubts about personal status to rest—including the doubts and anxieties of the person involved.

In these situations, some Reconstructionists have utilized a traditional ceremony—developed in the Middle Ages—that removes doubt (*ḥashash*) about the status of Jews who had been coercively converted to the majority religion and who wished to return. The new ceremony may include immersion in a *mikveh* (ritual bath), a conversation with representatives of the community, and a statement affirming Jewish identity. The purpose of the ceremony is to provide a symbolic passage back into the Jewish community. It often serves as a moving and transformative experience for the individual.

Including Jews with One Jewish Parent: Matrilineal and Patrilineal Descent

The Reconstructionist movement's policy is that conversion is unnecessary for a person born of one Jewish parent. (If that one Jewish parent is the father, the child must additionally be raised and educated as a Jew.) In the first centuries of our era—*only* nineteen or twenty centuries ago—the rabbis decided that Jewish identity would be transmitted only through the mother (matrilineal descent). Current research indicates that before that time, Jewish identity had been transmitted through the father. When the rabbis made that reversal, they lived in a Roman empire in which the matrilineal principle was the norm for all matters of personal status. Moreover, they were addressing a Jewish community in which a Jewish mother was a virtual guarantee that a child would be Jewish, and a non-Jewish mother similarly would determine that her children would not be Jewish.

The Reconstructionist movement, since 1968, has recognized the Jewishness of the child of a Jewish father and a non-Jewish mother when that child is raised and educated as a Jew (patrilineal descent). We have done so for a number of reasons that we believe are compelling.

First, we believe that the circumstances of an open society render the traditional norm obsolete. Two millennia ago, when the rare intermarriage occurred, the children followed the religion of the mother. Thus, the rabbis' matrilineal principle was not an edict pronounced in a vacuum; it responded to the social realities of the time. Today, that is not the case. Jewish children are being raised by Jewish fathers and non-Jewish mothers.

The effects of this discrepancy between Jewish law and the de facto realities are, we believe, injurious to the health of Jewish civilization. Children who have been raised as Jews are sometimes forced to undergo halakhic conversion prior to their bar/bat mitzvah ceremonies, thus communicating to them that Jewishness is a matter of formalistic—almost magical—ritual, rather than the living of a Jewish life. Divorced Jewish fathers find that they have no legal basis to ask the civil courts to allow their children to receive a Jewish education. This illustrates that the rigid upholding of halakhah in this case can be counterproductive. It sanctifies a human, historically-conditioned rabbinic ruling, with consequences that were unforeseeable to those rabbis. It denies the evolving nature of Jewish civilization.

Second, the matrilineal principle is based on assumptions about gender roles that are no longer viable. It is no longer automatic in our society that the mother is the primary provider of child care. Jewish fathers are also involved in raising their children in ways unheard of in previous eras. While most of the gender-related disabilities imposed by the Jewish tradition are suffered by women, in this case it is the father who suffers. Inasmuch as we are dedicated to the removal of all such disabilities and to the cultivation of a community in which men and women can choose their roles freely, patrilineal descent must be restored alongside matrilineal descent.

Third, we believe that Jewish identity is cultivated by living a Jewish life, and is not something that is automatically inherited. At a time when having *two* Jewish parents is no guarantee that a child will be raised as a Jew, it is counterproductive to insist that a person raised as a Jew and identifying as a Jew is not a Jew because his or her mother did not convert before the birth. We understand rituals as deriving their power and efficacy from the way they symbolize real transformations. Thus, conversion rituals "work" when they express an actual entry of a non-Jew into our community. When they are imposed arbitrarily, however, in the belief that the edicts of generations long gone must be obeyed, the very meaning of ritual conversion is undermined.

Fourth, we are dedicated to the reconstruction of Jewish civilization because we believe that there are countless Jews who are alienated from traditional forms of Jewish life but who are seeking means of spiritual fulfillment. Many of those Jews have already chosen non-Jewish spouses or will do so in the future. Intermarried Jews represent a sizable percentage of the North American Jewish population. We believe that a reconstructed Judaism can meet the needs of many of those Jews. In our open society, it is easy to leave the Jewish community. It is therefore imperative that we avoid increasing the difficulty of the return of those who are so inclined.

Finally, we believe that a revitalized Jewish civilization must be sensitive and humanitarian if it is to be worth preserving. It enriches our lives because it provides us with insights into the human condition, with means of expressing our deepest aspirations, and with a community of Jews with whom we can share our quest for meaning and integration. We value Jewish traditions because they offer us wisdom from past generations that helps us to achieve these ends. We do not value all traditions unconditionally. To the contrary, we reject the interpretation of Judaism that insists it is a static system to which Jews must submit no matter what, relinquishing their autonomy. When the matrilineal principle is used in this way, we believe it must be changed.

Including Intermarried Couples

North American Jews today live in an open society. We share much in common with our non-Jewish neighbors, including the assumption that individuals should have the liberty to choose the course of their lives and that marriage partners should be selected based on loving relationships. Yet we want our children to marry Jews, to have partners with whom they can fully share the cycle of Jewish living, and to pass on their Jewish heritage to yet another generation. Often, these values are in conflict.

We could, of course, withdraw from the open society by choosing *aliyah* to Israel or by screening out the secular society as Hasidim do. Or we could continue to recite the Mourner's Kaddish over a son or daughter who has intermarried, marking him or her as one who is leaving the fold. That we don't advocate these options indicates our acceptance of the open society.

For several generations, we relied on the slowness of Jewish acculturation. Jews may have been equal under the law, but we remained different from our non-Jewish neighbors. Living in Jewish neighborhoods and sending our children to Jewish camps and teen and college programs, our insistence that Jews marry only Jews was largely effective. Up until the early 1960s, an intermarrying Jew was most likely one whose action demonstrated his or her conscious and active desire to abandon Jewish identity.

Today, however, that is no longer an accurate assumption. Jews regularly marry non-Jews while simultaneously maintaining positive identification as Jews. Studies show that it is most often the case that they choose non-Jewish partners who are lapsed and uncommitted Christians, and that it is often the case that these mixed couples want to raise Jewish children. Even when they are indifferent to their Jewishness, they are no more indifferent than large numbers of Jews who are married to Jews.

Faced with these new circumstances, we seek new solutions. We view our primary responsibility as revitalizing Jewish life. In so doing, even indifferent Jews—no matter whom they have married—will, we hope, want to join us in our quest to Judaize our lives. And when we are faced with the common case of intermarried couples and families who want to be involved in Jewish life, we believe the sensible course is not only to welcome them, but to seek them out. Thus, Reconstructionist groups across the continent are involved in active outreach—sponsoring "Introduction to Judaism" courses, facilitating peer groups in which mixed couples can share their distinctive predicaments, developing communal forms of Jewish celebrations that help Jews become familiar with our inherited treasures. Our goal is to bring increasing numbers of Jews—and their partners and children—into the Jewish orbit.

For too long, the Jewish community has focused its efforts on convincing the non-Jewish partner to become Jewish before the wedding. While conversion best supports and sustains a couple's declared intent to a Jewish home and Jewish children, it is not the only authentic way to pursue these goals. Nor need conversion be limited to before the wedding; many non-Jewish partners in an interfaith marriage come to conversion later on, sometimes after many years. And the period immediately preceding the wedding, when the couple is involved in creating a relationship independent of their respective families, may not be the best time to bring uninvited pressure to bear upon them. In any event, while interest in conversion may be sparked initially by a *relationship,* the authenticity and integrity of any conversion ultimately depends on the *individual's* personal choice and commitment.

While the majority of Reconstructionist rabbis do not officiate at mixed-marriage ceremonies, all Reconstructionist rabbis are committed to making themselves available for counseling and guidance. The decision not to officiate is based on the belief that it is inauthentic to use Jewish symbols in a ceremony that unites a Jew and a non-Jew, understanding that even without *ḥuppah* and *ketubah,* the rabbi is perceived as a living Jewish symbol. Nevertheless, Reconstructionist rabbis convey to couples that they are interested in working with them to explore their Jewish options and will not pass negative and hostile judgments. Under appropriate circumstances, some will attend civil ceremonies and, although not officiating, will offer remarks welcoming the couple's intentions to create a Jewish home. Reconstructionist groups are open to the participation and membership of mixed couples.

The Reconstructionist rabbis who do officiate at mixed-marriage ceremonies do not challenge the movement's perspective on this issue. They argue only that, faced with a couple committed to creating a Jewish home and interested in joining the Jewish community, a rabbi can be most effective in cultivating this commitment by officiating. For some rabbis, this consideration supersedes their belief in maintaining Jewish symbols for Jews only. The Reconstructionist Rabbinical Association respects the minority of colleagues who reach this conclusion.

We adopt this spirit of welcome in our conviction that we have no basis to stand in judgment. Those who condemn intermarriage as if it were sinful really are condemning the fruits of the open society to which they are otherwise dedicated. It is not necessarily true that intermarried couples have a higher rate of divorce or that it is always the case that a Jew would be better off marrying a Jew than a non-Jew. Until we face those facts, we are likely to miss the opportunity to help alienated Jews return to the community and tradition. Our task is thus not to condemn the intermarried, but rather to make Judaism compelling.

Such a welcoming attitude leads us to uncharted terrain. It challenges us to consider the roles of the unconverted partners in our synagogues. Should they be members? Can they chair committees or hold office? In which rituals is it appropriate for them to participate? A committee of the Jewish Reconstructionist Federation on the Role of the Non-Jew produced a report, *Boundaries and Opportunities* (1996). In typical Reconstructionist fashion, the report articulates the Jewish values on the basis of which such questions ought to be answered. The report makes recommendations about the process by which each community should reach its own conclusions. The active presence in our midst of non-Jews who are partners of Jews and/or parents of Jews challenges us to find ways of including them in our definition of membership in the Jewish community. It also enables them to feel included and respected by the Jewish community, making official conversion more attractive.

The Unity of the Jewish People

Many Jews—including many Reconstructionist Jews—are concerned about the danger of schism. Now that Reconstructionist and Reform Jews accept the patrilineal principle, and non-Jewish partners who have not officially converted are welcomed, our definition of Jewish identity departs from that of more traditional Jews who are now proclaiming that, without halakhic conversion, they will not allow their children to marry ours.

Let it be stated clearly at the outset that our intentions are not schismatic. We advise parents that a patrilineally descended child will not be recognized as Jewish by halakhic authorities, and we facilitate the formal conversion of infants when parents so desire. We maintain our devotion to the ideal of a Jewish community that is united *and* diverse.

We are faced, however, with a majority of Orthodox rabbis who do not even accept the conversions non-Orthodox rabbis do perform according to halakhic procedure, merely because those rabbis perform them. They seek to deny us the right to make any definition of who is a Jew, claiming that authority for themselves alone. But the issue runs deeper. At stake is the very survival of the Jewish people. We adamantly reject the version of Jewish history that suggests that there has always existed a normative, halakhic Judaism that has survived unchanged despite the challenges of Jewish heretics in every generation. A careful look at Jewish history reveals the fact that Jews have been divided in *every* generation. Every period of our history has been witness to competing interpretations of Judaism, whose advocates often condemned one another. It has never been possible, in advance, to determine which group would emerge victorious to tell the tale. The only certainty has been that each victorious faction —incorporating aspects of its competitors' programs and itself altered by that very competition—has portrayed the alternatives in retrospect as heresy.

Any serious attempt to account for the survival of the Jewish people must include the resilience of Jewish civilization—its remarkable ability to adapt to new conditions by developing new forms and reinterpreting once-sacred beliefs. It has never been the case, however, that the most effective means of adaptation could be known in advance. In fact, we must assume that most innovations have not survived or even been recorded for posterity.

As we face the unprecedented challenges to Judaism of our ever more rapidly changing world, it is imperative that we be bold. We cannot be certain which of our reinterpretations will survive. We can be certain, however, that Jewish civilization will survive as a vital way of life only if it continues to adapt. In North America, that means that Jews living in an open society must be offered interpretations of Judaism that will facilitate their becoming more involved. In such circumstances, we believe that the rigid adherence to halakhic forms —themselves once developed innovatively to meet past challenges— is a recipe for doom. Embracing the open society, we are committed to cultivating a Jewish renaissance that will welcome all Jews who are interested in participating.

Including "Others"

While some have felt excluded because they do not fit into traditional definitions of who is a Jew, others have experienced alienation from the Jewish community because of philosophical commitments or personal attributes. They are excluded because they belong to a sub-group that does not conform to the common images of the Jew. Feminists, gay men and lesbians, people with disabilities, Sephardic and *Mizrahi* Jews in North America, working class people, single people, and, sometimes, older people are among those who have felt like outsiders to the organized Jewish community. Mainstream Jews often fail to understand their special needs or are threatened by their differences. Reconstructionist Judaism has made an important contribution to the task of including members of these groups as part of our communities.

Including Feminist Jews

Since its inception, Reconstructionist Judaism has been committed to equality for women. An examination of the steps Reconstructionist Judaism has taken throughout the twentieth century illustrates the early and fundamental Reconstructionist commitment to inclusivity.

Women's equality would not be an issue for us if we did not live in two civilizations; for it is in the secular civilization that changes in women's roles have been initiated. It was in the 1920s that the women's suffrage movement gained prominence, raising the issue of women's equality and personhood. Aware of this trend, Kaplan strongly advocated that Judaism keep up with those changes in perception, both from a pragmatic and a moral point of view: pragmatic, because many women would lose interest in Jewish life if they were excluded from it in the public realm; moral, because the equality of all persons is a value espoused by the democratic tradition that Kaplan wished to introduce into Jewish life in new and unprecedented ways.

Of course, that is not to say that the position of women in Jewish life was static prior to Kaplan's time. Throughout Jewish history women were subject to varying levels of economic, social, political, and religious disabilities. Most frequently, the status of women in Jewish life fluctuated with the status of women in those civilizations with which Jews came into contact.

The changes that have taken place in most recent times, however, are qualitatively different. For the first time, women themselves have sought to speak in their own voices, not allowing their roles and status to be defined for them by men. Kaplan foresaw that this would happen as early as 1946 when he urged the Jewish woman to "demand the equality due her as a right to which she is fully entitled."

An example of giving women equal access to roles that previously were performed exclusively by men is the training of women to be rabbis. The Reconstructionist Rabbinical College opened its doors in 1968. During its first year, a woman (Sandy Eisenberg Sasso) applied and was accepted to begin her studies the following fall. Significant numbers of others followed in her footsteps, and by the mid-1970s, half of each entering class at the RRC was female. Woman students have always been treated as equals by faculty, administration, and by male colleagues. The RRC has been in the vanguard in opening full-time faculty and administrative posts to women.

Will the presence of women performing traditionally male roles radically alter Judaism? On one level, the answer is no, or at least no more than any other measure that increases the number of people who are eligible to take active roles in Jewish life. Yet, in a deeper sense, women in public roles will make a profound difference. That a girl can now grow up assuming that she has a rightful, public place in the synagogue makes an enormous difference in the consciousness of children. And equality for women often leads to asking new questions. Women may also bring different sensibilities to Jewish life—making public such concerns as sexual harassment, domestic violence, family planning, child-rearing, and human sexuality. Women undoubtedly will also bring a greater awareness of "sexism"—how power gets divided within institutional structures, often to the disadvantage of women.

In this way, feminist consciousness goes beyond equality for women to raise other questions. It brings to the foreground the way Judaism has defined and limited people based on gender. From this perspective we begin to examine the role gender played in determining values and structures throughout Jewish history, leading us to new understandings and interpretations of the Jewish past.

Therefore we ask questions not only about women's roles, but about men's roles. We believe that just as women's roles have been broadened in contemporary society, men's roles must also be re-examined. If women are to take a more active role in public expressions of Judaism, so men's roles in the home and family must be enhanced. Only in this way can people freely and equally express what it means to them to be Jewish.

From a feminist perspective, we concern ourselves with the conduct of *all* human relationships and include *all* people—restoring the ancient prophetic dream. This is the ultimate, if yet unrealized, potential of the changes which we began to initiate many years ago.

Inclusive Liturgical Changes

Feminist perspectives have influenced Reconstructionist approaches to liturgical change in order to make the experience of communal prayer more welcoming to people who have been marginalized. The English translations in Reconstructionist prayer books are gender neutral. If women and men are full and equal partners in the Jewish community, then there is no excuse for the use of masculine nouns and pronouns to signify all people, no reason not to mention the matriarchs with the patriarchs.

But Reconstructionists ask a deeper question: Why does Jewish liturgy always refer to God as He? Why are the vast majority of our metaphors for God—King, Shepherd, Father—set in male language? We have responded in several ways to this feminist challenge. The first possibility is to include feminine God language—to begin to refer to God also as She, Mother, strong and radiant Woman. This way has several advantages. It gives women an opportunity to experience themselves as made in the image of God. It broadens our conception of how God works in the world. It challenges us to be clear that our anthropomorphic images are just that—that God can fit comfortably into all of them, yet can't be contained by any. So God can be addressed as He or She—reminding us that God is neither one.

Yet there is another Reconstructionist approach to this question. Perhaps feminism has come to remind us that our metaphors cannot approximate our concept of God. Perhaps God is best addressed as Power or Process. If so, we might think, with Rabbi Harold Schulweis, about reformulating some of our prayers to read *Berukhah haElohut,* Blessed is Godliness, or with the poet Marcia Falk, *Nevarekh et Ein Ha-Ḥayyim,* Let us bless the Source of Life.

This does not imply that Reconstructionists reject the use of male God language. We recognize the mythic power and the metaphorical truth of the traditional liturgy. The language of our ancient prayers resonates in ways that transcend literal intellectual affirmation. Thus, it is possible for some to accept feminist insights, avoiding idolatrous attachment to a literal male image of God while retaining traditional prayer forms.

For others, it is *also* important to change the language of the traditional Hebrew words as well. Reconstructionist prayer books offer alternative names of God and forms for blessings. Some blessings provide gender-neutral metaphors for God; others, feminine metaphors. The challenge here is linguistic rather than theological. Unlike English, Hebrew does not have gender-neutral nouns and verbs, so that gender neutrality must be achieved by alternating masculine and feminine. To alternate the gender of the Hebrew text requires a sophisticated knowledge of Hebrew grammar, a skill that is beyond most worshipers, whose ability to translate the meaning of the Hebrew is limited. Thus, our prayer books do not vary Hebrew verb forms, but in groups where the meaning of the Hebrew can be understood, the gender of God is alternated in the Hebrew as well.

Including Gay Men and Lesbians

The feminist perspective about bringing in all marginalized people has led the Reconstructionist movement to take a bold stand on the inclusion of gay and lesbian Jews. To be sure, Mordecai Kaplan never envisioned that men and women would be able to choose to make primary life commitments to same-sex partners. In Kaplan's time, those who recognized their erotic attractions to members of their own sex hid those feelings and relationships from public view. But with the advent of the Gay Liberation movement in the 1960s and 1970s, gay men and lesbians began to speak out publicly, to combat prejudice, and to form a political and cultural movement.

Reconstructionists have prided ourselves on our willingness to tackle unpopular issues. This is the legacy of Mordecai Kaplan. Welcoming gay and lesbian Jews has been a slow and painstaking process for the Reconstructionist movement. In 1984, under the leadership of President Ira Silverman, the faculty of the Reconstructionist Rabbinical College voted to become the first rabbinical school in history to admit openly gay and lesbian students to the rabbinate.

The RRC took a courageous step in admitting gay and lesbian students. The decision opened up the discussion of the role of gay and lesbian Jews for the whole Reconstructionist movement. In 1992, a joint Reconstructionist Commission on Homosexuality, which included rabbinic and congregational representatives, published a lengthy document in support of gay men and lesbians in Jewish life. The report emphasized the ways in which gay men and lesbians are like others in the Jewish community who are involved in loving, long-term relationships. The statement welcomed gay men and lesbians into the community as leaders and teachers. The movement gained much recognition and withstood many attacks as the first Jewish denomination, and one of the first of any religious groups in North America, to be open to lesbians and gay men.

The Commission encouraged all Reconstructionist groups to become "welcoming communities," and published a six-part workshop syllabus to take each group through a process of addressing this goal. A significant number of Reconstructionist congregations have held workshops on lesbian and gay issues and welcome gay and lesbian members. Many Reconstructionist congregations have made strong efforts to include gay men and lesbians. Rabbis speak frequently on gay issues, and discussion about gay and lesbian families is included in religious school curricula. Heterosexual members of congregations often become involved in gay pride events, and many have written and spoken publicly about the profound effect the presence of gay and lesbian members has had on them.

The Reconstructionist movement's emphasis on the ways in which lesbians and gay men are similar to other Jews and fit into communal norms has set a pattern for other Jewish organizations that have become increasingly accepting of gay and lesbian Jews.

Including Singles

How do you create an atmosphere in which *individuals* are comfortable sharing their stories in community? There are so many impediments. Aspects of North American culture encourage a level of autonomy and privacy that can make it embarrassing to expose yourself at vulnerable moments. Similarly, the experience that so many people have of Jewish communities is that they promulgate norms by which people are judged and made to feel inadequate.

In no area of our lives have we been subjected to judgmental norms more than in the area of family. Adult Jews are supposed to get married, have children, and remain together. *Be fruitful and multiply,* the rabbis taught, is the first of the commandments. As Jewish communities have evolved in the last two centuries, synagogues have been organized on the basis of these assumptions: men's clubs and sisterhoods, religious schools and youth groups. "You aren't married?

What a pity! Let me try to fix you up (because, of course, you'll be happier married than single)." Despite the best of intentions, most synagogues inadvertently make it very difficult for an unmarried individual to feel welcomed and accepted for what she or he is. Even singles services and programs don't get at the challenge if their overt or covert intent is to make matches.

Reconstructionist communities are committed to changing this situation, however uphill the struggle. Welcoming same-sex couples and families has actually been *relatively* unchallenging, inasmuch as the traditional "married" paradigm can be transferred. We respect and affirm members' decisions, for the short term or long term, *not* to get married, *not* to raise children, to bear and raise children as single parents or to end unhappy marriages without urgently seeking another partner. We seek sensitively to avoid affirming marriage and parenting as the ultimate in the hierarchy of circumstances, but it is not so easy—not at b'nai-mitzvah services or *aufruf* (pre-wedding) *aliyot,* not in the lists of congratulations in synagogue bulletins. We do so by *also* celebrating passages and *simhas* that are not traditionally marked in the Jewish life cycle, by counting membership units by "households" rather than by "families," by formulating policies and planning programs that are maximally inclusive and do not penalize those who do not fit the married-with-children mold.

The goal, in the end, is to celebrate the *values* embedded in traditionally sanctified relationships, rather that the *form* of those relationships alone. Jewish marriage is called *kiddushin* (sanctification) because of the belief that covenanted, loving relationships bring holiness into the world. And so, Reconstructionists celebrate such relationships, whether straight or gay. Raising children has been a central Jewish value because of the way it involves parents as partners in creation, taking responsibility for the next generation, humbly acknowledging the limits of the degree to which they have control over their own and their children's destinies. Again, there are other, critically important ways to "parent" the next generation. People who do not have children of their own may engage with the next generation by teaching, leading youth groups, or functioning as "additional" parents to support friends and family who are engaged in the process of raising children. Furthermore, we are all involved in contributing to the next generation when we participate in building nurturing Jewish communities. Without negating the value of marriage and child raising, Reconstructionists refuse to use them as a hurtful means to exclude the many, many Jews who do not embody our ancestors' ideals.

Including Jews with Disabilities

The Reconstructionist emphasis on accepting difference has drawn us to be particularly sensitive to Jews with special needs. As is true of the other groups that we have sought to include, we realize that the Jewish tradition does not necessarily mandate our goal. Ancient Judaism excluded people with physical disabilities from acting in the priestly role. And our people does put a premium on learning and intellectual achievement, which disproportionately disadvantages those people with learning or developmental disabilities.

But as Reconstructionists we acknowledge that the tradition is imperfect, and that we ourselves often lack sensitivities to people with whom we do not have the opportunity to come into contact. And we also find in our tradition a mandate for inclusion of people who are different from ourselves. We interpret the idea that we are all made in God's image, *tzelem Elohim,* to acknowledge the great variety of gifts that difference brings to Jewish life.

As with the other issues of inclusion, we cannot only *say* that we are being inclusive, but must *act* on our principles. For that reason, the Jewish Reconstructionist Federation established a Task Force that made recommendations about how we can come into compliance with the guidelines of the Americans with Disabilities Act, even though religious institutions are not required to do so by law. We have begun to eliminate the barriers to full inclusion of people with disabilities:

- the physical barriers that make our buildings inaccessible to people who use wheelchairs or canes;

- the communication barriers that prevent us from providing interpretation services for the blind and hearing impaired;

- and the attitudinal barriers that keep us from providing programming for children with Down's syndrome or Attention Deficit Disorder in our synagogue schools, from using sensitive language when talking about the differently abled, and from being comfortable around people who may not talk or look or act like us and who may need special attention from us.

Including Jews of Color

Jewish communities in North America often assume that Jewishness entails European ancestry. Of course, anyone who has spent time in Israel quickly becomes aware of how far that is from the truth. Jews are not only European. We are Middle Eastern, Asian, African, and Latin American. Yet Jews of European ancestry are not always sufficiently sensitive to the feelings of exclusion experienced by Jews from non-European backgrounds in the context of North America.

Some of these Jews are Sephardic or *Mizrahi*. Some are converts. Others are the partners or adopted children of European Jews. Reconstructionist communities pay special attention to the cultural interests and needs of Jews from around the world who participate in our congregations.

We are careful, for example, not to assume that all Jews eat lox and bagels rather than fritada, had relatives who spoke Yiddish rather than Ladino, or name their children after dead relatives rather than living ones.

We are open to incorporating Chinese calligraphy or Guatemalan blankets in the naming ceremonies for children whose parents have adopted them from those countries. We add words of welcome in Vietnamese, Spanish, or Arabic into weddings and funerals. We are moved when African-American Reconstructionists weave the patterns of Kente cloth into their *tallitot*.

It is important to us that our communities remain conscious of these differences, learning as much as we can about the varieties of cultural heritages that combine to create the Jewish people today.

Reconstructionists believe that *belonging* must precede *behaving* and *believing*. First, a Jew must belong to a Jewish community; only through the process of being a full member of the group does a person become Jewishly acculturated, assimilating Jewish perspectives and beliefs, values and practices. It is for this reason that we are so committed to expanding the range of those who feel included in our midst.

All of the groups we are committed to including have experienced invisibility in Jewish life. Our main goal as Reconstructionists is to educate ourselves about the specific differences of others and about the need to remain vigilant to include the formerly disenfranchised. We do this primarily through education about the issues involved. But our efforts only succeed when people with disabilities, gay men and lesbians, feminists, patrilineal Jews, Jews by choice, and the intermarried themselves become involved and feel comfortable enough to take leadership roles within our movement. This is the ultimate goal of inclusion.

10
The Reconstructionist Movement

The fundamental principle upon which all aspects of the Reconstructionist program are based is the need to continue the adaptation of Judaism to meet the unprecedented circumstances of the contemporary era. That reconstruction applies not only to traditional Jewish beliefs and practices, but also to the very *structure* of Jewish communities.

Jews were once linked together across national boundaries by shared loyalty to halakhic authorities or talmudic academies. Today, new mechanisms are required through which we can interact. Individual communities once were governed by Jewish law; in today's open societies, new communal forms have been developed. Synagogues of the past were part of autonomous, halakhically governed communities in which rabbis were authorities. Today synagogues function differently in order to serve Jews who live in secular society, and rabbis learn to lead without traditional authority. This chapter discusses the Reconstructionist approach to the reorganization of these Jewish institutions.

The Organic Jewish Community

All of the aspects of Mordecai Kaplan's original program can be viewed as different dimensions of one grand concern: how the Jewish people might become one in spirit and reality. The political transformations of the modern world created a situation in which Jews are divided not only by distances, but also by their widely divergent relationships to their governments. In the United States, with no established religion, Jewish denominations have been free to develop in their diversity and to attract Jews who voluntarily associate with them. In Israel, there is an established Orthodox rabbinate that exercises a legal monopoly on religious practice. In Europe, there are Chief Rabbinates that function in yet other ways. Under such circumstances, Kaplan perceived a pressing need to develop an umbrella under which all Jewries and all committed Jews could be united.

Kaplan's understanding of religion led him, as discussed in chapter 2, to the insight that the primary way of expressing oneself as a Jew is to belong—to identify as a member of the Jewish people. He wanted to make that indefinite sense of belonging concrete, and he sought to develop a single governing apparatus through which the Jewish people could once again function as a whole.

Kaplan envisioned a democratically elected congress of representatives of the Jewish people. Such a congress would have created a constitution and government of individuals who would join voluntarily. The people's representatives would then have begun to struggle with defining what it means to be a Jew in our times. This organic Jewish community would also have provided an international basis for the Jewish people to help, support, and defend one another in times of crisis.

Of course, this reconstituted Jewish people would not have defined beliefs and practices. Kaplan firmly believed in the concept of unity, but not uniformity. The key to the connection is belonging; believing and behaving are matters left up to smaller units of the Jewish people to define.

Jewish Centers

Kaplan sought to apply the same model to specific Jewish communities around the world. He deplored the competitive and antagonistic attitudes that Jewish institutions sometimes display towards one another. A goal of his proposed organic Jewish community was to put an end to such in-fighting.

Kaplan's plan was that in each neighborhood or area there would be one central Jewish address. Democratically elected officials would run the philanthropic, educational, religious, and social aspects of the community, collecting and using funds to benefit all. There would be a central staff of leaders representing all perspectives. People would be able to choose their preferred kind of worship service and education for their children, but all the options would be housed under one roof. Even if people chose to worship in different services, they could still come together for an Oneg Shabbat, for example. Resources would be used more efficiently. The advantage of an efficient body would thus be combined with the creativity of small, independent groups.

In this model, people would be brought together by what they share in common—their belonging to the Jewish community. Yet it would give them the freedom to express their Jewishness in a variety of ways.

Today, the vision described above remains only a vision. These ideas have had their impact, though. The Jewish Center movement broadened synagogue commitments beyond religious services to include educational, social, and philanthropic concerns. The Jewish Federations in most cities have become central funding agencies for most nondenominational Jewish organizations concerned with the welfare of the Jewish community.

Yet these changes, while a vast improvement over the competitive and loose arrangements in Kaplan's time, are not yet "organic" in the sense he described. Federation boards are not democratically elected by all givers. This would not be as serious a flaw in Kaplan's view as their primary failure—their continuing inability to unite the religious and secular dimensions of Jewish life today. In essence, the synagogue has expanded its functions to include activities that parallel many supported by the secular establishments (philanthropic efforts on behalf of Israel and local communities, adult education classes, athletic facilities, social services for older people). On the other hand, Federations see themselves as the central address of the Jewish community and seek to cultivate quasi-religious commitments in the Jews who are involved in their efforts (Young Leadership programming and missions to Israel, feminist Passover Seders). Nonetheless, there have been significant attempts to bridge the secular-religious divide, especially in light of concerns about Jewish continuity. Federations increasingly fund synagogue outreach efforts, require their own board members to be members of synagogues, and fund regional consortia of congregations that undertake joint programming. Yet there is still a sense that the secular and religious elements of Jewish civilization do not fit together organically.

There is competition among the different religious groups as well, and a lack of organicity exists there too. Though most local Boards of Rabbis include Reform, Orthodox, Conservative, and Reconstructionist participants, they do not provide the unity Kaplan desired. And while we perceive that in some ways, the boundaries between groups have become less clear than in times past, institutional considerations still divide loyalties. Indeed, the rift between Orthodox and non-Orthodox is wider today—and growing, often fueled by political and organizational motives.

It is clear from the state of the Jewish community today that hopes for organicity are "utopian"; a desired goal perhaps, but impractical to realize. One might compare Kaplan's vision to that of the United Nations, where self-interest has overshadowed universalistic concerns. Like other dreams, the organic Jewish community stands out as an ideal that is unlikely to be realized.

Reconstructionists today may derive a lesson from Kaplan's vision. We must maintain our own vision of the organic Jewish community, reconstructed for the next generation. Kaplan taught us that we should not only work for the Jewish people today, but must look ahead to the needs of the Jewish people tomorrow. Planning for the future means dreaming dreams, setting goals, and developing concrete plans on the basis of which we launch creative efforts to build for the future. Rather than abandoning Kaplan's hope for an organic Jewish community, we devote our efforts toward that end even if it is not realizable in our day. Indeed, if we believe that Judaism is a civilization—that belonging to the Jewish people is of utmost importance, that what draws us together as Jews is more basic than what divides us—then we can't abandon Kaplan's desire to express those ideas in practical terms.

The Reconstructionist Federation

Kaplan's goal of Jewish unity was a major factor that discouraged him from devoting most of his energy to the institutional establishment of the Reconstructionist movement. He sought instead to convince all Jewish groups of the veracity of his analysis of Jewish civilization and his program for the reconstruction of Jewish life. To that end, in 1940 he organized the Jewish Reconstructionist Foundation in New York. The Foundation served to publish his works and implement his program. Since then, many basic Reconstructionist ideas have been accepted by most non-Orthodox American Jews: the civilizational nature of Judaism, the primacy of belonging, the legitimacy

of pluralism, the importance of ritual to non-halakhic Jews, the synagogue as community center.

Another factor that inhibited the growth of the Reconstructionist
movement through the 1950s was the anti-institutional bias of
Reconstructionists. The other movements had developed unwieldy
national organizations and large synagogues that were obstacles to
the active involvement of individual Jews. Policy statements and halakhic rulings were issued from above, rendering individuals and
congregations passive recipients. The American rabbinate developed
a style of formality and authority that encouraged worshipers to become peripheral observers at services.

Eventually, however, Kaplan's followers overcame their reluctance
to translate Reconstructionist ideas into institutional structures. They
saw that they could not rely on other movements to implement the
Reconstructionist program—a program needed to revitalize Judaism
for disaffected, thinking Jews. That program required living communities. And so in 1955 the Federation of Reconstructionist Congregation and Havurot (later renamed the Jewish Reconstructionist Federation [JRF]) was formed, at first a group of only four congregations
that has now grown to over 100 congregations and havurot with over
50,000 members.

The JRF coordinates the policies and activities of all Reconstructionist congregations and havurot. The JRF staff provides consultation
on such areas as by-laws and education, budgeting and liturgical innovation. Regional and national programs include lectures, leadership
and organizational workshops, educational programming and consulting, retreats, intercongregational exchanges, a biennial North American
convention with regional kallot in alternate years, youth programming,
and policy statements. The Federation helps in the creation of new
congregations, reaches out to unaffiliated groups, and conducts an
ongoing program of public relations and outreach to unaffiliated

individuals. It maintains the Reconstructionist Press and publishes *Reconstructionism Today.*

Reconstructionist Congregations

Reconstructionist communities are diverse. Specific policies are determined by each congregation. Nevertheless, they share many important characteristics:

- *Gender Equality.* All aspects of community life are open equally to women and men—for example, leadership positions, roles in liturgy and ritual, and community service responsibilities.

- *Participatory Decision Making.* Synagogue policies are determined through democratic processes in which interested members are invited to participate. Decisions are preceded by periods of study in which traditional as well as modern Jewish texts and contemporary dilemmas are explored and values are clarified.

- *Institutional Values.* There is an ongoing effort to scrutinize procedures and policies in light of the congregation's shared and articulated values and to modify them when they fall short.

- *Shared Leadership.* Part of the way that rabbis, cantors, and educators lead is by helping members learn how to lead. While the knowledge and skills of professionals are important and respected, communities also seek to involve as many people as possible in leading services, chanting Torah, delivering *divrei Torah* (Torah commentaries), visiting the sick, chairing committees, and a host of other community roles.

- *Welcoming Atmosphere.* It is the hallmark of Reconstructionist congregations that they define themselves as inclusive and welcoming—both to guests and to members. Aware that many Jews feel excluded and alienated, communities go beyond atmospherics and cultivate a welcoming attitude in the way that they create programs.

- *Ongoing Education.* There is an expectation that members will continue to learn and grow. Jewish education is not conceived as something exclusively for children and teens.

- *Liturgical and Ritual Creativity.* There is an openness to experimentation with new forms of prayer and ritual practice that make traditional themes come alive in a contemporary idiom.

- *Serious Embrace of Tradition.* Nevertheless, traditional forms are retained whenever possible—songs, liturgical melodies, Hebrew, rituals—and are often re-introduced when they have been abandoned in other parts of the non-Orthodox world.

- *Social Action.* Reconstructionist groups exemplify the conviction that Jewish communities must provide Jewish contexts for members to engage in political and social action, working towards *tikkun olam* (repair of the world), as well as in ritual and ethical practice.

- *Mutual Support.* Some congregations institute formal and informal support networks that help members to help one another in all facets of their lives. The shared principle is that when members of communities are interconnected in many aspects of their lives, the power and meaning of their religious connections are enhanced immeasurably.

Prayer Book Revisions

The first series of Reconstructionist prayer books, edited by Kaplan, along with Rabbis Ira Eisenstein, Milton Steinberg, and Eugene Kohn, was published in the 1940s. It was groundbreaking and controversial because of the way that the Hebrew words of traditional prayers were altered to reflect Reconstructionist beliefs. References to the Chosen People and to the resurrection of the dead, for example, were eliminated. *The New Haggadah* (1941) shifted the focus of the Passover Seder from God's deliverance to the human struggle for freedom.

The most recent series of prayer books published by the Reconstructionist movement is called *Kol Haneshamah*. Edited by Rabbi David Teutsch and translated by poet Joel Rosenberg, it includes separate volumes for Shabbat and holidays, weekdays, home ceremonies, and the High Holy Days. In addition, Rabbis Joy Levitt and Michael Strassfeld have edited a new Passover Haggadah, *A Night of Questions*. The approach of these prayer books illustrates the Reconstructionist approach to communal worship.

Rabbinic-Lay Collaboration. The Prayer Book Commission that produced these volumes was composed of both rabbinic and lay leaders of the movement. This reflects the Reconstructionist commitment to shared, participatory decision making. It also insures that the diverse approaches of different affiliated congregations are reflected in the prayer books.

Transliteration. Countless Jews today are interested in communal Jewish worship but cannot participate fully because of the Hebrew skills needed to do so. Reconstructionist communities seek to be welcoming and inclusive, but Reconstructionist worship generally includes a lot of Hebrew. The prayer books provide English transliteration of all Hebrew that is commonly sung or chanted to allow everyone to participate. The transliteration is provided on the same page as the Hebrew, so that the reader can move gradually to reading the Hebrew as the words become more familiar.

Gender Neutral Language. Reconstructionists avoid the use of masculine pronouns to refer generically to people *and* to God. Therefore, all English readings and translations are expressed in gender-neutral language. In the Hebrew text, references to the patriarchs are supplemented by references to the matriarchs, and a variety of gender-neutral names for God are included.

Changes in Traditional Prayers. In line with the principle that we should not say words that we find objectionable or false, references to the chosenness of the Jewish people are changed or deleted, as are mentions of the resurrection of the dead. Unlike the first series of prayer books published by the movement, however, this series often either provides the traditional wording at the bottom of the page, or it notes and explains the changes. In this way, Reconstructionists retain their familiarity and connection with the traditional texts even if they choose not to pray these words. This also reflects the fact that Reconstructionists can and do disagree about which liturgical changes are necessary, and which parts of the traditional liturgy are best left unchanged and interpreted metaphorically—and that decisions are not legislated by a central body but are rather left to each local group.

Study as a Form of Prayer. Reconstructionists continue to believe that *Talmud Torah*—sacred study—is a primary mode of worship, allowing us to receive revelation as our ancestors did. It is thus no accident that most pages of the prayer books include multiple explanations and interpretations of the prayers that enable the worshiper at a service to pray by studying—and to deepen the experience of prayer by broadening the worshiper's understanding of the prayers. The format also reflects the commitment of Reconstructionists to ongoing learning for everyone.

Supplementary Readings. The interpretive poems and prayers included in the prayer books range from medieval to contemporary. Their authors are women and men, rabbis and non-rabbis, Jews and non-Jews. Reconstructionists seek wisdom and inspiration from all people and peoples; we believe that a deeper rootedness in our own traditions is best combined with other voices of struggle and seeking.

Jewish Education

The vision and direction for Jewish education programs in the Reconstructionist movement is established by a joint Education Commission of the Jewish Reconstructionist Federation and the Reconstructionist Rabbinical Association. The Commission has 45 members who are drawn from the ranks of lay and professional leaders in Jewish education. The Commission is composed of six committees that focus on Professional Development, Congregational Services, Adult Learning, Youth and Camping, Reconstructionist Day Schools, and Family Education.

The movement's most intensive work in Jewish education is done through the Cooperating Schools Network, a group of 22 affiliates of the JRF that have committed themselves to ongoing communication and professional development designed to integrate family, adult, and children's Jewish education into more holistic learning communities. Reconstructionist work in adult education has included the development of *Aytz Ḥayim We,* a project that links 33 JRF affiliates together in the ongoing study of Jewish texts.

The JRF works closely with other national agencies, particularly with Jewish Educational Services of North America. Together, JRF and JESNA have produced *Targilon: A Guide for Charting the Course of Jewish Family Education,* a book that has been widely praised for its impact on the field of family education. Much of JRF's most exciting and successful work in this field is contained in the volume

Growing Together: Programs, Experiences, and Resources for Jewish Family Education. The movement also works closely with the Teacher's Educators' Institute of the Mandel Foundation, where rabbis and educators attend intensive institutes on the mentoring and supervision of Jewish teachers.

Pursuing a New Rabbinic Model

As should be apparent, Reconstructionist communities diverge substantially from the structure of most other congregations—primarily in their expressed and fervent commitment to participatory Judaism. The nature of liturgical and ritual observance is normally determined by group consensus after collective study. Leading services, reading Torah, and delivering *divrei Torah* and sermons are rotated among capable members, while others study until they too are able. These communities are devoted to experimenting with traditional forms based on the conviction that, as an evolving civilization of the Jewish people, Judaism will survive only if it is reconstructed to speak to the needs and in the idiom of contemporary Jews. Congregations are centers for Jewish culture and Jewish community.

For all of these reasons and others, when the time came to plan for the establishment of the Reconstructionist Rabbinical College (RRC), it was clear that such a school would need to train rabbis for new roles. Rabbis had to be educated to understand the evolving nature of Judaism, to serve Jews in a variety of new settings, and, most important, to become teachers and facilitators—leaders who would encourage their congregants to assume many of the roles and responsibilities that rabbis often retain as their own.

Reconstructionist rabbis don't function as halakhic authorities, since Reconstructionist Jews do not regard the halakhah as authoritative. Instead, Reconstructionist rabbis are trained to be teachers—

Jews who have devoted years to the study of Jewish civilization so that they can serve as unique resources who can help others to learn about, understand, and empathize with Judaism and to grow into increasingly Judaized lives. Reconstructionist rabbis do not assume that solutions to complex issues can be found unambiguously within Jewish tradition. Rather, they struggle with the dilemmas confronting contemporary Jews, and they attempt to help in resolving those dilemmas in ways that enrich Jews' lives. Rather than perpetuating traditional liturgical and ritual forms regardless of congregants' understanding of them, Reconstructionist rabbis help Jews to understand the basis for traditional ritual and to practice in meaningful ways—ways that turn out sometimes to be traditional and sometimes not.

In addition to their roles as teachers of Torah, rabbis are professionals who also play pivotal roles in bringing Jewish values to their communities. It is not sufficient to *talk* about the importance of justice and caring, respectful listening and welcoming, honesty and openness. Jewish communities must embody the values they espouse if they are to be taken seriously and if they are to serve as places where Jews can sanctify their lives. In the course of their training, Reconstructionist rabbis are therefore taught the skills that enable them to inspire and strengthen such caring communities. Furthermore, the culture of the Reconstructionist Rabbinical College seeks itself to model these values and to provide students with the opportunity to participate in the kind of community that they will help to shape and lead.

Rabbis themselves must first cultivate spiritual lives of their own before they can lead others on their journeys. A central goal of the RRC program, therefore, includes guidance for students—in prayer, in sacred study, in social action, in meditation, in community celebration and support. No one mode of spirituality is favored over others. Rather, the RRC community seeks to support diversity and pluralism, so that future rabbis will be well-practiced in leading communities of diverse Jews.

The RRC Curriculum

Students who enter RRC (a bachelor's degree is required; many students already have prior graduate degrees or professional experience) study Judaism as an evolving religious civilization. Their course work is structured so that, in each year of the program, the religion, language, law, literature, history, social organization, and culture of the Jewish people in a given era are presented. Students begin with a year concentrating on the biblical era (Abraham to Ezra), then study the rabbinic era (Babylonian exile to codification of the Talmud), medieval era (the founding of Islam to the Reformation), modern era (the discovery of America to the Holocaust), and conclude with the contemporary era (the founding of Israel to the present). Through the College's core civilization program, students develop a clear awareness of the evolution of the Jewish people.

The core civilization program is augmented by the requirement that students learn about other religions. RRC students develop an appreciation of living in two civilizations and an understanding of how the social scientific study of other religions and cultures can enhance their study of Judaism.

The third element of the RRC training program is required work in practical rabbinics. Through coordinated course work and supervised field work, students develop the many skills needed in the rabbinate from counseling to administration, education to community organizing. The goal of the practical rabbinics program is to train rabbis to be leaders in all settings in Jewish life—congregations, schools, and agencies. Because Judaism is a civilization, the rabbinic role should not be limited to the performance of religious functions only. In fact, students may opt to specialize in campus work, chaplaincy, geriatric chaplaincy, education, or community organization, as well as in the congregational rabbinate. The development of new rabbinic roles does not replace the need for rabbis to function within congregations, and approximately half of RRC graduates choose to become congregational rabbis. In principle, however, the RRC trains rabbis to serve anywhere that Jews seek to live Jewish lives.

The *Reconstructionist*

Founded in 1935, the *Reconstructionist* has served to facilitate the processes of learning and involvement that are at the heart of all Reconstructionist undertakings. It assists group discussions and activities that seek to bring a liberal Jewish perspective to bear upon contemporary issues. It offers reviews of recent books of Jewish interest, interpretations of ritual practices and traditional beliefs, surveys of Jewish cultural developments, introductions to fields of Jewish study, and updates on issues relating to Jewish communities around the world. In all of these ways, it assumes the intelligence and seriousness of its readers, as it attempts to provide Jews with the information they need to make intelligent choices about personal and global issues. The journal is now published by the Reconstructionist Rabbinical College twice each year. Each issue focuses primarily on a single topic, which is explored from a variety of different viewpoints. It thus facilitates communication among Reconstructionists across the continent and provides a continuing forum for the intellectual development of the movement.

Reconstructionist Rabbinical Association

The Reconstructionist Rabbinical Association (RRA) was established in 1974 by the first graduates of RRC. The Association provides collegial support, serves as a forum for the discussion of issues facing rabbis, and is a resource for the continuing Jewish, professional, and personal development of its members. Comprised primarily of graduates of RRC, the RRA also includes rabbis trained elsewhere who have chosen to identify with the Reconstructionist movement.

Aware that rabbis daily face important questions of Jewish identity and ritual procedures, the RRA has focused on issues of personal status, such as conversion, patrilineality, intermarriage, and divorce. In addition to guidelines formulated for such issues, the RRA *Rabbi's Manual* (1997) contains life-cycle liturgies created to embrace tradition as well as innovation.

The RRA approaches issues with the same commitment to process and principle evidenced elsewhere in the movement. Traditional sources are consulted and studied, debated and discussed. Contemporary concerns, values, and circumstances are incorporated into the conversation. Forums are created in which diverse perspectives can be expressed. Policies and positions emerge as a consensus is shaped.

In keeping with the Reconstructionist approach to halakhah and the commitment to pluralism, many of the positions arrived at by the RRA become guidelines for rabbis (and for the Reconstructionist movement) which provide information as well as creating norms and expectations. Rabbis, and the various types of communities they serve, interact with these guidelines as they arrive at their own application of them. An individual rabbi may take a position which is more or less stringent than a given guideline. The RRA is aware that the contemporary Jewish community often changes rapidly; guidelines, rather than fixed laws, provide a stable yet flexible framework within which to work.

In addition to working on issues specific to rabbis, the RRA participates in the wider conversations of Reconstructionist commissions, committees, programs, and projects, representing rabbis' unique combination of learning and leadership.

II
Envisioning the Future

It is the fate of our generation of North American Jews that many of us are *ba'alei teshuvah*—people returning to Judaism whose practice of and commitment to Judaism exceed those of our parents. A generation or two ago, our parents and grandparents struggled to Americanize; today, we struggle to be Jewish. The efforts of Jewish immigrants and their children to shed their Jewishness have taken their toll. Our efforts to Judaize our lives are made with difficulty. The tradition and its forms often feel alien.

Nevertheless, our position as outsiders to the tradition also has its advantages. We are not Jews by inevitable momentum; for the most part, we do not practice Judaism because of an unarticulated nostalgia. Our commitments are made against the natural flow. They are self-motivated and authentic, filled with an energy and creativity that impel us to reconstruct the tradition to speak in the contemporary idiom.

Those of us who have returned by the Reconstructionist path find that the Jewish tradition is often exciting and enriching in ways that we could not have anticipated. Comfort with Jewish ritual comes only with practice—with an understanding of its meaning, but most importantly with an ease that is earned by regular repetition. Whatever the lighting of the Shabbat candles, for example, is *supposed* to mean according to rabbis, philosophers, and mystics, its true meaning to an individual is discovered at the moment when the flickering of those candles and the resonance of the accompanying *berakhah* (blessing) signify a real, internal transformation from workday concerns to the peace of the Shabbat. There are no shortcuts to that moment; it is earned by practice no less demanding than the meditation leading to Zen enlightenment, or the training that leads to the effortless swing of a consummate ballplayer. Judaism is a spiritual discipline.

Reconstructionist Jews have in common our acknowledgment that this Jewish mastery is as elusive as it is desirable. We struggle in the space between natural certainty and zealous skepticism. We share the quest to recover the beauty and power of our traditions without abandoning our commitment to modernity and intellectual integrity. As a result, our Jewish commitments inevitably are full of questioning and doubts. There are no easy answers.

Nevertheless, we pursue our Jewish commitments. There are rewards to be earned short of complete ease and fluency. In a de-personalizing, alienating, mobile society, a community of Jews seeking meaning is a priceless commodity. In a week devoted to the pressures of work, it is good to congregate in a common pursuit of the transcendent. In a world that often seems valueless at best and corrupting at worst, it is enriching to study and act on the basis of the values that past generations have designated as ultimate and sacred. In an environment that tends to reduce everything to scientific utility and economic expediency, we find it imperative to ask the larger questions about the meaning of life. And as we do all these things, we find Jewish tradition to be a particularly fertile field to seed our aspirations. Indeed, living with the threat of environmental disaster, there is some comfort to be found in rediscovering a tradition that, in its timeless commitment to our struggle with hubris, activates us to behave in sane and life-saving ways. Beyond the excitement of technological advances, beyond the pleasures of gourmet food and the satisfaction of professional success, Jewish living is a vehicle for cultivating our common humanity. Through it, we can become better people.

And so we study our history, celebrate the cycle of the Jewish year, speak and contemplate inherited prayers, and listen in the stillness for the whispers of eternity heard by our ancestors. We strive to transform Jewish civilization into a way of life through which we can become more fully human and more nearly divine. We seek to reclaim our ancestors' faith that this world is divinely created and holy, that God's presence within us and around us awaits our efforts to make it manifest. We are taking a double risk. We are deviating from accepted agnostic secular norms *and* from the traditional supernaturalism that demands a subservient faith. We believe it is possible to be religious without being fundamentalist, to be devoted to our traditions without losing human sensitivity and intellectual openness, to be the beneficiaries of the past without becoming subordinate to it.

We do not pretend that any of this is easy. It may be easier either to accept the tradition without question or to reject it entirely as outmoded, easier to accept an authority—whether the Torah or the *New York Times*—than to reach independent conclusions. But as Reconstructionist Jews, we are comfortable with our questions and doubts. The process of admitting and confronting our uncertainty has itself become part of our norm. Our study of traditional texts is undertaken not so that we can accept them uncritically, but so that we can confront their meanings and wrest from them the part of their message that speaks to us. We sing our songs to recapture a celebratory state of consciousness and an attitude of gratefulness that we often find difficult to generate. We often pray and practice in the hope that we will understand afterwards what is unclear at the outset. We continue to do so because our frequent successes outweigh our inevitable failures.

In all of this, we believe that our approach to Jewish life speaks to many contemporary Jews who are seeking avenues of return to their Jewish identities. We like to think that we represent a Judaism for those who are willing and ready to engage the post-modern world. We acknowledge that most things in life are gray, not black or white. Our commitment to balancing individual autonomy with communal commitment is at odds with the commanded, authoritarian nature of inherited traditions, but we are convinced that Jewish civilization is sufficiently resilient to be transformed successfully yet again, as it has evolved time and time again in our past. It is that faith that enables us to continue our struggle to reconstruct Judaism. That reconstructed Judaism is the necessary condition for Jewish vitality in our time.

12
Suggestions for Further Exploration

This book is meant to be an introduction to Reconstructionism and an invitation to further exploration. The suggestions for further reading below are organized to follow the sequence of chapters in the book. The Resource Guide at the end of this chapter provides information about Reconstructionist institutions.

The Reconstructionist Bookshelf

The Best Place to Begin

The Reconstructionist movement has put together an anthology for its "Introduction to Judaism" course that serves as a good place to continue exploring the Reconstructionist approach: *Jewish, Alive and American: A Student Resource Book,*[*1] Sheryl Lewart, ed. (Philadelphia: RRC Press, 1998).

CHAPTER 1: *Basic Introductions to Mordecai Kaplan's Life and Thought*

The definitive biography of Mordecai Kaplan is Mel Scult's *Judaism Faces the Twentieth Century: A Biography of Mordecai M. Kaplan*[*] v. 1 (Detroit: Wayne State University Press, 1994). Scult has also published Kaplan's

---

1. All publications marked with an asterisk are available through the Reconstructionist Press, 1 877 JRFPUBS.

diaries, *Selections from the Diaries of Mordecai M. Kaplan: Communings of the Spirit 1913–1934* v. 1 (Detroit: Wayne State University Press, 2000). *Dynamic Judaism: The Essential Writings of Mordecai M. Kaplan,** edited by Mel Scult and Emanuel Goldsmith (New York: Reconstructionist Press and Fordham University Press, 1991) includes extensive excerpts from Kaplan's works (both his books and less well-known writings) and general introductory essays on his life and thought. Richard Libowitz wrote a study of Kaplan, *Mordecai M. Kaplan and the Development of Reconstructionism* (New York: E. Mellen Press, 1984). Jeffrey Gurock and Jacob Schachter have written about Kaplan's relationship to Orthodoxy in *A Modern Heretic and a Traditional Community: Mordecai M. Kaplan, Orthodoxy, and American Judaism* (New York: Columbia University Press, 1997). Kaplan's influences and contributions are discussed in Emanuel Goldsmith, Mel Scult, and Robert Seltzer, eds. *The American Judaism of Mordecai M. Kaplan** (New York: NYU Press, 1990). See especially Part 2, "Stages in a Life" and Part 3, "Intellectual Contemporaries." You will find Kaplan's autobiographical statement, "The Way I Have Come" in *Mordecai M. Kaplan: An Evaluation,* Ira Eisenstein and Eugene Kohn, eds. (New York: The Jewish Reconstructionist Foundation, 1952). The Fall 1995 issue of the *Reconstructionist* (60/2) "Kaplan and Us" is a retrospective on Kaplan's influence on contemporary Reconstructionism.[2]

CHAPTER 2: *An Evolving Religious Civilization*

For further discussions of "An Evolving Religious Civilization," it is best to consult Kaplan's writings directly. See *Judaism as a Civilization** (1934), chapters 25 and 26, and *The Future of the American Jew** (1948), chapters 3 and 4. Kaplan's concept of peoplehood has been explained clearly by Ira Eisenstein in *Judaism Under Freedom* (New York: Reconstructionist Press, 1956), chapter 4, and by Jack Cohen, "Peoplehood" in *Mordecai M. Kaplan: An Evaluation.* See also "The Spiritualization of Peoplehood and the Reconstructionist Curriculum of the Future" in *Creative Jewish*

---

2. Back issues and subscriptions to the *Reconstructionist* are available through the Jewish Reconstructionist Federation, 215 782 8500.

Education: A Reconstructionist Perspective, Jeffrey Schein and Jacob Staub, eds. (Chappaqua, N.Y.: Rossel Books/Reconstructionist Rabbinical College Press, 1985) and Jacob J. Staub, "Evolving Definitions of Evolution," *Reconstructionist* 61/2 (Fall 1996): 4–13.

CHAPTER 3: *God*

Kaplan's theology is most clearly presented in Kaplan's *The Future of the American Jew* (1948), chapters 10 and 14, and *The Meaning of God in Modern Jewish Religion* (1937). The latter is a magnificent study of the method of functional reinterpretation of the God idea as applied to the Jewish holiday cycle. A clear application of Kaplan's thinking is available in Harold Kushner's *When Bad Things Happen to Good People* (New York: Schocken Books, 1981). Other important theological studies from a Reconstructionist perspective are Harold Kushner, "Why Do the Righteous Suffer?" *Judaism* 28/3 (Summer 1970): 316–323; Harold Schulweis, "From God to Godliness: A Proposal for a Predicate Theology," *Reconstructionist* 41/1 (February 1975): 16–26; Jacob Staub, "Kaplan and Process Theology," in *The American Judaism of Mordecai M. Kaplan,* 283–293; and "God as a Source of Comfort," *Reconstructionism Today* 7/1 (Fall 1999).

Chosenness

To learn more about chosenness, see Kaplan, *The Future of the American Jew,* chapter 13; Richard Hirsh, et. al., "The Chosen People Reconsidered: A Symposium," *Reconstructionist* 50/1 (September 1984): 8–28; Arnold Eisen, *The Chosen People in America* (Bloomington: Indiana University Press, 1983), and George B. Driesen, "Revisiting the Chosen People," *Reconstructionist* 60/2 (Fall 1995): 78–84.

---

3. For back issues and subscriptions of *Reconstructionism Today,* contact editor Larry Bush, c/o the Jewish Reconstructionist Federation, 215 782 8500.

CHAPTER 4: *The Past Has a Vote, Not a Veto*

To find out more about what is meant by "The Past Has a Vote, Not a Veto" see Kaplan, *Judaism as a Civilization,** chapter 29, and *The Future of the American Jew,** chapter 19. Kaplan's explanation of transvaluation and revaluation is in *The Meaning of God in Modern Jewish Religion.** (See the first nine pages.) The Reconstructionist Rabbinical College Press published a complete volume on Jewish Law in the series, *Jewish Civilization: Essays and Studies,* v. 2, Ronald Brauner, ed. (Philadelphia, 1981). Of particular note are the studies by Mel Scult, Jacob Staub, Jack Cohen, Ira Eisenstein, and Richard Hirsh. A further development of decision-making procedures is Rebecca Alpert's "Ethical Decision Making: A Reconstructionist Framework," *Reconstructionist* 50/7 (June 1985): 15–20. Also of interest is Sidney Schwarz, "Reconstructionist Halaḥa," *Reconstructionist* 58/2 (Spring 1993): 20–23.

CHAPTER 5: *Living in Two Civilizations*

The subject of "Living in Two Civilizations" is approached by Kaplan in *The Religion of Ethical Nationhood* (1970), chapter 7. Further discussion of the subject is found in articles in the *Reconstructionist:* Nancy Fuchs-Kreimer, "The Thanksgiving Dilemma," 49/1 (October 1983): 22–24; Daniel Nussbaum, "Two Civilizations or Three? Halloween as *Yom Yeladim,*" 40/6 (October 1979): 17–21; Jacob Staub, "Living in Two Civilizations: Preliminary Notes Towards a Reappraisal," 48/5 (Winter 1983): 23–28; Arthur Hertzberg, "Kaplan on the Promise of America," 50/3 (December 1984): 13–16; Sheila Peltz Weinberg, "Renewing Thanksgiving," 57/1 (Autumn 1991): 9–12; and Herb Levine, "Jewish Boundaries & American Openness," 59/2 (Fall 1994): 12–17.

Interfaith Dialogue
On interfaith dialogue, see volume 3 of *Jewish Civilization: Essays and Studies,* (1981) which is devoted to that subject. See also the following articles in the *Reconstructionist:* David Klatzker, "The 'Ecumenical' Kaplan," 47/5 (July–August 1981): 7–17; Sandra Lubarsky, "Kaplan, Plu-

ralism & Transformative Dialogue," 60/2 (Fall 1995): 71–77 and Cy Swartz, "When Jews Celebrate with Christians," 59/2 (Fall 1994): 44–48. In *Reconstructionism Today*, see Steven Carr Reuben, "A Black-Jewish Covenant in L.A.," 2/1 (Autumn 1994).

Jewish Education

On the subject of Jewish education, see *Creative Jewish Education: A Reconstructionist Perspective,** especially the essay by Nancy Fuchs-Kreimer, "Teaching about Other Religions," and Harold Kushner, *When Children Ask About God** (New York: Reconstructionist Press, 1971). See also Jeffrey Schein, *Tiṭhadesh: Renewal and Reflection in Jewish Education** (Wyncote, Pa.: Federation of Reconstructionist Congregations and Havurot, 1992), Jeffrey Schein and Leah Mundell, *Reconstructionist Curriculum Resource Guide** (Elkins Park, Pa.: Jewish Reconstructionist Federation, 1996); Jeffrey Schein and Leora W. Isaacs, Targilon, *A Workbook for Charting the Course of Jewish Family Education** (Philadelphia: Jewish Reconstructionist Federation and Jewish Education Service of North America, 1999) (reprint); Lisa Silberman Brenner, "Creative Creation," Toba Spitzer, "New Explorations in *Shemot*/Exodus," Daniel Silberman Brenner, "Rabbi Wayback's Adventure" in *Three Innovative New Curricula**(Elkins Park, Pa.: Jewish Reconstructionist Federation, 1997) and the following articles from the *Reconstructionist* by Jeffrey L. Schein, "Moral Education in Jewish Schools: Pt.1," 50/5 (March 1985): 15–19; "Pt.2," 51/3 (Dec. 1985): 9–13, 22; "Reconstructionist Education: Present & Future," 55/6 (July–August 1990): 14–17 and "A Reconstructionist Educator in China," in *Reconstructionism Today*, 5/4 (Summer 1998).

Public Policy Issues

On public policy issues, see Rebecca Alpert, "The Quest for Economic Justice" in *The American Judaism of Mordecai M. Kaplan,** and "Kaplan's Challenge to Us: A Vision of Social Justice," *Reconstructionist* 60/2 (Fall 1995): 41–46. See also the following articles in *Reconstructionism Today*: Ron Goldwyn, "The Welcoming Congregation of Mishkan Shalom," 1/1 (Autumn 1993); Betsy Tessler and Jeffrey Dekro, "Tzedakah and Social Action," 1/2 (Winter 1993/94); Jane Susswein, "Projecting Our Values into the Political World," 3/2 (Winter 1995/96); and Brian Walt, "God of Transformation," 5/2 (Winter 1997/98). See also Lawrence Bush and Jeffrey Dekro, *Jews, Money and Social Responsibility: Developing a "Torah of Money" for Contemporary Life* (Philadelphia: The Shefa Fund, 1993).

CHAPTER 6: *Zion as a Spiritual Center*

The Reconstructionist approach to "Zion as a Spiritual Center" is presented by Kaplan in *The Future of the American Jew,** chapters 7 and 17, and *The Religion of Ethical Nationhood,* chapter 6. See also Jack J. Cohen, "Reflections on Kaplan's Zionism" in *The American Judaism of Mordecai M. Kaplan,** and the following articles in the *Reconstructionist*: Jack J. Cohen, "Congregation Mevakshei Derech," 53/6 (April–May 1988): 12–14, 26; the Spring 1998 issue (62/2), especially articles by Elliot Skiddell, "Reflections of a Reconstructionist *Oleh,*" 20–27, Jacob J. Staub, "Interpreting Jewish History in Light of Zionism," 36–41, and David A. Teutsch, "Israel & the Diaspora: A Reconstructionist Reconsideration of Zionism," 48–54. Amy Klein writes about "The Struggle for Religious Pluralism" in Israel in *Reconstructionism Today,* 5/3 (Spring 1998). See also the Israel issue of *Reconstructionism Today* (Spring 1996).

CHAPTER 7: *Living as a Reconstructionist*

Prayer and Ritual
The Reconstructionist approach to prayer and ritual is discussed in Kaplan's *The Future of the American Jew,** chapter 21. See also articles by Jacob Staub, "The Sabbath in Reconstructionism," *Judaism* 31/1 (Winter 1982): 63–69; Rebecca T. Alpert, "The Reconstructionist Approach to Prayer: Some Questions and Answers," *Response* 13/1–2 (Fall–Winter 1982): 127–131. See also the following articles in the *Reconstructionist*: Ruth F. Brin, "On Writing New Prayer Books," 47/10 (February 1982): 7–17; Robin C. Goldberg, "Seeing and Seeing Through: Myth, Metaphor, and Meaning," 50/7 (June 1985): 9–14; Marcia Falk, "Notes on Composing New Blessings: Toward a Feminist-Jewish Reconstruction of Prayer," 53/

3 (December 1987): 10–15, 22; Steven G. Sager, "Fixed Forms and Fluid Meanings: A Format for the Sabbath Amidah," 53/4 (January–February 1988): 9–12, 16; "New Blessings: A Symposium," 53/7 (June 1988): 13–22, 30; Arthur Green, "Twin Centers: Sacred Time & Sacred Space," 55/5 (May–June 1990): 16–22; David Teutsch, "Seeking God in the Siddur: Reflections on *Kol Haneshamah*," 59/1 (Spring 1994): 12–20; and Richard Hirsh, "Spirituality & the Language of Prayer," 59/1 (Spring 1994): 21–26. On spiritual types, see Tilden Edwards, *Spiritual Friend: Reclaiming the Gifts of Spiritual Direction* (New York: Paulist Press, 1980).

Liturgy

The Reconstructionist movement has also published a series of prayer books, *Kol Haneshamah,** edited by David Teutsch that update the original series published by Kaplan in the 1940s. See *Kol Haneshamah: Shabbat Eve* (Wyncote, Pa.: The Reconstructionist Press, 1989); *Kol Haneshamah: Shirim Uvrahot* (Wyncote, Pa.: The Reconstructionist Press, 1991); *Kol Haneshamah: Nashir Unevareh* (Wyncote, Pa.: The Reconstructionist Press, 1992); *Kol Haneshamah: Shabbat Vehagim* (Wyncote, Pa.: The Reconstructionist Press, 1994); *Kol Haneshamah: Limot Hol/Daily Prayer Book* (Wyncote, Pa.: The Reconstructionist Press, 1996); *Kol Haneshamah: Mahzor Leyamim Nora'im* (Elkins Park, Pa.: The Reconstructionist Press, 1999); and *A Night of Questions: A Passover Haggadah,* edited by Joy Levitt and Michael Strassfeld (Elkins Park, Pa.: The Reconstructionist Press, 2000). See Jeffrey L. Schein, Joseph M. Blair and Leah M. Mundell, eds., *Connecting Prayer and Spirituality: Kol Haneshamah as a Creative Teaching and Learning Text* (Wyncote, Pa.: The Reconstructionist Press, 1996) for a guide to the prayer books.

Kashrut

Rebecca T. Alpert and Arthur Waskow, "Toward an Ethical Kashrut," *Reconstructionist* 52/5 (March–April 1987): 9–13 and Richard Hirsh, "A Reconstructionist Exploration of Dietary Law," *Reconstructionism Today* 5/4 (Summer 1998).

The Arts

See the following articles in the *Reconstructionist*: Judith Kaplan Eisenstein, "Protecting Jewish Creativity," 56/2 (Winter 1990–91): 12–13; Elizabeth Bolton, "Toward a Jewish Theology of Creativity," 62/1 (Spring–Fall 1997): 16–22; and Bob Gluck, "Jewish Music or Music of the Jewish People?" 62/1 (Spring–Fall 1997): 34–47. You might also consult Judith Kaplan Eisenstein, *Heritage of Music: The Music of the Jewish People** (Wyncote, Pa.: The Reconstructionist Press, 1981).

Embodied Spirituality

See Andrea Hodos, "Turn It Over and Turn It Over: Using Movement as an Exegetical Tool," *Reconstructionist* 62/1 (Spring–Fall 1997): 48–56 and the Spring 1999 (63/2) issue which is devoted to the subject of "Caring and Healing."

CHAPTER 8: *Marking the Life Cycle*

See the following articles in the *Reconstructionist*: Nancy Fuchs-Kreimer, "Bar-Yovel: Creating a Life-Cycle Ritual for Retirement," 53/2 (October–November 1987): 21–24 ; Saul E. Perlmutter and Shoshana Zonderman, "Preparing for Childbirth: A Ceremony for Parents to Be," 54/2 (October–November 1988): 18–21; and Barbara R. Penzner and Brian P. Rosman, "A Reconstructionist Engagement Ceremony," 52/3 (December 1986): 18–21. See also the following articles in *Reconstructionism Today*: Leah Mundell, "B'nai Mitzvah in Reconstructionist Communities," 4/3 (Spring, 1997); Cy Swartz, "A Reconstructionist Hevra Kadisha," 4/4 (Summer 1997). "B'rit B'not Yisrael" is found in *Moment* (May–June 1975): 50–51, and "Covenant of Washing" in *Menorah* 4/3–4 (April–May 1983): 5–6. See also *The Rabbi's Manual*, edited by Seth David Riemer (Wyncote, Pa.: Reconstructionist Rabbinical Association, 1997).

CHAPTER 9: *Becoming an Inclusive Community*

Discussions on the subject of intermarriage and patrilineal descent are found in the "Symposium on Intermarriage," *Reconstructionist* 49/2–3

(November–December 1983), and in the following articles: Richard Hirsh, "Jewish Identity and Patrilineal Descent: Some Second Thoughts," *Reconstructionist* 49/5 (March 1984): 25–28 and Jacob Staub, "A Reconstructionist View on Patrilineal Descent," *Judaism* 34/1 (Winter 1985): 97–106. The Reconstructionist Rabbinical Association's Guidelines on Conversion and Intermarriage are available from the RRA (see Resource Guide). The Intermarriage Guidelines of the JRF are in the newsletter insert within the *Reconstructionist* 50/1 (September 1985). For a lucid, scholarly survey on the history of matrilineal and patrilineal descent, see Shaye J. D. Cohen, "The Matrilineal Principle in Historical Perspective," *Judaism* 34/1 (Winter 1985): 9–13. See also the following articles in the *Reconstructionist*: Richard Hirsh, "Beyond Who is a Jew," 55/1 (September 1989): 9–11; David Dunn Bauer, "In at the Deep End: Immersion & Affirmation of Jewish Identity—A Personal Account," 63/1 (Fall 1998): 73–80; Jacob J. Staub, "Rituals of Return and Reaffirmation," 63/1 (Fall 1998): 67–72; and Carol Towarnicky, "Boundaries and Opportunities," *Reconstructionism Today* 5/2 (Winter 1997/98) on the role of non-Jews in the Reconstructionist synagogue. See also *Boundaries and Opportunities: The Role of Non-Jews in JRF Congregations. The Report of the JRF Task Force* (Wyncote, Pa.: The Reconstructionist Press, 1998).

Welcoming Feminist Jews

The original statement by Kaplan on women and Judaism is in *The Future of the American Jew,* * chapter 20. Kaplan's feminist perspective has been explored by Lori Krafte-Jacobs in chapter 5 of her *Feminism and Modern Jewish Theological Method* (New York: Peter Lang, 1996) and by Carole Kessner in "Kaplan and the Role of Women in Judaism" in *The American Judaism of Mordecai M. Kaplan,* * 335–356. Issues pertaining to women's roles have been discussed in the *Reconstructionist* by Joy Levitt, "Woman Rabbis: A Pyrrhic Victory?" 50/4 (January–February 1985): 19–24; Sandy Eisenberg Sasso, "Women in the Rabbinate: A Personal Reflection," 49/5 (March 1984): 18–21; Deborah Brin, "Up Against the Wall: How We Answered Our Own Prayers," 54/7 (June 1989): 13–16; and Rebecca T. Alpert, "A Feminist Takes Stock of Reconstructionism," 54/8 (July–August 1989): 17–22. See also Lori Lefkovitz, "Shaping the

Jewish Future," *Reconstructionism Today* 5/1 (Autumn, 1997) and Rebecca Alpert and Goldie Milgram, "Women in the Reconstructionist Rabbinate" in *Religious Institutions and Women's Leadership: New Roles Inside the Mainstream,* ed. Catherine Wessinger (Columbia, S.C.: University of South Carolina Press, 1996), 291–310.

Welcoming Gay and Lesbian Jews
See the Judaism and Homosexuality issue of the *Reconstructionist* 51/2 (October–November 1985) and *Homosexuality and Judaism: The Reconstructionist Position. The Report of the Reconstructionist Commission on Homosexuality* (Wyncote, Pa.: Federation of Reconstructionist Congregations and Havurot, 1993) and *Homosexuality and Judaism: A Reconstructionist Workshop Series,* ed. Robert Gluck (Wyncote, Pa.: The Reconstructionist Press, 1993). See also Rebecca T. Alpert, *Like Bread on the Seder Plate: Jewish Lesbians and the Transformation of Tradition* (New York: Columbia University Press, 1997).

CHAPTER 10: *The Reconstructionist Movement*

Kaplan's view of organic Jewish community is presented in *The Future of the American Jew,** chapter 6. On the havurah, see Jacob Neusner, "Fellowship and the Crisis of Community," *Reconstructionist* 26/19 (January 1961): 8–15 and Steven Stroiman, "A Practical Guide in the Formation of a Havurah" in *Creative Jewish Education.** See also Arnold Eisen, "Reimagining Jewish Community in America," *Reconstructionist* 60/1 (Spring 1995): 5–13 and David A. Teutsch, "Shaping Communities of Commitment," *Reconstructionist* 60/2 (Fall 1995): 16–23.

Training the Reconstructionist Rabbi
Rabbinic education from a Reconstructionist perspective has been treated by Kaplan, *The Religion of Ethical Nationhood,* chapter 8; Ivan Caine, "Teaching Biblical Civilization" in *Shiv'im: Essays and Studies in Honor of Ira Eisenstein,* ed. Ronald Brauner (Philadelphia and New York: RRC Press and KTAV Publishing House, 1977) 3–14; Rebecca Alpert, "The Making of a Rabbi: The Reconstructionist Approach," *Encyclopedia Judaica*

Yearbook 1985; and the following articles in the *Reconstructionist*: Mel Scult, "Mordecai Kaplan on Spiritual Leadership," 52/5 (March–April 1987): 18–19 and Jacob J. Staub, "The Rabbi: Past Images, Future Visions," 55/4 (March–April 1990): 9–12.

Reconstructionist Congregational Life

On Reconstructionist congregational life, see the following articles in the *Reconstructionist*: Harriet A. Feiner, "The Synagogue as a Support System," 50/4 (January–February 1985): 25–30; Sidney Schwarz, "Reconstructionism as Process," 45/4 (June 1979): 14–18, "A Synagogue with Principles," 50/7 (June 1985): 21–25, and "Operating Principles for Reconstructionist Synagogues," 53/4 (January–February 1988): 28–31, 34; the symposium on Lay-Rabbinic Relations, 51/1 (September 1985); Dennis C. Sasso, "The Rabbi's Role in a Participatory Community," 54/7 (June 1989): 21–23; Mordechai Liebling, "The Non-Jew in the Synagogue," 59/2 (Fall 1994): 30–35; and Adina Newberg, "Boundaries in Reconstructionist Synagogues," 59/2 (Fall 1994): 80–87. See also the Spring 2000 issue on the "Role of the Rabbi."

CHAPTER 11: *Envisioning the Future*

For some further thoughts on the future see the following articles in the *Reconstructionist*: "The Future of Reconstructionism: A Symposium" 56/3 (Spring 1991): 8–27; Jacob Staub, "A Vision of Our Future," 50/4 (January–February 1985): 13–18; Ira Eisenstein, "Back to the Future: After 40 Years," 54/2 (October–November 1988): 24–25; and *Imagining the Jewish Future*,* David A. Teutsch, ed. (Albany: State University of New York Press, 1992). An important though dated study of the Reconstructionist movement itself is in Charles Liebman, *Aspects of the Religious Behavior of American Jews* (New York: KTAV Publishing Co., 1970) 189–285.

The Resource Guide

For further information about the Reconstructionist movement, contact the following people and places:

The Jewish Reconstructionist Federation

7804 Montgomery Avenue, Suite 9
Elkins Park, PA 19027
Phone: 215-782-8500
FAX: 215-782-8805
E-mail: info@jrf.org
Website: www.jrf.org

Founded in 1955, the Jewish Reconstructionist Federation is the rapidly growing synagogue organization of the Reconstructionist movement. The more than 100 affiliated JRF congregations and havurot are spread across North America. The JRF provides a wide array of services to its affiliates and is the voice of and for Reconstructionism in the greater Jewish world.

JRF is continually developing resources and programs to serve and support affiliates. The broad spectrum of services provided to congregations includes:

- Rabbinic placement services in cooperation with the Reconstructionist Rabbinical Association
- Guidance and resources in key areas of congregational life
- Educational support, resources, and programming
- Participation in a unique, nationwide network rich in creativity, spirituality, intellect, and practical skills that is most evident at the biennial convention
- Specialized local support from regional offices throughout North America
- Youth activities

FOR INFORMATION ON:

Affiliation (group, individual)	Director of Outreach
Education	Director of Education
Congregational Consultation	Coordinator of Congregational Resources
Music and Liturgy	Director of Music and Liturgy
Marketing and Communications	Director of Marketing and Communications
Reconstructionism Today	Subscription Manager

Contact the JRF Central Office at 7804 Montgomery Avenue, Suite 9, Elkins Park, PA 19027, 215-782-8500 (voice), 215-782-8805 (fax), info@jrf.org (E-mail)

REGIONAL OFFICES:

MidAtlantic	c/o JRF Central Office
Midwest	5050 W. Church Street, Skokie, IL 60077 (847) 679-1964 (voice), jrfmidwest@aol.com (E-mail)
New York	165 E. 56th St., New York, NY 10022 (212) 752-5411 (voice), jrfny@aol.com (E-mail)
West Coast	6310 San Vicente Blvd., Suite 350 Los Angeles, CA 90048 (323) 933-7491 (voice), jrfwcreg@aol.com (E-mail)

The Reconstructionist Press

7804 Montgomery Avenue, Suite 9
Elkins Park, PA 19027
1-877-JRFPUBS (voice),
press@jrf.org (E-mail)
www.jrf.org (Web)

Many of the titles listed in "The Reconstructionist Bookshelf" are available from the Reconstructionist Press, which features Kaplan classics, resources for educators and congregational leaders, and the *Kol Haneshamah* prayerbook series.

The Reconstructionist

Editorial offices:

1299 Church Road
Wyncote, PA 19095
Phone: 215-576-5210

Subscription information
and requests should go to:

The *Reconstructionist*
JRF
7804 Montgomery Avenue, Suite 9
Elkins Park, PA 19027-2649

The *Reconstructionist,* which began publishing in 1935, serves as a medium for the continuing development of Reconstructionist ideas, practices, and institutions, by addressing religious, political, social, and moral issues of contemporary Jewish life. By focusing on a theme in each issue, examined from a variety of perspectives, the *Reconstructionist* is a forum for significant dialogue and fresh approaches within the Jewish community.

The *Reconstructionist* is published two times a year by the Reconstructionist Rabbinical College. Subscriptions are $40/four issues ($36 for members of JRF affiliates). Individual copies are $10.00.

The Reconstructionist Rabbinical College
1299 Church Road
Wyncote, PA 19095
Phone: (215) 576-0800
FAX: (215) 576-6143
Website: www.rrc.edu

Founded in 1968 to serve the Jewish people, the Reconstructionist Rabbinical College is dedicated to studying and teaching Judaism as an evolving religious civilization, and to advancing the universal freedom, justice, and peace that are Judaism's core values. Our mission is to train rabbis and other Jewish leaders to teach Torah in its broadest terms and strengthen leadership in congregations and other settings throughout the Jewish community in North America. The College provides scholarship and training to strengthen that community, advance the growth of the Reconstructionist movement, and spread its ideas and ideals throughout the Jewish world.

The College prepares men and women for leadership and service in every aspect of Jewish communal life and confers the Master of Arts in Hebrew Letters and Title of Rabbi, the Master of Arts in Jewish Studies, and Cantorial Investiture. The College's practical rabbinics program permits rabbinical students to pursue additional certification in the campus rabbinate, chaplaincy, community organization, and congregational life. In recent years the College has added joint degree programs in Jewish Music and Jewish Education in conjunction with Gratz College, and a joint certificate program in Women's Studies in conjunction with Temple University.

Although the students and faculty come from diverse personal, intellectual, and professional backgrounds, and represent a wide spectrum of religious observance and theological belief, the men and women of the Reconstructionist Rabbinical College are united by a firm commitment both to the Jewish people and their heritage, and to Judaism's ongoing renewal. The College seeks to create a mutually concerned community in which dreams and visions, doubts and aspirations are expressed freely, and through which the renewal and celebration of Judaism is shared meaningfully and joyously.

To find out more about the College's program, or to inquire about applying for admission, see the College web site at www.rrc.edu, call 215-576-0800, or write to RRC, 1299 Church Road, Wyncote, PA 19095.

The Reconstructionist Rabbinical Association
1299 Church Road
Wyncote, PA 19095
Phone: (215) 576-5210
FAX: (215) 576-8051
E-mail: rraassoc@aol.com

The Reconstructionist Rabbinical Association (RRA), established in 1974, is the professional association of Reconstructionist rabbis. Comprising over 200 rabbis, the RRA has three primary missions. First it serves as a collegial community, in which professional and personal support and resources are provided to rabbis. Second, the RRA represents the rabbinic voice within the Reconstructionist movement, bringing the teachings, stories, and traditions of Judaism to bear on contemporary issues and challenges, and helping to define Reconstructionist positions on Jewish issues for our time. Third, the RRA represents the Reconstructionist rabbinate to the larger Jewish and general communities, through participation in programs, commissions, and other activities. The RRA establishes rituals, documents, liturgy, and policies around moments of the Jewish life cycle. It publishes a Reconstructionist rabbi's manual, documents and procedures for egalitarian Jewish divorce, life-cycle certificates, and a series of ketubot. Regional events as well as the annual RRA convention serve to connect colleagues with one another and provide ongoing education and professional development.